Frances Gerard

**Some fair Hibernians**

Frances Gerard

**Some fair Hibernians**

ISBN/EAN: 9783337125011

Printed in Europe, USA, Canada, Australia, Japan

Cover: Foto ©Andreas Hilbeck / pixelio.de

More available books at **www.hansebooks.com**

# SOME FAIR HIBERNIANS

BEING

## A SUPPLEMENTARY VOLUME TO "SOME CELEBRATED IRISH BEAUTIES OF THE LAST CENTURY"

BY

FRANCES A. GERARD

AUTHOR OF

"SOME CELEBRATED IRISH BEAUTIES OF THE LAST CENTURY,"
"ANGELICA KAUFFMAN: A BIOGRAPHY," ETC.

LONDON
WARD & DOWNEY
*LIMITED*
12 YORK BUILDINGS ADELPHI W.C.
1897

# PREFACE

SAYING good-bye to friends is always sad, and as I part from my Irish beauties a feeling of regret comes over me. They have been my constant companions for many months; they have been tiresome at times —what woman is not? On the other hand, they have cheered many a dull day, and have lightened in some degree the hours of sorrow. So much for myself. The more important issue is now at hand—the verdict of my readers. They have been kind before, and I trust that to them the record of these lives may again give pleasure. Some are well known, others presented for the first time; all possess the interest that underlies human life. As we look at the portraits of these beautiful women, they seem to say, "We were once like you—we, too, dwelt in Arcadia."

In connection with this subject, I would wish to

make honourable mention of several Irishwomen whose claims as regards personal beauty were equal to, if not greater, than those presented in this volume. Happily, for themselves, they had no story to tell —that is, so far as is known. The first place in this category must be accorded to a Mrs Dillon, who has been introduced to me by no less a person than Mr Gladstone. "I have not found in the book," he writes,[1] "any notice of Mrs Dillon, nor indeed of anyone in her position. In case you should not have touched it, I will mention the slight story as I have heard it. Mrs Dillon was the mistress of a haberdasher's shop in a fashionable street of Dublin. One day, without any notice, the beautiful Duchess of Rutland,[2] in a grand equipage, drove up to the door; she went into the shop, gazed hard at Mrs Dillon, who was behind the counter, and cried, 'Yes, you are the most beautiful woman in the three kingdoms!' and thereupon quitted the shop."

I have given this story in Mr Gladstone's own words, and I fancy my readers will think I have

[1] Alluding to the preceding volume, *Some Celebrated Irish Beauties*.

[2] The Duchess was "the beautiful Isabella," daughter to the Duke of Beaufort. The Duke of Rutland was Viceroy in Ireland, 1784.

done right. It is a model of what a short story should be. I must add that the Duchess of Rutland's visit proceeded from conjugal jealousy, excited by the Duke of Rutland's praises of the fair haberdasher's loveliness. This, however, does not suggest any imputation against Mrs Dillon's conduct, which was above any suspicion of the kind.

Another celebrated beauty was Lady Elizabeth Stratford, daughter to John,[1] last Earl of Aldborough. She married Admiral Delap Haliday, eldest son of John Delap Haliday of the Leasowes and Lady Jane Tollemache, second daughter and co-heir of Lionel, third Earl of Dysart. One of her descendants, Mr Tollemache, has a lovely portrait of her by Romney, of which the engraving is in the possession of the Miss Vernon Harcourts, grandchildren to Lady Emily Stratford.

Those who can carry their memory back to the early forties will recall the commotion caused by the marriage of the Prince of Capua to Miss Smith of Beltrae. This Irish beauty hailed from Westmeath, and, judging from her portraits, must have been

[1] Lady Aldborough was a well-known character in the early part of this century.

exceptionally lovely. She had, however, somewhat of a chequered life, her husband's royal relatives refusing to accept her as a *royalty.* Although they could not succeed in setting aside her marriage, they relegated her to the quasi-royal position of a morganatic wife, and she was allowed no share in her consort's official dignity. There is something pathetic in the manner in which, in most of her portraits, the poor princess puts forward her left hand with the wedding-ring on the third finger. Her sister was likewise a beauty. She married Lord Dinorben, and was well known in London society.

Coming down to our own time, one could name a host of lovely Irishwomen — some of whom may well deserve the attention of future chroniclers.

In conclusion, I have the pleasant duty of offering my cordial thanks to those who have kindly helped me with portraits, family letters and other information.

FRANCES A. GERARD.

# CONTENTS

# LIST OF ILLUSTRATIONS

# SOME FAIR HIBERNIANS

## ERRATA.

Page 43. For Fréseli, read Fuseli.
" 60. " Gormon, read de Gernon.
" 65. Footnote should be on page 66.
" 72. For Mademoiselle ——read Mdlle. de Thun.
" 109. " Boreas, read Brocas.
" 176. " Borall, read Boxall, R.A.
" 177. " Lady Clarke died 1859, read 1845.
" 184. " idea, read statement.
" 185. " Dacres, read Davies (Lady Clementina.)
" 190. " Shiel, read Sheil.
" 192. " peroration, read aspiration.
" 200. " Careene, read Careme.
" 214. " Denan, read Dénon.
" 218. " manner, read superiority.
" 274. " Chevenix, read Chenevix.

[1] The history of Wilkinson, who was the son of the chaplain of the Savoy Chapel, is not without interest. "He had worked his way from the ranks of the hangers-on about the stage door, and through some gifts of mimicry and a vast deal of impudence had become a favourite with the Galleries. He had made himself useful in a small way to men like Foote and Garrick, and when he found his hold on them failing, made it strong again by the inconvenience and awkwardness they felt would ensue from the enmity of such a creature. As an instance of this, there is the scene in his memoirs where he describes how he took off Foote in reluctant obedience to the call of the audience, the actor himself being present. In his managerial life he was good-humoured and popular, and as bombastic as Mr Crummles himself."

# SOME FAIR HIBERNIANS

## DOROTHEA JORDAN

### (1762-1816)

WHEN that pleasant and, to a certain extent, truthful chronicler, Tate Wilkinson,[1] made his first venture on the Dublin stage in 1758, he played Othello to the Desdemona of a certain Miss Grace Phillips, one of three sisters who were all in the profession. These young ladies, who never rose above mediocrity, came of a genteel family, being daughters to a Welsh clergyman in the enjoyment of a small living near Chester. The dulness of the family circle, or the Sunday ministrations of their excellent father proved too much for the youthful spirits of the Misses Phillips. They wanted to try their wings away from the paternal preachings, and one by one they took flight from the dull vicarage house, and found their way to the stage. Miss Grace Phillips was lively and pretty, and although she made a somewhat unsatisfactory Desdemona, she was very well suited in light comedy parts, and was extremely popular with her audience, having her choice of admirers. Amongst these was Lieutenant, after-

[1] The history of Wilkinson, who was the son of the chaplain of the Savoy Chapel, is not without interest. "He had worked his way from the ranks of the hangers-on about the stage door, and through some gifts of mimicry and a vast deal of impudence had become a favourite with the Galleries. He had made himself useful in a small way to men like Foote and Garrick, and when he found his hold on them failing, made it strong again by the inconvenience and awkwardness they felt would ensue from the enmity of such a creature. As an instance of this, there is the scene in his memoirs where he describes how he took off Foote in reluctant obedience to the call of the audience, the actor himself being present. In his managerial life he was good-humoured and popular, and as bombastic as Mr Crummles himself."

wards Captain Bland, a young naval officer descended from an old Yorkshire family, a branch of which had settled in the County Kerry, where Lieutenant Bland's father was well known as a practising physician.[1]

Grace Phillips's early training made her resolute to have the sanction of the Church upon any engagement she entered into, and her lover, finding he could in no other way prevail, married her. The ceremony, unfortunately for her, was performed by a Catholic priest, and so, however satisfactory it might be from a religious point of view, was not binding in the eye of the law. Moreover, Captain Bland was under age at the time. Of these circumstances his family took advantage to obtain a dissolution of the marriage, not, however, until there were two children, if not more, of whom Dorothea was the elder, being born in Waterford in 1762. It has been stated that Captain Bland married again, and that either he or his family allowed a small pension to his first wife and her children, which would account for the constant fear Mrs Bland expressed of offending her husband's family, and for the number of aliases she adopted. She was undoubtedly left in poor circumstances, for Dora and her sister were apprenticed to a milliner in Dublin, where they remained until the first reached her sixteenth year.

The future actress had a soul above ribbons; acting, moreover, is in the blood, and the children of actors seldom settle down to private life, the stage seeming to draw them with irresistible force—much as the magnet does the needle. This strong passion now seized upon Dora. Her mother, who had returned to her old calling, but no longer played juvenile leads, imparted the first necessary lessons to a very apt scholar.

[1] The Dictionary of National Biography in the notice on Mrs Jordan considers that there is *grave* inherent improbability in the statement that Bland was a gentleman. "There is reason to suppose that he was merely a stage underling." This would seem to be a mistake on the part of the writer of the notice, as will be seen from the following communication from one of the descendants of Captain Bland's family still residing in Ireland. "Her father was Captain Bland, R.N., a scion of one of the oldest families in Yorkshire, who settled in Kerry many centuries ago, and now rank amongst the largest proprietors in Ireland." From another source we learn that Captain Bland was first cousin to General Johnson and to Sir Francis Lunn. A great deal of uncertainty surrounds the whole story of the "Bland marriage."

Ryder was at that time manager of Crowe Street Theatre, Dublin, and a friend of the family. With the usual *bonhomie* of the profession, he was willing to give the young girl a chance.

She appeared in the trifling part of Phœbe in "As you Like It," her stage name being Miss Francis, not to shock the prejudices of her father's family, it being for some reason—probably the potent one of money—Mrs Bland's earnest desire not to offend the Bland family. Beyond her small circle of friends, Dora's *début* does not seem to have excited the least attention, her mother ascribing this apparent failure to the inferiority of the part, which afforded no chance of attracting the notice of the house. Nothing daunted, Mrs Bland, who believed in her daughter's talent, approached Daly, the manager of Smoke Alley Theatre, whose stock company, being inferior in strength to that of Crowe Street, was more likely to afford the desired opening.

A more careful mother than Mrs Bland might have hesitated to place her child in the hands of such a man as Daly,[1] whose character was of the worst. The need, however, was pressing. The manager's keen eye detected at once promise in the undeveloped beauty and immature performance of the young girl whose very freshness was to him a charm. He engaged her for the new farce then in preparation, "The Duenna," in which she appeared as *Lopez*, in male attire, followed by "The Romp." She was more successful as the *Tomboy* in the last than in *Lopez*. Later on, she appeared in Captain Jephson's play, "Adelaide."

This first season in Dublin gained her the reputation of an attractive actress. Her next appearance was at Cork, where an incident occurred very similar to that which happened to Peg Woffington in her early days. Heaphy, the manager of the Cork Theatre, had engaged her on Daly's representations of her talent at a salary of one pound a week. She was

[1] Daly was a gentleman by birth, and had a good education. When a Fellow Commoner at Trinity College he had distinguished himself by bursting into an actress's dressing-room (Miss Pope) at the head of a party of collegians. He was a handsome man, but of a coarse, excitable and quarrelsome nature. He forced a duel on Kemble.

universally admired and a great attraction; nevertheless, her benefit turned out a failure from the want of the proper patronage. The young bucks of Cork espoused her cause, just as did the collegians of Trinity College that of Woffington. They were headed by a certain Mr Smith, son to a banker in the town, and were resolved that their favourite should have another chance. They shouted for Heaphy, and when he would not appear proceeded to wreak their displeasure by tearing up the benches. A regular row was imminent when Heaphy's son-in-law came forward. To him the young men, through Mr Smith, made known their pleasure—Miss Phillips should have another benefit. In vain he objected: they would listen to no other terms: and the manager had to agree. The actress had a crowded house, and netted forty pounds, an immense sum in her eyes; and what was even more important, when she returned to Dublin her salary was raised to three guineas a week.

On her visit to Cork, the young actress was accompanied, it is said, by her father, who performed the duties of scene-shifter. This could not have been Captain Bland, but it has been suggested that this was Francis, who by many writers has been mentioned as Mrs Bland's second husband.[1] Why any secrecy was kept as to this marriage seems strange, unless it was that Mrs Bland was afraid of losing the small allowance made to her by Captain Bland or his family. She had no other possible reason for concealing a marriage she had every right to make. The aliases in which Mrs Bland delighted are, however, extremely confusing, she appearing sometimes as Mrs Phillips, again as Bland and occasionally as Francis.

Dora's next provincial engagement was at Waterford—a singular choice considering the fuss that was made as to offending her father's family. The adoption of the "alias" was, it must be supposed, sufficient to soothe their suscepti-

[1] Boaden speaks of Mrs Bland more than once as Mrs Francis. Tate Wilkinson mentions the Francis family as apart from Dora and her brother. The Dictionary of National Biography gives the name as *Frances*.

bilities. Here, however, occurred the first crisis in our heroine's life. Admirers she had already in dozens, but a genuine offer of marriage is a more stirring event, and always forms an epoch in a woman's life. Lieutenant Charles Doyne was, like Captain Bland, a gentleman by birth and education, and his attachment was both honourable and sincere: it, however, found no favour with Dora's mother. The fact that the lover had no fortune but his profession, and that he made it a condition that Dora should leave the stage, weighed heavily against him. Mrs Francis's knowledge of acting told her that in her daughter she possessed what, if well developed, might be a mine of gold, and she had no fancy to lose such a treasure by burying it in a marching regiment. Moreover, her own experience of a man's passion was not conclusive as to its being very lasting. In her own case, she had experienced how easily love can be weakened and how, after a little while, nothing remains of all the vows and protestations but a sense of their burden, and what had happened to her might be repeated in Dora's case. Mrs Francis placed all these considerations before her child, asking her to weigh well before she decided whether she was willing to sacifice a possibly great career for certain poverty and uncertain happiness. Like all mothers, she understood talking down a daughter's heart—not that in this case the young girl's affections were really engaged. She relinquished her lover without a struggle. Not so Lieutenant Doyne. He pleaded for an engagement warmly, passionately, and his friend, Sir Jonah Barrington, dilates upon the misery the young man suffered when finally dismissed.

After this episode, the young actress returned to Dublin, where the news of her success in Cork had preceded her. Her popularity was much increased by her performance of *Sophia* in "the Lord of the Manor," written by General Burgoyne,[1] in which her singing of "A Rose Tree in Full Bearing" trans-

[1] General Burgoyne was a meritorious and gallant officer, unfortunate in one instance, and for this was somewhat ungenerously persecuted by the ministers of the day. In private life he was an accomplished gentleman and a sincere friend, "a fellow of infinite jest, of most excellent fancy." He died, 1792, at his house in Hertford Street. See 1st Series *Memoirs of Miss Farren*.

ported her audience.[1] Another favourite part was *Patrick* in "The Poor Soldier," which she played seventy-five nights, which was then thought an extraordinarily long run.

Irish audiences were critical and enthusiastic, and if they approved heartily, their verdict was considerd certain to throw open the doors of the London houses. This idea filled the mind of Mrs Francis, who was, like all mothers, more ambitious for her daughter than she had ever been for herself. It is not likely, however, that she would have carried her wishes so speedily into effect unless the continuance of Dora's engagement had been rendered impossible by the unpleasant circumstances in which she found herself placed. Daly had lately married a clever and well-known actress, Miss Barsanti, who was accustomed to play with much applause some of the leading parts at Covent Garden Theatre. This lady naturally felt aggrieved at the evidence of popular favour towards a "chit of a girl who, in her, Mrs Daly's, opinion, did not know how to act." To add to her offences, Mrs Daly chose to conceive, rightly or wrongly, that Dora was favouring *her* husband's attentions in order to advance her own interests. Mrs Daly's jealousy caused her to circulate all manner of vile reports against the young girl.

This complication hastened Mrs Francis's decision. Although she was not so watchful of her daughter's reputation as was Mrs Farren, she was thoroughly in earnest in wishing to remove her from such dangerous surroundings, and in July of the year 1782 severed her connection with Daly's company.

[1] In Dublin she introduced "Melton Oysters." Another favourite song with the Dublin audience was "The Rose Tree in Full Bearing" and "The Camp Medley," composed by Major Lebellier, then quartered in Limerick, where he fell in love with a beauty of the locality, one Miss Mounteford Bown, or Bowen, who married William Henn of Paradise, whereupon the Irish, who are given to apt naming of their friends, called her the Bird of Paradise. Amongst the audience on one occasion was Mrs Lefann (Sheridan's sister). "Do you observe," she said to her uncle, Mr Chamberlaine, "that young lady standing by the wing nearest the stage door." "The little, young lass do you mean? "Yes," said she, "that little girl if she lives will be some time or other the first comic actress in England or Ireland ; she is a Miss Francis ; she has not been long on the stage, but for chastity of acting, *naïveté* and being the character she represents, young as she is, she surpasses what could have been expected of so young a performer."

In those days, London was the goal of all aspirants to fame and fortune. There was plenty of money to be had, and a popular actress who once hit the fancy of the town could make her own terms—but an opening of some sort was necessary. There was no hope of an introduction from Daly, who, irritated at the withdrawal of the popular young actress, threatened to demand a penalty for the infringement of contract. In this rather hopeless condition, Mrs Francis bethought herself of the Othello to whom she had acted Desdemona twenty or more years ago. Tate Wilkinson, who formerly had been well buffeted by ill fortune, was now an important personage as the manager of a country circuit, of which the large city of York was the centre. Provincial towns in the last century held higher social status than they do nowadays when railroads have made such short work of distance from the capital. We who have never known it otherwise can hardly grasp the difference steam has made in everyday life, and yet with all the undoubted advantages afforded by this quick transit there is something to regret in that tranquil ease and daily round of small occupations which was a noticeable feature in the lives of our forefathers. Remaining so much at home, they had plenty of time for that wonderful correspondence in which many of them indulged: those delightful letters, folded in four, sealed with the big coat-of-arms which hung at their fobs, and written in a copperplate hand, are so many pictures of life and society, which are of far more value than any amount of society papers and Kodaks of which we are so proud. When they did travel, which was generally once a year, they did not rush at break-neck speed through steam-laden air, bent on reaching their journey's end in the quickest possible time, but packed themselves and family into the roomy coach and jogged along the roads lazily, stopping when they liked at same comfortable roadside inn, and arriving, without turning a hair, at their destination, which was not only London, but York or Bristol or Bath. At any of these towns there was no lack of good society and sufficient gaiety to satisfy the limited desires of the squire's family, who did not aspire to going to Court, but liked a good dance and a chance of seeing Mrs Siddons or any other star. A man like Tate Wilkinson was on excellent terms with the principal gentry in the towns where his circuit took him. He had in his youth known Garrick and Woffington, Cibber and Foote, and a long list of kings and queens of the stage, most of whom he had deeply offended by his clever mimicry of their different peculiarities. In his memoirs, he gives the pleasantest account of his own mortifications as well as his triumphs. In this amusing record, we find the following record of his first meeting with his former Desdemona and her family. This interview took place at Leeds, to which place the York manager had brought his company, then on circuit.

*July* 1782.—"Miss Francis suddenly starts upon me, with her mother, Mrs G. Philips, Master and Miss Francis, her brother and sister, all in hand—recognised her mother as my first Desdemona in Dublin 1758. She then played as Miss G. Philips. Her younger sister, who was also in Dublin, had been for some years after in the York company and was then, 1782, dying. When I first met them at the inn, I cannot say they were so well accoutred as I could have wished, for my own sake as well as theirs, the mamma, like all other mammas, and especially actresses' mammas, talked so fulsomely of her daughter that I was almost disgusted and very near giving a flat denial to any negotiation. Now, had I given a determined 'No!' to Mrs Jordan at that flurried instant, it might have been unfortunate for her and her dependants."

It speaks much for the kindness of Wilkinson's heart that he did engage her without any previous knowledge of her powers beyond what he could judge from the few lines which she spoke from "Calista," but although she was weary with travelling and dejected in mind and body, the keen ear of the manager detected a plaintive tone in her melodious voice, which from experience he knew to be of the right ring to touch an audience. "Calista" was therefore fixed upon for her *début*, to be followed by the "Virgin Unmask'd." The rehearsals strengthened Wilkinsen's first impression that Miss Francis would prove a success, but he had not the faintest idea that her gifts lay in a totally different direction from plaintive heroines. Great, therefore, was his consternation when, on the day of the first appearance, her mother asked that it should be announced in the bills that after the play Miss Francis would sing "The Greenwood Laddie." One can hardly imagine that the astute manager acceded to this request without first testing her capabilities in this line, otherwise he would certainly have had a bad moment when *Calista*, just risen from the dead, rushed before the still tearful audience in a frock and little mob cap, and with a smile that no other comic actress ever was blest with set them all laughing. Her success was assured, and when she took her benefit a month later, the house was crowded. She was then permanently engaged, and her appearance at York was heralded by the usual amount of puffing, and likewise by the usual fuss made as to the name she should assume. Mrs Francis, who seems to have had a passion for aliases, came to the manager with a story as to her not taking the name of Phillips which she had used at Leeds, as her aunt, one of the clergyman's daughters, was dying, and it would hurt her feelings and likewise injure the chance of a legacy of stage dresses. This being a valid reason, the manager suggested Bland or Francis, but to both there were objections. Ultimately, she adopted the one by which the actress was ever after known. This third change has been ascribed to different reasons, too long and unpleasant to give here. The one given by Tate Wilkinson is as satisfactory as any other. "She was talking to me one day of all she had suffered in Daly's company. 'I shed tears enough,' said she, 'to overflow the Jordan.' From that time I called her little Jordan, and when she went to London, she kept the name as being more imposing."[1]

[1] Tate Wilkinson always took to himself the credit—"I gave her that name; I was her sponsor." "You!" "Yes: when she thought of going to London, she thought Miss sounded insignificant, so she asked me to advise her a name. 'Why,' said I, 'my dear, you *have crossed the water, so I'll call you Jordan*,' and by the memory of Sam! if she didn't take my joke in earnest, and call herself Mrs Jordan ever since." On the other hand, Boaden, who, the *Quarterly Review* says, was candle-snuffer behind the scenes, persists, "The *baptism* had no reference whatever to London. Mrs Jordan was three years with Tate Wilkinson before she quitted him for Drury Lane Theatre."

From whatever the cause, all must allow that the change from Miss Francis to Mrs Jordan was a manifest improvement. One would not like to controvert the authority who lays down the dictum that "a rose by any other name would smell as sweet," yet one cannot deny that some names carry more weight than others, and, as a rule, Christian names do not make satisfactory surnames.

The race week at York was the gayest meeting of the year, and the theatre was nightly crowded. Amongst the visitors to the town was a well-known actor of Drury Lane Theatre, William Smith, generally known by the name of Gentleman Smith, on account of his very polished manners. Mrs Jordan's performance of *Priscilla Tomboy* in "The Romp" pleased the London actor, and as he was a kind-hearted man, he did not limit his admiration to mere words, but, as will be seen, exerted himself to do her a service.

MRS JORDAN AS "THE ROMP."

Meantime, she was very well content with her first season. Her salary had been raised to thirty shillings a-week, and at Sheffield, Hull and Leeds she had enthusiastic receptions. The York audiences were never very warm admirers; they were accustomed to the courtly grace of Miss Farren, which, nevertheless, was not touched with one spark of genius, and they looked doubtfully upon Mrs Jordan's delightful romping. They were, however, very appreciative of her singing, and whenever they were out of humour from any cause, the manager would entreat Mrs Jordan to give them a song, which was certain to restore their serenity. Her singing was one of her greatest charms, her voice untaught, as it was, producing more effect than that of many cultivated musicians. "The Camp Medley" was a favourite with the York audience, and her singing of "Let not Age Thy Bloom ensnare," in the part of *Miss Juniper* in "Summer Amusements," completely captivated the Duke of Norfolk, who was a great lover of the stage.

It is not to be supposed that Mrs Jordan's rise in public favour did not raise up for her the usual amount of enemies that are born of success, for it is only the mediocre that have troops of friends. The theatrical profession, moreover, is one where success is so evident and failure so overwhelming that one can hardly be surprised that the losers in the game are tempted to some overt demonstration of their rage and jealousy.[1]

In Mrs Jordan's case what seems to have excited the greatest amount of envy was her appearing in male attire as *William* in the opera of "Rosina." This drew upon her the anger of Mrs Ward, a somewhat veteran actress, who had hitherto the monopoly of such parts. This lady, who was more jealous of the youthful appearance of her rival than of her decided superiority as an actress, organised amongst her own set of friends a conspiracy to disconcert the popular favourite whilst she was on the stage. The conspirators placed themselves near the stage doors, and used all their ingenuity to disturb and annoy Mrs Jordan by laughing at her, making rude remarks on her appearance and being otherwise offensive. Appeals to their mercy were of no avail, and to have drawn the manager into the quarrel would have been to make matters worse. In this situation, Mrs Francis's stage experience came to her daughter's assistance. By her instructions, the young actress appeared before her audience with every sign of disturbance upon her charming face, tears in her lovely eyes, an appeal for help and sympathy in every

[1] Mrs Barry was so jealous of Mrs Boutell that when the latter played *Statira* in the "Rival Queens," she struck at her with a dagger and although the point was blunted, it made its way through Mrs Boutell's stays and entered a quarter of an inch into the flesh. Different causes were assigned for this outbreak on the part of Mrs Barry, who, it was said, really wanted to destroy her rival.—Genest, *History of the Stage.*

glance. Her admirers at once wanted to know the cause of their favourite's distress. This led to inquiry into the annoyance, and the manager's attention being drawn to the matter for the future the doors were locked when Mrs Jordan was on the stage. To Mrs Ward's further mortification, her detested rival appeared as *Patrick* in "The Poor Soldier," a part she played to perfection. In this she transported her audience by her singing of—

> "How happy the soldier who lives on his pay,
> And spends half-a-crown out of sixpence a day."

The decided animosity shown towards her, in addition to the necessity of making more money to support the number depending upon her, made it desirous for Mrs Jordan to change the scene. She had already been in correspondence with the managers of Drury Lane, to whom Mr Smith had given a most flattering account of her talents, but nothing was actually settled until the season of 1785. Meantime, the uncertainty gave the actress that restless sensation which always precedes a coming change in our condition of life. This state of mind influenced her whole conduct. The manager complained she had grown careless and indifferent to pleasing either him or the public. On one occasion when called upon to sing between the acts, she flatly refused. The audience insisted, the manager stormed, while the young lady sullenly continued her obstinate refusal. At last the storm outside the curtain grew too strong even for her audacity, and so, almost crying with annoyance, she came on and warbled out "In the Prattling Hours of Youth," a somewhat inane ditty, composed by Doctor Arne. Tate Wilkinson, who tells this story, adds that if the actress had taken her benefit she would never have submitted, but, as that was still to come, her poverty and not her will consented. The petulance she exhibited on this and other occasions was hardly wise; it alienated her friends and admirers.[1] Her benefit at Leeds

[1] All through her life, Mrs Jordan was subject to these fits of sullenness and ill-humour.

was, in consequence, thinly attended, and Mrs Siddons, who saw her in this mood, formed no great opinion of her powers, and thought she would do better to stay where she was than venture on the London boards. Yates, likewise, received the same impression, and while praising the lovely Miss Wilkinson, afterwards Mrs Mountain and Mrs Browne, adds that Mrs Jordan was merely a piece of theatrical mediocrity. Both these good judges were in a few weeks to find how short-sighted had been their verdict.

A fine commotion took place when, later on, the news leaked out that the Jordan was actually engaged to appear at Drury Lane. All manner of spiteful prophecies were at once let loose. Mrs Robinson, one of her rivals, told the manager that when he had lost his "great treasure" (a favourite term of Wilkinson's in addressing Mrs Jordan), "*it* would soon be turned back upon his hands, and *it* would be glad to come if he would accept it." In return for this low witticism, Mrs Jordan's mother begged Mr Wilkinson to let her know when that fright (Mrs Robinson) had done acting, for *it* was so horrid, she could not look at *it*. All this was contemptible in the extreme, but it did not tend to soothe the actress's troubled spirit. She was, indeed, setting out on an unknown sea, where many dangers were likely to swamp her little bark, and few friendly hands were ready to help her to a safe harbour. One can imagine in what a perturbation of mind she made this momentous journey to London. Everything depended upon the success of this experiment—if it had resulted in failure she would have had to return to York with her value considerably lowered. As to the salary, there was not much gained there, four pounds a-week was all Mr Smith could obtain for her. The oft-quoted saying of Sir Walter Raleigh however holds good in theatrical as in all other ventures, and the event justified our heroine's endeavour to climb the ladder of success.

At the moment of Mrs Jordan's arrival, Drury Lane was crowded with actresses, all of them popular and of remarkable merit. This circumstance rendered the advent of the new-comer singularly unpropitious. Established favourites, like

Mrs Siddons, Miss Farren and Miss Pope, filled all the leading parts in tragedy and comedy, and this so ably as to render it difficult for the *débutante* to secure even the crumbs of public favour. Mrs Jordan wisely took a line utterly different, and one in which she could in no way clash with the popular idols. The youthful heroines of Shakespeare's dramas, and the whole class of romps in modern comedy were unoccupied, except by inferior actresses, and here she resolved to make her mark. To this proposal, the acting managers, Sheridan and King, made no objection, and it only remained to settle in what character she should make her first appearance.

During her York experiences, she had been much impressed by a Mrs Browne's acting of *Peggy* in "The Country Girl." Mrs Browne was an actress of great comic power, her mature years, however, and large person were ill-suited to playing a vivacious girl in her teens. Nevertheless, as she was a perfect mistress of the "business," she pleased her audience by her well-meant efforts. Mrs Jordan was quick enough to see that, with more seasonable graces and a natural, not assumed, girlish hilarity, the part could be made altogether one to captivate the public, and the result showed how true was her estimate. In her hands, "The Country Girl" became the rage of the town; it seemed as if it had been written expressly for her, although composed by Wycherley[1] many years before she was known on the stage. It was said that she had studied the part under its original producer, Mrs Browne; this, however, is not at all probable, and in any case the especial charms which Mrs Jordan brought before her audience, "the elastic step, the artless simplicity, and, if the expression may be used, the juicy tones of her melodious voice, these were Nature's gifts, and never could have been imparted." Mrs Jordan's laugh is insisted upon by all her critics. Most actresses are distinguished for certain qualities which are lacking in others. Miss O'Neill, we are told, was great in a *cry*, Mrs Jordan unrivalled in a *laugh*, which was so infectious as to communicate itself at once to the whole

[1] Wycherley wrote it as the "Country Wife," and Garrick altered the title to the "Country Girl."

house. Playgoers of the present day are not in a position to understand the effect produced by a laugh or a cry: either from a defect of training or a natural inability in modern players, the actresses of our time indulge in that most unpleasant of artificial sounds, the stage laugh, which is only equalled by the stage cry. We are told that the laughter of Mrs Jordan was perfectly genuine in all its branches, from the juvenile giggle to the full, joyous burst; it would break out in the most uncontrollable manner, "sparkling like bubbles in the water."

It was on the 18th October 1785 that Mrs Jordan made her first appearance at Drury Lane in the part of *Peggy* in "The Country Girl." The outside world had heard little of her beyond that she was a new addition to the company. For some reason, she had not been heralded by any puff preliminary; the house, therefore, was only moderately full. The actress, a prey to nervousness, stood trembling at the wing. It was a terrible moment for her, and now that she was in face of the ordeal, the magnitude of the undertaking seemed almost overpowering. The moment, however, she touched the boards her self-possession returned. Mrs Jordan at this time was in her twenty-third year: of middle height, her figure, which was exquisitely moulded, was somewhat inclined to *embonpoint*, which, later, developed into corpulence; her face was oval—not strictly beautiful, the charm lying principally in the expression, which was so altogether fascinating that no one thought of considering the question of her beauty. Looking at the portraits Romney painted of her, one can hardly realise this. The jaw is long almost to heaviness, and the eyes have a melancholy expression, which, in reality, was dissipated by her wonderful smile, which was her real charm. As she came on the stage, her youthful appearance (she did not look more than nineteen) and enchanting face took the house by surprise. This favourable impression was strengthened by the first sound of her melodious voice, with "its peculiar fulness, as if she had some delicious, ripe peach in her mouth," while her laugh, tinged with "exquisite humour, exhibited at once merriment and delight." In the scene where *Peggy* writes the clandestine letter to her lover, the house burst into applause at her indescribable *naïveté*, and the applause became a tumult of acclamation when she sang with her usual archness—

> "Do you, papa, but find a coach,
> And leave the other to me, sir,
> For that will make the lover approach,
> And I warrant we sha'n't disagree, sir.
> No sparks will talk to girls that walk,
> I've heard it and I confide in't.
> Do you then fix my coach and six,
> I warrant I'll get one to ride in't."

At the conclusion, she was recalled again and again. Mrs Inchbald, who was in the house, describes the scene.[1] "She came to town with no report in her favour to elevate her above a very moderate salary (four pounds a-week) or to attract more than a very moderate house when she appeared, but here moderation ceased. She at once displayed such consummate art, with such bewitching nature, such excellent sense, and such innocent simplicity, that her auditors were boundless in their plaudits and so warm in their praises when they left the theatre that their friends at home would not give credit to the extent of their eulogiums." One can imagine with what feelings Mrs Jordan returned home on this eventful evening: the congratulations of her friends and the plaudits of the house ringing in her ears, and the knowledge that her success was a solid one, in proof of which her salary was to be rated at twelve instead of four pounds a-week, with two benefits.

The part of *Peggy* was undoubtedly one of the best Mrs

[1] It is interesting to find, in a letter from Mrs Tickell to her sister, Mrs Sheridan, an account of the new actress. "I went last night to see our new "Country Girl," and I can assure you, if *you* have any reliance on my judgment, she has more genius in her little finger than Miss Brunton in her whole body. . . . But to this little actress—for little she is, and yet not insignificant in her figure, which, though short, has a certain roundness and *embonpoint* which is very graceful —her voice is harmony itself in level quiet speaking (we had an opportunity of judging this in a few lines she spoke in the way of epilogue like Rosalind), and it has certain little breaks and indescribable tones which in simple archness have a wonderful effect, and I think, without exception (even of Mrs Siddons), she has the most distinct delivery of any actor or actress I ever heard. Her face I could not see owing to the amazing bunch of hair she had pulled over her forehead, but they tell me it is expressive, but not very pretty. Her action is odd, a little *outré*, probably affected for the characters."

Jordan ever played, and it is admitted that no one has ever given the same witchery to the rustic heroine. Some of the critics found fault with her on the score of vulgarity. This accusation, however, could not be brought against her impersonation of *Viola* in "Twelfth Night," in which the mere melody of her voice brought tears to the eyes, while, in the popular comedy, "She would and she would not," her *naïveté* again enchanted the town. *Miss Tomboy* in "The Romp' was another success. Mrs Jordan revelled in such parts as *Miss Tomboy* and *Miss Hoyden* (in "A Trip to Scarborough"). She brought to them her whole treasury of fun. Those who knew her in her prime always maintained that in such parts she never has had any competitor that could in the remotest degree be compared to her. Her comic style was peculiar, and had the decided stamp of genius; it was emphatically natural, but such nature as is rarely seen, and it was the most consummate art. *Miss Hoyden* tickling, which Mrs Jordan in her romping so felicitously practised, was amongst the extremest sallies of a happy nature. Had the effervescence of her familiarity been stronger, it might have offended delicacy, but its joyousness increased the pleasure without ever in the least outraging propriety. The *European Magazine* of 1789 declares, ' that as *Miss Tomboy* she excelled every performer at present on the English stage, and almost equalled Mrs Clive."

The brilliant beginning made by Mrs Jordan on her first night was not followed by continued success. This was from no decline in popular esteem; when she did appear she was received with every demonstration of favour. Her appearances were, however, few and far between. Rapid success is not always so desirable as slow progress, which does not alarm the jealous fears of others as does the greater triumph.

The hitherto established favourites at Drury Lane did not care to have a younger and fresher favourite so near their thrones, and great efforts were made to suppress the dangerous new-comer. It was said that no conspicuous success attended her *début*. Mrs Siddons, whose words were listened to with reverence, mistrusted the wisdom of putting her forward;

she was told that in tragedy she did not rise above mediocrity, and advised to confine herself to characters within her range. These remarks and the unkind criticisms that appeared in the papers were, for a time, depressing, especially as she was given so few chances of ingratiating herself with the public, who were already partial to her. Gradually, however, the management began to awake to her unparalleled excellence in certain plays. The leading comic parts, and those called in stage language "breeches parts," were assigned to her.

Mrs Jordan, being now an established favourite bethought herself of presenting to the public Farquhar's "Constant Couple." The part of *Sir Harry Wildair* had never been approached since Mrs Woffington had succeeded Wilks. More than forty years had passed since the inimitable Peg had strutted her brief hour on the stage, and her name was to most playgoers *merely* a name. Very few living remembered her acting. That the part of the dashing young rake was as well suited to Mrs Jordan as to Peg Woffington would be perhaps saying too much; moreover, it is impossible to institute comparisons between a dead and a living actress. Memory plays strange tricks, and none is more common than the golden hues in which it envelops the idols of our younger days. "Youth," says a contemporary writer, "resembles a Claude Lorraine glass, which imparts to all objects its own beautiful tints; but age is like a magnifying lens, which leaves no defect unseen."

When, in May 1788, Mrs Jordan challenged comparison with the dead actress, she was pretty certain to have a few old gentlemen making the usual grumble as to her inferiority to the great Mrs Woffington. "Egad! sir, she can't hold a candle to her—you should have seen her in the dilemma"—and so on. To those, however, who had no past to remember, the new *Sir Harry* gave unqualified satisfaction. She was charmingly dressed and provokingly at her ease. One of her critics, writing on her assumption of masculine dress, says, "For a female to assume male attire with propriety requires a symmetry of person and perfection of shape ill-suited to the costume worn at the time our heroine flourished. Mrs

Jordan, however, was an exception, as to a careless, easy manner of deportment, she added the most perfect elegance of form, so that, while the actress excited our admiration, we were no less captivated by the woman." The *Morning Herald* of the day applauded her penetration in assuming so often a costume which suited her so perfectly. As an instance of the actress's perfect at-homeness in her male character, at the end of the performance she stepped before the curtain and gave out the play for the next night. This, says her faithful chronicler, took the audience by surprise, but they applauded vociferously.

Another success was *Rosalind* in "As You Like It," also *Nell* in "The Devil to Pay," which she acted after *Rosalind*. In both parts she again challenged comparison with the Woffington, and again (there being only a few old grumblers left who remembered the merits of the departed actress) she came out triumphant. Having finished her first season victoriously, Mrs Jordan took her holiday amongst her former friends.

MRS JORDAN AS *ROSALIND* IN "AS YOU LIKE IT."
[*From Painting by Satchwell.*

There is an amusing account of her visit to her old manager, Tate Wilkinson. The company were at Leeds when Mrs Jordan with her mother and sister arrived, and after dinner went to the theatre. By a singular chance, it so happened that it was the benefit of Mrs Robinson, the lady who had talked of the *treasure coming back* on the manager's hands, and, much to Mrs Francis's pleasure, the house was a poor one. Mrs Jordan was speedily recognised, and, it would seem, made no effort to conceal herself, feeling, we are told, "an honest joy in the buzz that turned every eye to the balcony box." During the farce, she came behind the scenes, making her compliments very gracefully to her former associates of the green-room. Having acquitted herself of this politeness, she walked forward to the very edge of the wing, and, leaning with a fashionable air upon her sister's arm, listened to poor Mrs Robinson struggling with "the Widow Brady" (a part made famous by her own acting), while the attention of the audience was entirely diverted to the London star. One can imagine the scene—the mortification of Mrs Robinson, and the triumph of Mrs Jordan and her family. To complete their satisfaction, Mrs Jordan was solicited to appear, if only for one night, which she consented to do, appearing in "The Romp" and "Country Girl," and so great was the effect of her fashionable reputation that every place was taken long before the play began, and seven rows of the pit had to be laid into boxes.

Each part she undertook seems to have added to her reputation as an actress. In "The Spoiled Child" she scored an immense success, playing *Little Pickle* in the most delightful manner. There was a rumour, without any certainty, that she had written this popular farce which held the stage for many years, the part of *Old Pickle* being a favourite with such actors as Mathews, Liston and Elliston. "The Spoiled Child" was ascribed to various people—Isaac Bickerstaff, Mr Ford.[1] Cumberland founded his opinion that it was written by Mrs Jordan, on certain hints in the prologue. It was while acting *Little Pickle* in 1788 at Cheltenham[2] that Mrs Jordan, unfortunately for herself, attracted the attention

[1] Mr Ford was the son of Sir Richard Ford, chief magistrate at Bow Street, in succession to Sir John Fielding.

[2] On this occasion, she played before the King and Queen. She secured the favour of their majesties, and was presented by the manager of the theatre with an elegant medallion locket richly set on one side with fine pearls, in the centre of which was a beautiful enamel of the Comic Muse from the painting by Sir Joshua Reynolds. On the reverse, there was an oval in blue enamel and fine brilliants, and in the centre an inscription in gold letters, "Presented to Mrs Jordan Thalia's sweetest child, September 11, 1788." Glasgow and Edinburgh paid her similar compliments.

of the Duke of Clarence: the young prince, who had just landed from his ship, being, like all sailors, ready to fall in love with the first woman he saw. There is little doubt she would never have listened to him had Mr Ford, when his father died, fulfilled his promise of marrying her.[1] This he was reluctant to do, and Mrs Jordan's relations with the Duke of Clarence became a matter of history.

At Richmond, where she lived, Mrs Jordan had been upon as Mr Ford's wife, the marriage not to be acknowledged until after his father's death. In this supposition she was received at houses of unimpeachable morality, her supposed husband always accompanying her. Mrs Inchbald talks of Mrs Ford warbling ballads at Lady Lunn's. "Do you know," writes Horace Walpole to Miss Berry, "that Mrs Jordan is acknowledged to be Mrs Ford," but, later, Miss Berry writes to a friend, "Mrs Jordan, whom Mr Ford had declared his wife and presented as such to some ladies at Richmond, has resumed her former name, and is said to be much at a *Princepal Villa* at Petersham."

Horace Walpole, in his usual gossiping fashion, has a good deal to say about the new scandal in his letters to his correspondents. Writing to Sir Horace Mann in 1789, he chronicles:—

"The Duke of Clarence has taken Mr Hobart's house at Richmond point blank over against Mr Cambridge's, which will make the good woman of that mansion cross herself piously and stretch the throat of the blatant beast at Sudbrook (Lady Greenwich) and of all the other pious matrons *à la ronde*, for his Royal Highness, to divert some loneliness, has brought with him Mrs Jordan, who, being still more averse to solitude, declares that any tempter would make even Paradise more agreeable than a constant *tête-à-tête*." Mrs Jordan was at this time playing at the Richmond Theatre, which has "raised its character immensely," writes Walpole—"Jews and Gentiles throng it. I have not been there, for, though I think *her* perfection in her walk, I could not sit through a *whole* play ill

[1] A few years later, Mr Ford married Miss Booth.

performed." During this engagement, Mrs Jordan's usual prudence seems to have deserted her. On one occasion there appeared at the bottom of the play-bill an announcement that Mrs Jordan could not fill her part, as it was the Duke of Clarence's birthday, and she had to do the honours to the Prince of Orange who was to dine with him. Such a lack of judgment and delicacy was an affront to even a suburban audience, and must have accentuated the cantankerous clack of the gossips of Richmond and Twickenham Green. From this or some other cause, the Duke of Clarence was disgusted with living in the middle of a village with "nothing but a green apron to the river," and where he and his fair companion were marks for the scandalmongers; he, therefore, moved his establishment to the more retired and leafy Roehampton, then an altogether secluded neighbourhood. Walpole bears testimony to the sailor Duke's business-like habits which made him extremely unpopular. "He pays his bills regularly *himself*, locks his door every night, so that his servants may not remain out late, and drinks only a few glasses of wine. The connection between Mrs Jordan and the Duke caused a feeling of irritation which was kept up by the flood of pamphlets and paragraphs that were issued daily.[1] In the last century, the Press allowed itself a licence that would not be tolerated now; no one was safe from the most scurrilous attacks and the most outrageous personal remarks. Mrs Jordan's professional character was violently assailed. She was accused of absenting herself from the theatre on the nights when her name was in the bill in order that she might amuse herself elsewhere. Mrs Jordan was not the one to sit down under unmerited censure. She published a letter in the morning paper, denying these allegations. When she appeared the next night as

[1] Mr Ford contributed the following extraordinary letter which appeared in the *Morning Herald*:—"Lest any insinuation should be circulated to the prejudice of Mrs Jordan in respect to her having behaved improperly to her children in regard to pecuniary matters, I hereby declare that her conduct in that particular has been as laudable, generous and as like a fond mother as it was possible to be. She has indeed given up for their use every sixpence she has been able to save from her theatrical profits. She has also engaged herself to allow them £550 a-year, and at the same time has settled £50 a-year on her sister.

"RICHARD FORD."

*Roxalana* in "The Sultan," she was received with displeasure, and it was evident that a decided party against her had been organised. With considerable courage, she at once advanced to the footlights and, confronting her enemies, addressed them in that clear, melodious voice which could never be beard witnout giving pleasure:—

"Ladies and Gentlemen,—I should conceive myself utterly unworthy of your favour if the slightest mark of public disapprobation did not effect me very sensibly. Since I have had the honour and the happiness to strive here to please you, it has been my constant endeavour, by unremitting assiduity, to merit your approbation. I beg leave to assure you, upon my honour, that I have never absented myself one minute from the duties of my profession but from real indisposition. Thus having invariably acted, I do consider myself under the public protection."

It was agreed by all that nothing could have been better than her manner of delivering this spirited and yet humble address. "The little hardship that sat upon her brow and like a cloud kept back the comic smile that but waited their cheer to break forth into graceful obeisance." All was in perfect taste and completely captivated her audience, and so the matter ended.

In the green-room, however, it was still whispered that Mrs Jordan gave herself royal airs. Coming to rehearsal one morning, she was so *distraite* and indifferent that Wroughton, then acting manager, remarked drily, "Why, Mrs Jordan, you are grand, quite the duchess again this morning." "Very likely," was the reply, "for you are not the first person who has this very day *condescended* to honour me ironically with the title." And then she proceeded to recount, for the amusement of her hearers, how that morning, having occasion to discharge her Irish cook for impertinence, the woman had banged a shilling on the table, exclaiming, "Arrah, now, honey, with this thirteener[1] won't I sit in the gallery and won't *your royal grace* give me curtsey, and won't I give your royal highness a howl and a hiss into the bargain." Her biographer, in his accommodating fashion, admires the

[1] The Irish shilling was thirteen pence.

good-humour of the lady in thus relating the low impertinence of her servant, but it would appear to most people that in this case good-humour was another name for callous indifference as to her position. She gave a further proof of this when, at her benefit in 1791, she chose Fletcher's humorous Lieutenant, evidently for the reason that the heroine's situation resembled her own. To point this still more, in the epilogue written by Bunbury and spoken by Mrs Jordan, these curious lines occur:—

> "The manager his want of sense evinces
> To pitch on *Hoydens* for the love of princes."

During the years that had elapsed since Mrs Jordan's first appearance at Drury Lane, great changes had taken place in this time-honoured theatre, where Garrick and Woffington, Cibber and Clive had played to crowded houses. With the death of Garrick, the fortunes of Drury Lane seem to have changed. In 1776, Sheridan became the proprietor, and his management did not take the same steady course as did Garrick's. Both men were geniuses, but the one bound down the erratic flights of his Pegasus to one steady purpose, the other allowed his steed to caracole in every possible direction—addressing the House of Commons, regulating everybody's business but his own, writing brilliant plays, sitting up half the night with men of fashion, enjoying the friendship of the Prince of Wales, and altogether neglecting his own affairs. Truly a typical Irishman, and mark the conclusion; where Garrick amassed a considerable fortune, Sheridan accumulated nothing but debt, finally sealing his ruin by undertaking to build a National Theatre from the ruins of Drury Lane. The enormous building he erected was not so popular as the old house built by Wren and restored by the brothers Adam, and which to many playgoers was endeared by old associations.

The National Theatre, however, started with a strong company. Kemble and Mrs Siddons played Shakespearian characters, Mrs Jordan light comedy and Miss Farren the fine ladies. A series of indifferent plays, however, and the introduction of pantomimes alienated a critical audience, and a succession of failures put the public in bad humour. Manager succeeded manager without producing any salutary change in the financial condition of the theatre. Large sums of money were squandered upon grand spectacular pieces, while the salaries of the actors were left unpaid. Through all these troubles and vicissitudes, Mrs Jordan's popularity remained unchanged. Where others failed to draw, the house was always crowded when her name was in the bill. Some of this favour was no doubt due to her peculiar position, and the curiosity of the public to see the royal favourite. There was no doubt that it was this feeling that induced the visit of the long-absent royalties to Drury Lane, a theatre they had deserted in consequence of Sheridan being a warm partisan of the Prince.[1] On the 15th May 1800, however, their Majesties with the Royal Princesses signified their intention of honouring Drury Lane by being present at "She Would and She Would Not," in which Mrs Jordan played Hypolita. The event of the evening is historical. The King, but lately recovered from one of his attacks, had just entered the box and was bowing with his usual bland courtesy to the company, when a maniac fired straight at him from the pit. His aim, happily, missed, but the consternation was terrible. After an interval of uproar and excitement, the King, who was quite cool (and later took his usual sleep between the acts), requested that order might be restored and the play allowed to go on; but the audience, although they resumed their seats, could not calm down. As each actor came on he was interrupted by loud cries for the assassin, whom the people wanted to have brought on the stage. There was no calming them until Mrs Jordan came forward and assured them that he was properly secured and well guarded. Her voice acted like a charm, and the play was allowed to proceed, but, as may be imagined, was very little attended to.

The share Mrs Jordan had taken on this occasion, and her

[1] To mark their disapproval of Sheridan, the King and Queen went constantly to the Haymarket during the period the Drury Lane Company migrated to that house to allow of the National Theatre being rebuilt by Holland.

evident popularity, roused an intense feeling of jealousy. Unlike Miss Farren, who cautiously steered her way without any green-room squabbles, the more open-hearted Mrs Jordan had enemies by the score. The situation between her and Mrs Siddons became especially strained, and as the Kembles were a large faction to contend against, Mrs Jordan began to think seriously of giving in her resignation. The manager of Covent Garden, hearing of this likelihood, offered her her own terms and *carte blanche* as to benefits: but Sheridan, getting alarmed at losing such an attraction, promised to redress all her grievances, and closed with her for thirty guineas a-week.

Tate Wilkinson, when he heard of this, remarked that "the Jordan at making a bargain was the cunningest devil of us all." If, however, she made money, she worked hard enough to deserve it. She never shirked her regular duty, playing on an average three nights in the week, and always to full houses.

Her engagement at Drury Lane had lasted for more than twenty years, with only occasional breaks, when in 1809 it came to a sudden conclusion on the 24th February, when the theatre was utterly consumed by fire. Only five months previous its great rival, Covent Garden, had met a similar fate to that which now befell the *chef-d'œuvre* of Holland. The fire commenced in what was called the coffee-room, on the first story in the front next Brydges Street, out of which the communication was direct with the first circle of the boxes, the woodwork of these feeding the ever-increasing body of fire. The iron curtain, upon which so much stress had been laid by Miss Farren[1] in her address to the audience on the opening night of the theatre, was powerless to keep off the flames, as it would not drop of itself; and when the fire seized upon the stage, with its mass of combustible matter, the scene became appalling. Soon all London turned out to see the sight, and all the approaches to the theatre were blocked by the multitude. The news reached Mr Sheridan when he was at the House of Commons, the windows of which were lit up by the reflection in the sky of the destruction

[1] See Memoir of Miss Farren, First Series.

going on across the water. It was proposed by Lord Temple that the House should adjourn as a fitting mark of sympathy with so distinguished a member as the manager of Drury Lane. Mr Sheridan, who was much affected by the kindness, said in a low voice that he could not consider the misfortune of such magnitude as to interrupt the business of the assembly. He hurried away with some friends to the scene of the disaster. His agony of mind was painful to witness, although he tried to show firmness and constantly expressed his thankfulness that no lives were sacrificed.

The actors, however, suffered considerable loss. Mrs Jordan was one of the greatest sufferers, she keeping for convenience much of her very handsome wardrobe at the theatre. Her jewels, it was said, were saved. This event, however, hastened her determination to retire from the stage. This step she took principally in accordance with the wish of the Duke, who disliked her subjecting herself to the gross impertinence of the Press. She did not, however, take any farewell of the public, her last appearance being at the Opera House, where she acted "The Country Girl" for the benefit of those who had suffered from the fire.

During the twenty years of her professional career, Mrs Jordan's income had never been under four or five thousand a year, and her savings were said to be over a hundred thousand pounds. Her relations, however, made heavy inroads upon her earnings. They were all her annuitants. As she wrote to an intimate friend in 1811, when troubles were beginning to close round her, "My professional success through life has indeed been most extraordinary, and consequently attended with great emolument, but from my first starting at the early age of fourteen, I have always had a large family to support. My mother was a duty, but on my brothers and sisters I have lavished more than can be supposed."

In addition to her family claims, Mrs Jordan was generous to those of her profession who had not experienced the same good fortune as she enjoyed; while to the poor she was a benefactress—in this resembling Peg Woffington.

An interesting anecdote is that of the Methodist preacher

who was an unseen witness of an interview between Mrs Jordan and one of the recipients of her charity, a poor washer-woman whose husband the actress had saved from being sent to prison. This was on a visit to Chester, where she was playing nightly at the theatre. In one of her morning walks she was overtaken by rain and took shelter under an arch-way, where the woman found her and poured forth her gratitude to her benefactress. When the touching scene was over, a thin, ascetic-looking clergyman came forward, and, tendering his hand, said with a deep-drawn sigh,—

"Lady, forgive the freedom of a total stranger, but would to God all the world were like thee."

The actress, at once seized the humour of the situation, and with a backward movement from the preacher, said, with a stifled laugh,—

"No, sir, I will not shake hands with you!"

"Why?"

"Because you are a Methodist preacher, and when you hear who I am, you will send me straight to the devil."

"The Lord forbid! I am, as you rightly judge, a minister of the Church which teaches us the grand precept, 'Clothe the naked, feed the hungry, relieve the distressed,' and do you think I can see a sister fulfilling the commands of my Master without offering her the hand of friendship and brotherly love?"

"Well, well, you are a good old soul; but I don't like preachers. And I tell you, you won't shake hands when I tell you who I am."

"I hope I shall."

"No, you won't. I am a player, and you can see my name on the door of the playhouse. It is Jordan. You have heard of Mrs Jordan?"

There was a pause, and then the preacher once more held out his hand.

"The Lord bless thee, whoever thou art, for the goodness of the Lord is unlimited. He has given unto thee a good spirit; and as to thy calling, if thy soul upbraid thee not, the Lord forbid that I should do so."

We gather that the preacher was but a man, and no doubt was won as much by Mrs Jordan's irresistible charm as by her charity, for, the rain still continuing, he offered her his arm and took her back to her hotel under the shelter of his umbrella.

Mrs Jordan's retirement from the stage, which was due to the constant attacks of the Press upon her connection with the Duke of Clarence, lasted only two years, during which time she resided principally at Bushy Park, where she seems to have led a quiet, domestic life.[1] Her friends seem to have considered that there was a similarity between her position and that of Mrs Fitzherbert. They hinted at a sort of left-handed marriage. Ridiculous paragraphs were circulated by these injudicious persons as to Mrs Jordan receiving persons of distinction at Bushy Park, and being placed at the head of the table between the Duke of Clarence and the Prince of Wales. These absurd reports, which had no foundation, had, in all probability, something to say to the breaking up of the establishment. Her return to her professional duties was naturally ascribed to a coolness having arisen between her and her royal admirer. The fact of her removing to a villa at Hammersmith seemed to lend colour to the report. Mrs Jordan, however, strenuously denied that any breach had occurred between her and the Duke. Writing to her old friend, Sir Jonah Barrington, she says, "With regard to the report of my quarrel with the Duke, every day of our past and present must give the lie to it. I will in a day or two avail myself of your kind offer to contradict these odious and

[1] Her retirement was the signal for a *fusillade* in the papers. The *Morning Herald* affecting to mourn the retiring actress as dead, headed its article with an inscription :—

Sacred to the Memory
of
Mrs Dorothy Jordan,
Late of Drury Lane Theatre.
Poor, injured mortality,
snatched
from the fostering embrace of
Public Admiration.

truly wicked reports. I am so ill that I can do nothing myself, but must wait for the assistance of a good and clever friend, who is at present out of the way, and who (if truth is not quite scared out of the world) will endeavour to do away with the ill impressions those reports were meant to make."

Notwithstanding this denial, it was evident to those who possessed her friendship that Mrs Jordan had a mind ill at ease. She had nothing to complain of in her reception by the public, who welcomed their old favourite with enthusiasm. She made her reappearance at Covent Garden in "The Country Girl," and, although the ease of retirement had added to her somewhat corpulent figure, still the matchless Thalia of the stage exerted her potent charm, and the theatre was crowded whenever her name was in the bill.

The papers still continuing to publish all manner of unpleasant reports concerning her and the Duke, Mrs Jordan was advised to cancel her London engagements and to go on a tour instead. This she did; but at Bath, where her first engagement took place, she found the whole town full of the separation between her and her royal admirer. From Bath she went to Dublin, which she had not visited since she ran away from Daly's company. Twenty years had passed since then, and a new generation had grown up who only knew her name by repute, while some of the older folk, who remembered her and her singing of "Melton Oysters," found it difficult to recognise in the large, handsome Mrs Jordan the slender girl who had won popular favour by her youthful vivacity. Her engagement was altogether a failure: scurrilous attacks were made upon her and her friends, while constant impositions from Jones, the manager, with whom she shared the house and got no profit, involved her in perpetual quarrels, until at last, wearied and sick at heart, she shook the dust of her native country from her feet and returned to England, where the final blow fell upon her.

It was when she was acting at Cheltenham to crowded houses that the closing scene in this miserable drama took place. The performance was for the manager's benefit, and

Mrs Jordan, with her usual good nature, had undertaken to play her famous part of *Nell* in "Devil to Pay," Jobson doing the cobbler. Every seat was booked. That very afternoon, the fatal letter came from the Duke of Clarence to inform her that all was over between them, and that their last interview was to take place at Maidenhead, where he would meet her. The unfortunate woman came to the theatre more dead than alive. She, however, struggled through her part until Jobson arrived at the passage where he has to accuse the conjurer of making her "laughing drunk": here the effort to laugh resulted in the overstrung actress bursting into tears. Jobson, with great presence of mind, altered the text, exclaiming, "Why, Nell, the conjurer has made thee crying drunk!"

The scene was got through, Mrs Jordan recovering herself, and the play ended with the usual wild enthusiasm for the popular favourite. After the performance, she was put into a chaise in her stage costume, and travelled all night to keep her appointment next day with the Duke.

What passed at this interview, at which the Prince of Wales was present, is not known, but can be easily imagined. The fact that, by the death of the Duke of York, the Duke of Clarence had advanced a step nearer to the throne, made it a matter of necessity that he should marry, and already several eligible alliances were under discussion. It was therefore necessary that the tie (whether of illegal marriage, as Mrs Jordan's friends asserted, or otherwise) should be severed. The actress's tears and supplications availed nothing, and the parting was final. The Duke never saw her again. Shortly after she removed from Hammersmith to Cadogan Place, from whence she wrote to Boaden, who was, all through her life, a staunch friend.

"CADOGAN PLACE, *Thursday*.

"MY DEAR SIR,—I fear I must have appeared unmindful of your many kindnesses in having been such a length of time without writing to you, but really, till very lately, my spirits have been so depressed that I am sure you will understand my feelings when I say it cost me more pain to write to those interested about me than to a common acquaintance; but the constant kindness and attention I meet with from the Duke, in every respect but personal interviews (and which depends as much on my feelings as his), has, in a great measure, restored me to my former health and spirits. Among many noble traits of goodness, he has lately added one more, that of exonerating me from my promise of *not* returning to my profession. This he has done under the idea of its benefitting my health and adding to my pleasures and comforts, and, though it is very uncertain whether I shall ever avail myself of this kindness, yet you, if you choose, are at liberty to make it known, whether publicly or privately.—Yours ever, etc., etc.,

"DORA JORDAN."

"*P.S.*—I wish I could see you, but it is such a long way for you to come."

A few days later, she again writes to the same friend :—

"ST JAMES'S,
"*Tuesday, 7th December.*"

"MY DEAR SIR,—I lose not a moment in letting you know that the Duke of Clarence has concluded and settled on me and his children the most liberal and generous provision, and I trust everything will sink into oblivion.—Yours ever,

"DORA JORDAN."

The terms of the settlement were,—For the maintenance of the Duke's four daughters, £1500; for a horse and a carriage for their use, £600; for Mrs Jordan's use, £2000; in all, £4100 per annum. It was made a special condition that, if Mrs Jordan returned to the stage, the care of his daughters and the £1500 a-year for their maintenance should revert to His Royal Highness. This statement, and the fact that a legal settlement of a very liberal character was effected, dispose of the insinuations constantly made by Boaden that part of Mrs Jordan's fortune was placed by her at the disposal of the Duke. Both Boaden and Sir Jonah Barrington seem to think there can be no other way of accounting for the sudden collapse of the large sum she had made by her profession. They forget that, like all those who make money easily, Mrs Jordan spent with the left hand what the right had received. Her Irish nature and indifferent training were likely to add to the easy squandering of money, and there were those about her only too ready to help her in such lavish expenditure. One is not surprised to find that difficulties began to gather round her.

To meet the demands made upon her, as well as to find excitement in the profession she loved, Mrs Jordan, in a very few months, resolved to return to the stage. Managers, however, were not so eager to engage her as formerly. No longer a royal favourite, but a discarded mistress, she had the mortification of experiencing that her position had something to say to her success. To this was added the always melancholy advance of years, which, unobserved by her, had stolen many of her greatest charms, had dimmed the lustre of her eyes and deadened the joyous echo of her infectious laugh, while her immense size made such parts as the Country Girl and Miss Hoyden singularly unsuitable. Mr Dyce, who saw her play the part of the heroine in Kenney's new comedy, "Debtor and Creditor," produced at Covent Garden, says her figure was ridiculously unsuited to the part of a young girl, and in consequence the piece ran only a few nights.

Fortunately for Mrs Jordan, the English nation has a tender reverence for bygone favourites. Witness their forbearance towards veteran singers and actors of the present day. This forbearance was extended to Mrs Jordan all the more generously from the indignation that was roused in her behalf by the unseemly and indelicate attacks made by the Press upon her. The audience, to show how much they valued so old a public servant, took every opportunity that afforded personal application to testify to her their sympathy.

The season at Covent Garden being over, Mrs Jordan went on tour, visiting most of the large towns in the provinces with the most extraordinary success. If London had shown her that her day was over, its sentence was reversed by Bath, Bristol, Leeds and York. The financial success of the tour was stated to be £7000. This would seem hardly credible. Her biographer considers it a gross exaggeration, in proof of which assertion he makes a calculation that to acquire such a sum, Mrs Jordan must have acted one hundred and forty nights in one year, which, when a lady is over fifty, would have been, in his opinion, too great a strain.

The strain, however, was a matter of necessity. It would take too long to enter into all the details (given in full by Boaden and her friend Sir Jonah Barrington) of Mrs Jordan's involved affairs. The failure of her son-in-law, Mr Alsop, a Calcutta merchant, precipitated matters, while her own carelessness in giving security for some friend whose name does not transpire, but who let her in for a large sum of money, seems to have completed her ruin. Mrs Jordan was at an end of all her resources when, in 1815, a sudden call was made upon her for £2000. Not having this sum at command, she had to pledge her annuity from the Duke, and, to avoid arrest, escaped to France, meaning to remain there until her affairs could be arranged. Month after month passed, however, and no settlement was made.

Meanwhile Mrs Jordan resided at Boulogne, a place very generally selected by persons who, in the language of the day, were in hiding. She lived a little way out of the town in a suburb called Marquetra, from the fortress close to it. Her residence was a small cottage, neat, clean and very cheerful. She passed as Mrs James, and one of her sons-in-law, Colonel Hawker,[1] was with her, as also her companion, Miss Sketchley. Here Mrs Jordan remained nearly a year, waiting for the recall from her lawyers which never came. On the contrary, there seemed some reason for further precautions and a more secluded residence. We gather this from Mrs Jordan's sudden flight to Paris, and likewise her change of name from James to Johnson. She did not remain in Paris, but went first to

[1] Colonel Hawker was married to one of the Miss Fords.

Versailles and afterwards to St Cloud, where she resided in one of the large, comfortless "hotels" adjoining the palace.

No more desolate dwelling could be imagined. There was no comfort in the large, ill-furnished rooms, and she had no friends to cheer her solitude. The companion, a former governess of her children, whom she had brought with her from England, had returned there to look after the complicated law business. Mrs Jordan spent her day lying on a miserable sofa, eating her heart out in her eager desire for news from England that never came. There is something terrible in this picture of the once matchless Thalia, the idol of the public, the spoiled and petted royal favourite, slowly pining away in her sad, self-inflicted exile. Boaden and her friend Sir Jonah Barrington would have us believe that the poor lady was the victim of a conspiracy; that someone, who is never named, had an object in keeping her away, and that this dark conspirator had the poor lady kept under restraint, not allowing any friends to have access to her, while impressing on her that she was surrounded by spies and enemies who deprived her of the necessaries of life. What the object of this dark conspiracy was we are not informed, but, using one's own common sense, we come to the conclusion that the conspiracy had existence only in the minds of her friendly biographers. The whole story is common enough. Mrs Jordan had contracted debts either for herself or others, and as in her time there was no such thing as sponging out liabilities in a Bankruptcy Court, her person would have been "attached" if she had not run away from her creditors, as was the fashion in the last century.

This is the explanation of the secrecy, the change of name and the flitting from one place to another. There was nothing mysterious, but the closing scenes of the laughter-loving Jordan were inexpressibly sad. She was in a strange country, ill in body and mind and evidently suffering from nervous delusions. The story told of the old friend who found her out goes far to prove that the poor lady was not in her right mind. This person, who had been a confectioner, or sweetmeat provider to the Royal Family, had left England many years before and had settled in Paris. He had known Mrs Jordan well, and was anxious to renew his old friendship and to be of service to her. He was not, however, allowed to see her. He later received a letter from her desiring him to repair at *midnight* to St Cloud, when she spoke to him from a casement window. The interview lasted two hours, during which time she told her friend that she was in actual want,[1] and implored him to return next day and to bring her twenty pounds. It was further arranged that he should help to get her away to England.

He did return in ten days' time, having made all the necessary preparations, but to his dismay he was told she had expired the previous day. The story of her death, as told by her biographer Boaden, is highly dramatic, but it somehow lacks consistency. According to this narrative, which was related to Sir Jonah Barrington by the master of the house —a certain Mr C—— (his name is all through jealously concealed)—Mrs Jordan, from the moment of her arrival, had appeared restlessly anxious for letters from England.

"An interval of some posts elapsed, during which she received no answers to her letters; and her consequent anxiety seemed too great for mortal strength to bear up against. On the morning of her death, this impatient feeling reached its crisis. The words used now by Mr C—— become of the greatest value. 'The agitation was almost fearful; her eyes were now restless, now fixed: her motion rapid and unmeaning: and her whole manner seemed to bespeak the attack of some convulsive paroxysm.' She eagerly requested Mr C—— to go for her *letters*, before the usual hour of delivery. On his return she started up and held out her hand, as if impatient to receive them. He told her, '*there were none.*' 'She stood a moment motionless; looked towards him with a vacant stare: held out her hand again, as if by an involuntary action; instantly withdrew it, and sank back upon the sofa from which she had arisen.

[1] At this time she had with her valuable jewels, and wore on her finger a diamond ring worth £100. These facts give the lie to her destitute condition.

Mr C—— now left the room to send up her attendant, but she had gone out; he, therefore, himself, returned to Mrs Jordan. On approaching her he observed some change in her looks that alarmed him. She spoke not a word, but gazed at him steadfastly. She wept not- no tear flowed. Her face was one moment flushed, another livid. She sighed deeply, and her heart seemed bursting, Mr C—— stood, uncertain what to do; but in a minute, he heard her breath drawn more hardly, and, as it were, sobbingly. He was now thoroughly terrified; he hastily approached the sofa, and, leaning over the unfortunate lady, discovered that those deep-drawn sobs had immediately preceded the moment of Mrs Jordan's dissolution. She was already no more!'"

She was buried in the churchyard of St Cloud, not without some difficulty on account of her profession; this, however, was got over, and nine English gentlemen followed her remains to the grave. For many years no memorial marked the spot where she lay. At length, however, a tablet was put up with a flourishing inscription in Latin. This states her death to have taken place July the 3d 1816—her age, fifty. All contemporary writers, including Boaden, date her birth 1762; consequently, she must have been at the time of her decease fifty-four years of age. There is no doubt that the strange narrative of Mrs Jordan's last moments leaves an unpleasant impression upon the mind of the reader; it, therefore, was not surprising that at the time in which this bygone tragedy occurred it caused a stir and sensation. Ridiculous stories got about, one being that she was not dead, but, with the help of Miss Sketchley and the kindly Mr C——, had managed to escape from the hands of her creditors: some people declared they had seen her in the flesh. One of these was her biographer, Boaden, who spins a lengthy and improbable yarn as to stopping to look into a print shop in Piccadilly. On a sudden, a lady stood by his side. She raised her veil to look at the prints, and his conviction was that she was no other than Mrs Jordan—strangely enough, the conviction was sufficient. His ardent friendship never prompted him to address his departed friend. Mrs Alsop[1] was likewise convinced that she met her mother walking in the Strand. Neither of these witnesses is very credible, and the whole story is marked by flagrant improbability.

The scandal connected with Mrs Jordan's name did not cease with her life. It took seven years to arrange her affairs, all the available assets being sworn as under £300. In 1823 a compromise was offered to the creditors through the public press. Hereupon, a perfect broadside of abuse opened upon the Duke of Clarence. Mr Barton, who had been thirty-six years in the Duke's service, replied with a full statement, exonerating his master from any share in the unfortunate mismanagement of Mrs Jordan's affairs. This brought on a crowd of letters, accusations and a revival of the whole unsavoury story, which should have been decently buried, now that the Duke of Clarence was a married man.[2]

Mrs Jordan's nine children—four daughters and five sons, of which the eldest was created Earl of Munster—were so many thorns in the flesh of their Royal father. The Duke of Wellington said, "They all want to be made dukes and duchesses."[3]

The best of them seems to have been Lord Adolphus Fitz-Clarence. Lady Morgan tells rather a touching incident creditable to the feelings of those concerned. She was dining with Lord Adolphus in 1837 at old St James's Palace. Her host took her into his boudoir. "We were alone, and he showed me a miniature set in brilliants. 'The King?' I said.

[1] Mrs Alsop, who had been known as Miss Jordan, followed her mother's profession for a few years, and, trusting to the kindly feeling of the public, appeared in some of her favourite parts, with, however, but little success. Mr Dyce in his notes says, "I saw her play in Murphy's comedy, and she played it well, singing a song accompanied on the harp by herself. She really possessed considerable talent as an actress. She was downright ugly." Hazlitt says, "She was no more like her mother than I am like Hercules, but she was a nice little woman." Her life and death were alike a tragedy.

[2] That the Duke of Clarence did not marry until 1818, two years after Mrs Jordan's death, is cited by the descendants of that lady as a proof that some sort of legalised tie existed between her and the Duke.

[3] The daughters were all handsome, they lived at Bushy Park, and were received in society as the Duke's daughters; they married well.

'Yes, my father,' said he, taking another picture out of the casket, 'and,' added he, with much emotion, 'this was—my mother.' After a pause I said, 'It is a great likeness as I last saw her.' 'Where was that? In Dublin—on the stage?' 'Yes, in "The Country Girl," the most wondrous representation of life and nature I ever beheld. I also saw her when she was on a visit to Sir Jonah Barrington's. She sent to my father to go and visit her. He did so. She called him the most amiable of managers.'" After a pause he added, "Sir Charles and you will accompany me to Chantrey's to-morrow to see her beautiful monument, which they have refused to admit into St Paul's, although Mrs Woffington's is still expected there."

Boaden cites a very generous letter from Lord Frederick Fitz-Clarence to his mother, when she was in hiding at Boulogne, offering her his quarter's allowance if that would help her in her difficulties.

In Miss Berry's Journal there is an entry (in the year 1839) of a curious conversation she had with Chantrey, who was her neighbour at a dinner-party. "William the Fourth sent for him (Chantrey) soon after his accession and told him he had a commission to give him for a monument to Mrs Jordan. The King desired the sculptor's opinion as to where it should be placed. His Majesty then went into a thousand particulars of her private life always ending each with an encomium that she had been such an excellent mother. He said he knew he had been much blamed for his conduct to her, but that from the time they separated, he had allowed her two thousand a-year, which was regularly paid. The monument in question was executed by Chantrey, and he was paid for it."

There would not be space here to go through Mrs Jordan's successes as an actress. Before, however, concluding this brief *résumé* of her life, we must take a glance at her professional career, and the claims she had to be classed with such actresses as Woffington, Clive and Abington.

It seems to have been agreed upon by all her critics, that Shakespeare was not her forte, neither could she be taken seriously as a tragic actress. Although she had been originally engaged by Smith to take second lead in tragedy to Mrs Siddons, her failure was so marked in any effort she made in that line, that the attempt was abandoned. Her last venture was in the character of *Juliet* in "Romeo and Juliet." This was in 1796, when both her age and increasing corpulence made her singularly unfitted for the part.[1] With strange pertinacity, however, she had fixed her mind upon playing one of Shakespeare's heroines for her own benefit. Her first selection had been *Ophelia*. Kemble, however, had selected Hamlet for his benefit, and would not relinquish the idea. Fierce battles were fought between the two. Mrs Jordan had in the end to give way; she went, however, from Scylla to Charybdis. The absurdity of the child-like, impassioned *Juliet* being represented by a middle-aged, stout woman, was bound to result in a farcical failure. The papers were unmeasured in their condemnation. The *Morning Herald* did not mince its words:—

"When it is recollected that Mrs Jordan was engaged by Mr Smith to play second to Mrs Siddons in tragedy, in consequence of the gentleman's great admiration of her talents in that line, the surprise into which many persons were thrown on seeing her name on the play-bills for *Juliet* will naturally diminish. We confess, however, that neither in conception nor in power is she adequate to the character. When she comes to scenes of impassioned dignity and violent declamation, where the stronger feelings are to be roused, she falls suddenly short and leaves the audience to supply the deficiency."

*Rosalind* and *Viola* were, on the other hand, thoroughly within her powers. She gave to them more of the author's

[1] The best critics have been for years calling attention to the want of the proper representation of this, the most difficult of all the great dramatist's creations. Every actor who has a tolerable share of good looks thinks himself qualified by that fact alone to play Romeo; and as for Juliet—she occasionally dispenses with even the qualification of good looks. It is not much of a wonder that the persons who so frequently attempt the representation do not succeed in giving us any idea of the Romeo and Juliet as they were drawn by Shakespeare's warmest and most delicate pencil, and the tender, generous enthusiasm which actuates them is widely different from the sentimental affectation of youthful love often presented by ladies and gentlemen whose years are alone inimical to any due representation.

conception than any actress has ever done, to quote the lines of "Peter Pindar":—

> "Had Shakespeare's self at Drury been
> While Jordan played each varied scene,
> He would have started from his seat
> And cried—'That's Rosalind complete.'"

Sir Joshua Reynolds, who had a sort of fatherly affection for a being, who, like the Jordan, ran upon the stage as a playground and laughed from sincere wildness of delight, talks of "her exquisite and tender *Viola*, where she combines feeling with sportive effect." When asked to decide between her and Mrs Abington, Sir Joshua declared that Mrs Jordan vastly exceeded everything he had ever seen, and really *was* what others affected to be. Genest says her *Rosalind*, *Viola* and *Lady Contess* will never be excelled.

Another wonderful impersonation was *Nell* in "The Devil to Pay." Here again she challenged competition with two departed actresses—Clive and Woffington—and once more the few who still remembered their early favourites grumbled. "We old folks," said Horace Walpole, "are apt to be prejudiced in favour of our first impressions." The senile grumblings of old age are, however, little regarded on any subject, and in the case of Mrs Jordan's *Nell*, we may be sure that her impersonation fully satisfied the play-goers of her own time. Miss Berry who saw her play it with Bannister as "Jobson," describes her performance as *incomparable*, but adds that in "The Wonder" she

MRS JORDAN AS *NELL* IN "THE DEVIL TO PAY," *after Romney.*

brought out her *oyster woman* notes too often, 'which destroys all the effect of her otherwise captivating voice."

The astonishing *naïveté* with which she delivered the words in "The Country Girl"—"Ay, but if he loves me, why should he miss?" never failed to charm her hearers, as also her clandestine composition of her letter to her lover, which was beyond all praise. In "The Romp" she displayed an astonishing power of holding her audience and commanding their applause. One of her best performances was the *Hoyden* in "The Trip to Scarborough:" it was admirably suited to her in every way. Her rusticity did not appear assumed, her vulgarity was not affected; she was for the time a young hoyden. Her awkward air when she first entered, the use she made of the piece of bread and butter, the silent show of surly discontent, her adjusting the dress of the nurse and refusal to be locked up, her dividing the cake and final approach to Lord Foppington,—these have never been equalled.

Severe critics denied that Mrs Jordan had actual beauty. She possessed, however, attractions which are superior to mere personal charms. Her countenance was full of expression and animated variety, her laugh was tinged with the most exquisite humour, exciting at once merriment and delight; her attitudes were expressive, her pronunciation was correct, and she represented in every way

> "Those nameless graces which no methods teach,
> And which a master hand alone can reach."

Hazlitt calls her a child of Nature, whose voice was a cordial to the heart, to hear whose laugh was nectar, whose talk was far above singing, and whose singing was like the twanging of Cupid's bow. Her person, he adds, was large, soft and generous like her heart. Her voice, that rare gift, says Leigh Hunt, had an extraordinary mellowness that delighted the ear with its peculiar fulness, and possessed a certain emphasis that appeared the earnest of perfect conviction. Lamb gives her the highest praise. Haydon speaks of her as touching and fascinating. Byron declared she was superb. Mathews talks of her as an extraordinary and exquisite being, distinct from any other being in the world as she was superior to all her contemporaries in her particular line.

Kemble said she was irresistible. "It may seem ridiculous," he once remarked to Boaden, "but I could have taken her in my arms and cherished her, though it was in the open street, without blushing." Such an expression from the frigid lips of Kemble was a compliment that spoke volumes in her praise. Lord William Lennox, who saw her when he was a lad, retained a lively recollection of her silver-toned voice, her unsophisticated manner, her tenderness and her exuberant spirits. Of her it was truly said:—

> "Her smile was by a thousand smiles repaid,
> Her art was Nature, governed by thy laws.
> To act of good full oft she bent her aid;
> Her talents gained her thus, with hands, the heart's applause."

The portraits of Mrs Jordan are numerous. She was painted as "The Country Girl," by Romney[1] (the original being now in the possession of the present Earl of Munster), and as *Nell*, in "The Devil to Pay"; by Hoppner as *Thalia* and as *Hyppolita*; by Steeden as *Sir Harry Wildair*; as *Beatrice* in a picture by Friseli with Mrs Siddons as *Hero*. It is also said that Romney painted her dancing in his picture of "Mirth."

[1] This picture was painted for the Duke of Clarence, and it hung in the dining-room at Bushy Park.

# LADY ANNE AND LADY GERTRUDE FITZPATRICK,

## DAUGHTERS TO JOHN, SECOND EARL OF UPPER OSSORY.

(1770-18—)

VISITORS to the exhibitions of old Masters, and frequenters of print-shops, are acquainted with Sir Joshua's charming portrait of the little girl Collina[1] as a mountaineer, with her skirt tucked up, and her large, wondering eyes drinking in the fresh air of the hills. The original of Collina was Lady Gertrude Fitzpatrick, and Lady Anne, her elder by four years, sat for another charming child-portrait. These children were the daughters of John, Earl of Ossory of the "benignant smile,"[2] while their mother is best known to this generation as the recipient of some of Horace Walpole's choicest letters. She was Anne Liddell, daughter to Lord Ravensworth, and when Walpole first knew her, she was Duchess of Grafton. Writing to his well loved Horace Mann, he makes a panegyric of her charms—"she is a passion of mine: she is my sovereign lady and 'my duchess.'" When she goes abroad he writes again to impress upon his friend, who was Minister at Florence, that he must pay her every attention, "for she is one of our first great ladies, and one of the finest women you ever saw; the Duke goes with her: a man of strict honour, and does not want sense nor good breeding, but is not particularly familiar nor particularly good-humoured nor at all particularly generous." On another occasion, Walpole, who was fitful in his opinions, described the Duke of Grafton as having an inherent want of principle, or, what came to

[1] "Collina" was begun in 1779 when Sir Joshua Reynolds was on a visit to Lord Ossory at Farming Woods, it was completed in 1780 and engraved 1782.

[2] "Ossory's benignant smile
Diffuses good-humour round our isle."

LADY ANNE FITZPATRICK AS THE "GIRL WITH THE BUNCH OF GRAPES."

*After Sir Joshua Reynolds—1775.*

the same thing, inattention, indolence and indifference to the interests of the country. "He is one of the most persuasive and pathetic speakers in the House of Lords; he delivers his speeches like a gentleman and a scholar, his language is well chosen and correct, while his judgment in arranging his matter is not excelled or even equalled by anyone. Slight circumstances, such as a change of seat, are apt to disconcert him; his temper is irascible and easily roused, especially by any coarse expression from his antagonists."

From a domestic point of view, the Duke of Grafton was perhaps not worse than the men of his time, but he flaunted his infidelities in a most outrageous fashion: his attentions to a St Giles's beauty, called Nancy Parsons, were carried so far as to escort her through the Houses of Parliament. His Duchess, who was high-spirited as well as beautiful, resented this public outrage, and revenged herself by encouraging the attentions of Lord Ossory. These attentions soon became so marked as to be talked of over teacups with much shaking of heads and hypocritical whisperings, which whisperings ended in the usual way. There was a scandal and a trial. The Duchess descended from her high estate, and her story was the common talk of the servants' hall.

That his sovereign lady should have climbed down the social ladder in this sorry fashion was a shock to her faithful admirer, Walpole. He had a fine sense of propriety, and drew the line at *divorcées*. He recovered his respect and regard, however, when, the day after the divorce was pronounced, she married Lord Ossory.[1] It is remarkable that he announces the

[1] The original name of the Earls of Ossorys was Mac-gill Patrick, softened into the more euphonious Fitzpatrick. According to Sir Bernard Burke, the Mac-gill Patricks belonged to the "ancient monarchy of Ireland." In later times, they were faithful adherents of the unfortunate House of Stuart, and suffered for their fidelity during the usurpation of Cromwell, and under the Act of Attainder, 1689. One of the family, however, was wiser in his generation. Richard Fitzpatrick fought under William the Third's standard, and in reward for his services received, after the battle of Aughrim, large grants of land—especially in the Queen's County—which had been the property of an adherent of James the Second, Edward Morris. Richard Fitzpatrick was also elevated to the peerage, with the title of Baron Gowran; his son John was advanced to be Earl of Upper Ossory. He married Lady Evelyn Leveson Gower, daughter to Earl Gower and sister to the first Earl of Stafford, and had two sons—John of the benignant smile who married Anne Liddell and was the father of "Collina," and Richard, the Secretary for War and Privy Councillor.

marriage to George Montagu without a word of comment. "The Duchess of Grafton is actually Lady Ossory." Not a jest, not a sneer, not an ill-natured story. Neither did he approach his divinity, now that she was reinstated on the social platform; he waited until she took the initiative and wrote to him, inviting him to Ampthill, Lord Ossory's seat in Bedfordshire. His answer is a triumph of *finesse*, for we must all acknowledge that to congratulate a lady in Lady Ossory's position on her second marriage was a difficult task. See how our Horace extricates himself from all entanglement:—

"1769.—You cannot imagine how pleased I shall be to be witness of your happiness, which undoubtedly does not surprise me. I have for some time known the goodness and sense of Lord Ossory, and your ladyship must be very partial to him indeed before I shall think your affection ill-placed."

From this time, a close intimacy existed between the witty and vivacious Horace and both husband and wife, a friendship which has given us the long and delightful correspondence which fills two volumes of his printed works, and which covers a space of twenty years. In this collection we have the tone of the day from a partaker in the frolics. Walpole photographs society with a light and brilliant touch. He is bright, sparkling, witty and serious by turns; he retails, for the amusement of his correspondents, every detail of the world he lives amongst, collects all the *on dits* of society, lavishes his most caustic sayings, and finishes the whole picture with a *verve* and lightness truly delightful. It seems somewhat of a pity that Lord Orford did not preserve Lady Ossory's replies to these letters. She was a woman of high endowments, with a lively imagination, quick discernment and a ready wit. Her letters would have been worth reading, for her style, we are told, was easy and negligent, perhaps intentionally calculated rather to elicit answers than to convey much information, or to express any decided opinion upon any subject.

There is one remarkable feature in this correspondence, a

feature which is likewise observable in the correspondence between Walpole and the favourites of his old age (Mary and Agnes Berry), that while the letters preserve a formality of address which no one nowadays would use to a friend, they contain certain allusions and anecdotes which would never be related to a lady in the present day. We must, however, remember that plain speaking was a marked feature of the eighteenth century, and that our grandmothers did not object to a doubtful story or a coarse joke.[1] This wonderful correspondence runs into over sixty letters, while to her husband (for whom he entertained a warm friendship) Walpole wrote double that number. To him, however, he wrote of politics, war's alarms and Cabinet councils, while to her ladyship he was a news purveyor and fashion-plate, telling her of Lady Powis's new damask, or "that certain invisible machines that one heard of a year or two ago, and which are said to be constructed of cork, are to be worn somewhere or other behind or before in emulation of the Duchess of Devonshire's condition." This is very amusing, but not very dignified; purveyors of news, however, cannot be too particular as to the quality of their contributions. His mention of a visit paid to him by Lord March, afterwards Duke of Queensberry, who was accompanied by La Rena, a celebrated opera dancer, would seem to be in questionable taste.

There is delightful reading in the brilliant *coup d'œil* he gives us of fashionable life in London. Nobody has ever touched such chronicles with so light a pen. So vivid is the portraiture that we who read feel as if we too had known these Lady Bettys and the Lord Georges who figure in his pages. We hear the ripple of their laughter, the sound of

[1] No better instance can be cited of the extraordinary frankness that prevailed in conversation than the anecdote related of Mrs Montagu of blue-stocking celebrity. On one occasion, when Charles Fox was visiting her, she exclaimed, in the heat of a warm dispute upon some question, that she did not care three skips of a l—se for his opinion, upon which Fox made the following witty impromptu,—

"Says Montagu to me, and in her own house,
I do not care for you three skips of a l—se,
I forgive it—for women, however well-bred,
Will still talk of that which runs in their head."

their voices, the *frou-frou* of their brocaded skirts as they go up and down the grand staircases, flirting their fans and ogling the macaronis. They were a terribly wicked set, men and women alike, but there was something grand about them for all their wickedness: and, after all, the world is not much better nowadays, only *we* do not flaunt our sins as they did. Walpole went here, there, everywhere, picking up his bits of news, with which he filled his letters to his different correspondents. "I was last night at the French Ambassador's, where the house was all arbours and bowers of roses, and where the heat reminded me of Calcutta, where so many English were stewed to death." At another fashionable assembly he saw the new French quadrille danced, and before going to bed writes to his sovereign lady a full account of this new dance.

"The quadrille was very pretty. Mrs Damer, Lady Sefton, Lady Melbourne and the Princess Czartoriski were in blue satin with blonde, and collets montés à la reine Elizabeth. Lord R. Spencer, Mr Fitzpatrick, Lord Carlisle, and I forget whom, in like dresses with red sashes, black hats with diamond loops and a few feathers; after which, Mrs Hobart, all in gauze and spangles, like a spangle pudding, a Miss—I forget—Lord Edward Bentinck and a Mr Corbet danced a *pas-de-quatre*, in which Mrs Hobart performed admirably. Of all the pretty creatures," he adds, "was Mrs Bunbury, one of Goldsmith's Hornecks."

Walpole's account of his daily life is worth reading, from the light it throws upon the ways of society a hundred and fifty years ago, when a man of fashion had to play so many parts. His nephew, Lord Orford's son, was dying at this time, and his affairs were in the utmost confusion.

"In the midst of this prospect must I keep up the tone of the world, go shepherdising with macaronis, sit up to loo with my Lady Hertford, be witness to Miss Pelham's orgies, dine at villas and give dinners at my own. Consultations of physicians, letters to Lady Orford, decent visit to my Court, sup at Lady Powis's on Wednesday, drink tea with all the fashionable world at Mr Fitzroy's farm on Thursday, blown by a north wind into the house, and whisk back to Lady Hertford's. This morning to my brother's to hear of new bills, away into my chaise and to Strawberry Hill, where come two Frenchmen to dinner. On Monday a man to sell me two acres, immensely dear. (To Philip, his valet: 'I cannot help it; you must go and put him off. I have not a minute to spare. I will be back to-morrow night to meet the lawyer.') Margaret, his housekeeper, comes in. 'Sir, Lady Bingham desires you will dine with her on Monday at Hampton Court.' 'I cannot!' 'Sir, Captain What-d'ye-call-him has sent twice for a ticket to see the house.' 'Don't plague me about tickets!' 'Sir, a servant from Isleworth has brought this parcel.' 'What the deuce is in it?' Only a printer's proposal for writing the lives of all British writers, and a letter to tell me that I would do it better than anybody else; but as I may not have the time, Dr Berkenhout proposes to do it, and will conclude the bargain if I will be so good as to write it first and send it to him and give him advice and point out materials and provide him with anecdotes. My dear madam, what if you should send him this letter as a specimen of my style? Alas! alas! I have already lost my lilac tide."

This is a good specimen of Walpole's most sprightly manner, and some of the touches are full of spirit.

Another very amusing letter contains a description of a visit to Nuneham, the residence of Lord Harcourt, where his pleasure was damped by the constant presence of a certain Sir William Lee with his wife and a prim miss, whose thin lips were "well stuffed into her nostrils." This trio are presented to us with a few graphic touches which make us feel as if we had known these wet blankets.

"They sat bolt upright, like macaws on their perches in a menagerie, and scarce said so much. I wanted to bid them call a coach. The morning and the evening was the first day, and the morning and the evening was the second day, and still they were just in their places."

Walpole's extraordinary faculty of identifying himself with every subject that interested his friend comes well to the front in these letters. He knows all that goes on at Ampthill, Lord Ossory's seat, and gives his correspondents little bits of its chronological history. Ampthill belonged to Elizabeth, Duchess of Exeter, sister to our Henry IV.; her second husband, Sir John Cornwall, Lord Fanhope, died there. "Their portraits," he adds, "in painted glass, were in the church, but I daresay I have told you all this before, *et que voilà de ma radoterie* it is a proof I dote on."

His letters photograph for us the family circle there, each personage being quite distinct (this being a peculiar feature of his graphic style). We have Ossory himself, amiable, benignant, "diffusing good-humour all around;" his countess lovely, with a certain air of a "*precieuse*," and her "maids of honour," as he calls the three beautiful Miss Vernons,[1] in whose praise he wrote the verses entitled "The Graces." He was very much taken with this charming trio, and suggests to Lady Ossory that Sir Joshua should paint an allegorical picture of them after the manner of Rubens. "You must hold Lady Anne on your lap. Our lord, like Mercury, introduces the three Vernons; and with so much truth, you could not want allegory, which I do not love." The Lady Anne mentioned here was the baby daughter of his friends, and two years later, the little Lady Gertrude made her appearance. The two children seem to have been singularly attractive, quaint, large-eyed little creatures, with that delicious baby roundness of limb so admirably portrayed by Sir Joshua. A dear little pair were Anne and Gertrude, and their confiding ways would have stolen into the heart of a misanthrope, which Walpole was not. He was genuinely fond of children, a good trait in his character. Unmarried himself, he had none of that cynicism affected by those who sneer

[1] Daughters and co-heirs of Richard Vernon of Hilton, by his wife, Lady Evelyn Fitzpatrick, widow of John, late Earl of Upper Ossory. The Miss Vernons were, therefore, half-sisters to the second Earl of Upper Ossory. The eldest married George, Earl of Warwick, in 1776. The second died young. The third, Caroline Maria, married, in 1798, Richard Percy Smith of Cheam, Surrey, who took the name of Vernon. His son, Robert Vernon, was created Baron Lyveden. Another charming trio of sisters formed part of the Ampthill circle. There were the Miss Fitzpatricks, cousins of the Earl, also his sisters, the beautiful Lady Louisa Fitzpatrick, who married William, first Marquis of Lansdowne, and Mary, Lady Holland.

LADY GERTRUDE FITZ-PATRICK AS "COLLINA, THE LITTLE MOUNTAINEER."

*After Sir Joshua Reynolds, 1779.*
*From the Original Picture.*

at blessings they do not possess. One can make a pretty picture in imagination of the old courtier with his friends' children at his knee, a thin varnish of sentiment overlaying his world-smitten soul, for surely there was never a more thorough worldling than this same Walpole, and yet with something like a heart, or what did service for such.

Lady Anne, although not such a pretty child as her sister, seems to have been Walpole's favourite. Poor little Lady Gertrude[1] incurred his displeasure, and probably that of her own parents, by coming into the world in place of the brother who, according to Walpole's ideas, should have succeeded Lady Anne. "I own I am vexed– I am disappointed," he writes, "but when Madame de Trop ceases to be the youngest of your race, I daresay I shall love her, especially when Lady Anne begins to love her less than her brother; but remember, a brother is the *sine quâ non* of my reconciliation."

There is an ill-humoured tone in his reply to the mother's description of Madame de Trop's lovely eyes and baptismal name. "I like the blue eyes, madam, better than the denomination of Lady Gertrude Fitzpatrick, which, respectable as it is, is very harsh and rough sounding. Pray let her change it for the first goldfinch that offers. Nay, I do not even trust the blueth of the eyes. I do not believe they last once in twenty years. One cannot go into a village fifty miles from London without seeing a dozen little children with flaxen hair and eyes of sky-blue. What becomes of them all? One does not see a grown Christian with them twice in a century, except in poetry."

It was for the Ampthill children that Walpole wrote the two fairy tales that appear in his works. The first of these, *The Peach in Brandy*, like all that came from his pen, is most elegantly written, but would hardly commend itself to children of tender years. Lady Anne, however, was somewhat of a blue stocking. When she was only ten years of age, she sent her old friend a regular poser in the shape of a riddle in *four quipos*. Walpole, who was then drifting some-

[1] Born 1774.

what into the crabbed humour of a sexagenarian, took this childish exhibition of pedantry in bad part, especially as he found it too hard a nut to crack. There is great ill-humour in his answer,—

"I cannot unsew a single stitch of such *millinery versification*, and though I will not contemptuously return such silken lines directly, I despair of unravelling them, and will only detain them till I have *effilé* them for a whole morning, since it seems that a mistake in a single shade may occasion a blunder or a double *entendre*." In his next letter he follows up this attack with another equally bitter,—

"I return the quipos, madam, because if I retained them till I understand them, I fear you would never have them again. I should as soon be able to hold a dialogue with a rainbow by the help of the grammar or a prism—for I have not yet discovered which is the first or the last verse of four lines that hang like ropes of onions."

Lady Ossory seems to have resented this ill-tempered criticism upon her little daughter's precocious efforts, for presently we find Horace crying *peccavi*,—

"In truth I am sorry I expressed myself so awkwardly that you thought I disapproved of the quipos. On the contrary, you see how much they have amused me." And then he goes into a lengthy dissertation upon the riddle, too long and unamusing to relate here. In spite of his little outburst of ill-humour, Walpole was undoubtedly very partial to Lady Anne. On her birthday he sent her a charming poem on "Shells," and, all through, his interest was more for her than for her prettier sister. He thought her "full of sensibility, although I am sorry she promises to have so much of a virtue, whose kingdom is not of this world, but, like patience, is ever tried with the greater disadvantage of wanting to remedy half the misfortunes it feels for. Sensibility is one of those mother springs on which *most* depends the colour of our lives, and determines our being happy or miserable. I have often said the world is a comedy to those who think, and a tragedy to those who feel; and sensibility has not only occasion to suffer for others, but is sure to have its own portion too."

This sensibility is noticeable in Lady Anne's portrait as the child with a bunch of grapes, while the quality is somewhat lacking in Collina's—Lady Gertrude's—dear, bright, sparkling little face, and yet there is an untouched wealth of love in those large, childish eyes, which we must hope preserved the grey-blue Irish tint. Walpole did not think the portrait did her justice, "although it is sweetly pretty; it has not half the countenance of the original." He adds, that the print is poorly executed, faint and unfinished.

As time goes on, we find Walpole still playing the part of family friend and general referee on all matters of importance, giving judicious and sincere advice to Lady Ossory to show herself more in society. "I doubt your ladyship's dislike of quitting Ampthill proceeds a little from your aversion to appearing in public, but do you know you must surmount this—nay, entirely." And then he adds, "There is no pleasure in being anybody's friend if one is not to tell them very disagreeable truths." Again, writing on this subject, he says, "Pray, madam, do not be so vulgar as to stay in the country because there is somebody or other here that you are afraid of meeting. What an old-fashioned prejudice! Does one like anybody the less because one dislikes that person? There is not a monarch in Europe who cannot conquer his aversion in seventeen days, and shall a subject be allowed greater latitude? I know your ladyship's are not antipathies, but very contrary awkwardnesses: but you must get over them. Lions and lambs, doves and serpents, now trot in the same harness, and it does one's heart good to see them." Again, when Lord Euston, her son by her previous marriage to the Duke of Grafton, displeased his father by engaging himself to Walpole's niece, Lady Maria Waldegrave, the old diplomatist counselled Lady Ossory as to the part she should take. "I agree with you that any fervour on your ladyship's part could but hurt: indeed, the only part I take myself, is to recommend perfect silence, which I shall strictly observe myself." On the subject of the little girls' education and their deportment, he has much to say, especially as to his favourite Anne, who was the cleverer of the two. He writes, in answer to her questions concerning the *Salique law*, a long and learned explanation, counsels her on her drawing, for which she had decided talent and criticises in an amiable manner her double heads, at the same time strongly advising her to cultivate music, which he considers a more fascinating art. He is deeply interested in the private theatricals at Ampthill, to which, however, he did not go. He sent a prologue, and is anxious for all particulars, especially of Lady Anne's acting of Kitty, in "High Life Below Stairs." He writes to Lady Ossory that he approves extremely of *her* good humour in acting and dancing, "for I should hate gravity, dignity or austerity in one's own house *in the country*." Who had not rather see Scipio playing at leap-frog with his children at his Ampthill than parading to St Paul's singing *Te Deum*?"

It was not in accordance with Walpole's usual tact thus to remind Lady Ossory that her day was over, and that of her daughters' was beginning. These reminders of advancing years are not well said. This was, however, in 1785, when Lady Anne was fifteen, her sister only eleven, yet Walpole, in a letter to her mother, gives her the agreeable information that the Province of Bedford, meaning the Duke of that name's son, admired her daughter, a somewhat premature announcement, considering her age.

This is about the last friendly act on Walpole's part to his former friends. He was growing old, and the waywardness of the spoiled child of fashionable society was beginning to show itself unchecked. A letter he wrote to Lady Ossory in 1787 was the beginning of a coolness in his affections for his sovereign lady. In it he takes exception to Lady Ossory having shown one of his letters to General Fitzpatrick, the Secretary for War. There is something irrepressibly sad in this letter. The subtle insight the old man of the world shows in reading the character of his equally worldly correspondent, the disgust he cannot conceal at her doses of flattery, while all the time he is quite conscious that she and Mr Fitzpatrick are amusing themselves at his expense. The bitter cry, too, that comes straight from his heart that he has *no friend* who will tell him the truth, is terribly real,

"You reprove me for not being perfectly humble, and then tell me you show my letters to Mr Fitzpatrick.[1] Do you think I can like *that?* and can I help suspecting that you are laughing at me for a credulous old simpleton. Indeed, I do suspect it, and am not such a gudgeon as to swallow the hook with which you tempt me to play. Mr Fitzpatrick has too much sense and taste to be amused with the gossiping babble of my replies to the questions you put me, and I can have no satisfaction in scribbling the trifles I send you, if they are to be seen, or if I am to ponder and guard them against being downright dotage. And how shall I discover that they are not so, if they are? Where is the touchstone on which old age is to try its decay? *It will strike seventy to-morrow, and who will be so much my friend as to tell me that it might as well strike fourscore?* With these convictions staring me in the face, do not imagine, my good madam, that I suppose I can entertain one of the liveliest young men in England, and who passes his time with Mr Fox, Mr Sheridan and Mr Hare."

The real rupture, however, in the friendship between him and Lady Ossory dates from the time Mary and Agnes Berry appear on the scene. "They are the best informed and most perfect creatures I ever saw of their age," he writes to Lady Ossory. This delightful family—"for the father is a little, merry man with a round face"—grappled the lonely sexa-

[1] Richard Fitzpatrick, celebrated as the friend of Charles Fox, as well as on account of his own accomplishments, was the son of John, first Earl of Upper Ossory, and was born on the 30th of January 1747. In his youth he served with some credit in the American War. In 1780, he was returned to Parliament as member for Tavistock; in 1782, he was appointed secretary to the Duke of Portland, Lord-Lieutenant of Ireland, and the following year was nominated to the office of Secretary at War. His person is said to have been extremely striking. He was tall and handsome, his manners were peculiarly prepossessing, and there was a charm in his conversation which rendered his society more courted than that of almost any other person of his day. As Secretary at War he gave general satisfaction. In the House of Commons he was admitted to have been an able, if not a powerful speaker, and his lighter poetical compositions have no mean merit. Like his friend Fox, he was a libertine in every sense of the word. Their friendship had commenced in early life, and they continued to be inseparably attached to each other to the last. The same love of pleasure, the same fatal attachment to the gaming-table, and the same redeeming taste for literature distinguished them both. In his later years, the mental as well as bodily faculties of Fitzpatrick appear to have been impaired by the excesses in which he had indulged. "I witnessed," says Wraxall, "the painful spectacle of his surviving almost all the personal and intellectual graces which Nature had conferred upon him with so lavish a hand." General Fitzpatrick died on the 25th April 1813, in his 67th year.

genarian with hooks of steel, and from this time the two pearls, as he designates Mary and Agnes, took complete possession of his capricious fancy; and as there was not room in his somewhat narrow heart for his new loves, Lady Ossory had to be content with a back seat. His last letter to her is very touching, as showing the embittered state of his mind:—

"*January*, 1789.

"MY DEAR MADAM,—You distress me infinitely by showing my idle notes, which I cannot conceive can interest anybody. My old-fashioned breeding compels me every now and then to reply to the letters you honour me with writing, but, in truth, very unwillingly, for I seldom can have anything particular to say. I scarce go out of my own house, and then only to two or three very private places, where I see nobody that really knows anything; and what I learn comes from newspapers that collect intelligence from coffee-houses—consequently, what I neither believe nor repeat. At home I only see a few charitable elders, except some fourscore nephews and nieces of different ages, who are only brought me about once a year to stare at me as the Methusaleh of the family, and they can only speak of their own contemporaries, which interests me no more than if they talked of their dolls or bats and balls.

"Must not the result of all this, madam, make me a very entertaining correspondent? And can such letters be worth reading, or can I have any spirit, when so old and reduced, to dictate?

"Oh, my good madam, dispense with me from such a task, and think how it must add to it to apprehend such letters being shown. Pray, send me no more such laurels, which I desire no more than their leaves when decked with a scrap of tinsel and stuck on Twelfth cakes that lie on the shop-boards of pastrycooks at Christmas. I shall be quite content with a sprig of rosemary thrown after me when the parson of the parish commits my dust to dust. Till then, pray, madam, accept the resignation of your ancient servant,

"ORFORD."

With the cessation of Horace Walpole's correspondence, we lose touch of the family at Ampthill. Here and there we catch glimpses of the names with which he has made us so familiar, but there is nothing tangible. We know that,

THE RIGHT HONOURABLE LADY GERTRUDE FITZPATRICK.
[*From a Picture by Hoppner.*

following the usual course of things, Collina and her sister grew up into beautiful young ladies, went to Court in high heads and hoops, and we may assume (for I here state nothing on fact) broke the heart of dozens of admirers.

Some sort of blight, however, seems to have followed their path. The portrait of Lady Gertrude, beautiful as it is, has a sad expression, as of one who had suffered somewhat from the buffets of evil fortune, and yet it would appear on the surface that nothing was wanting to make their lives happy and contented—who can tell? The more one has to do with the inner life of those who have gone before us, the more is the truth borne in upon us that it is not the circumstances in which our lot is cast, not the adventitious accident of birth or fortune, intellect or beauty, that make or mar the whole, but it is we ourselves who build up or destroy the airy fabric of our own happiness—this may have been the case with these two sisters. Anne's over-sensibility, perhaps, brought about the result predicted by her early friend, Walpole: while Gertrude may have turned out a *hard*, scoffing young person, laughing at her lover's protestations and weeping afterwards that she had driven him from her. This is all guess work, however, framed principally on looking at the beautiful but somewhat discontented face in the portrait before me. Poor little Collina, something went wrong in your life, but you are an independent soul, and, I dare swear, didn't sigh long for any false-hearted swain. . . . Then came the usual change, father and mother both dying—Lady Ossory of a painful disease which she bore with exemplary patience. Lord Ossory died in 1818, and, some years later, Ampthill was sold[1]—another landmark gone. This was when little Collina was nearly fifty.[2] She and her sister had a house in Grosvenor Place, and spent their time between London and Ireland, where they lived in a corner of the family mansion. The country people liked them, and it was told to me that they very much resembled the Ladies of Llangollen in their eccentricities and amiabilities. I know not how far this is true. As I said before, the interest which attaches to these ladies is not in their own lives, but in the link they make with the past century.

[1] Ampthill was sold to Baron Parke. [2] She died in 1841.

BOOK [illegible]

ANNE (COUNTESS OF CHARLEMONT).

[*From a Miniature in the possession of the Countess of Charlemont.*

# MARY BIRMINGHAM, COUNTESS OF LEITRIM; ANNE BIRMINGHAM, COUNTESS OF CHARLEMONT

THE Birminghams are of English descent, as their name denotes. They belong, however, to the earliest plantation of settlers under Henry II., when Robert, son to William de Birmingham of Birmingham Castle, accompanied Strongbow on his expedition to Ireland. Robert distinguished himself by his keen pursuit of the natives; no man showed more zeal in hunting them from rock, cave and thicket, for which zeal he was duly rewarded by large grants of land in the west. Such grants were but doubtful blessings, the first English settlers holding, so to speak, their lives in their hands. Their adversaries had certain advantages in carrying on the predatory warfare they indulged in: they knew the country, and could hide themselves in the hills for weeks and months, descending when the opportunity offered, slaughtering, pillaging and carrying off all they could lay their hands on. One famous instance of their success in such predatory warfare remains on record in the title "Black Monday," which owes its name to the fact that Henry II, presented the tract of country surrounding the River Liffey, upon which Dublin was afterwards built (the capital at this early period being only represented by the dusky river flowing from bog and turf with some few huts and a wicker bridge),[1] to his faithful subjects of Bristol. Five hundred of these crossed in rude boats the wide expanse of ocean which separates the smiling waters of the River Avon from the more turbid stream of the Liffey, and being well pleased with their new acquisition, they, on one Easter Monday, went

[1] Professor Dowden's "Dublin City."—*Scribner's.* 1884.

a-pleasuring in the fields, picnicing in their rough fashion,—when, lo! as the evening fell, down from the hills and woods, and from ambushes on all sides, rushed like a torrent the Irish, who had been waiting their opportunity, and of the luckless five hundred none, we are told, returned to the city to tell the tale of slaughter, which, however, was commemorated by the significant title of Black Monday, while the place where it happened was called "Bloody Fields."

These outbreaks on the part of the weaker party provoked the most sanguinary reprisals from the conquerors, and so the bloody record went on. The Birminghams, who were men of strength and purpose, seem to have been fitted by nature for this predatory warfare and to have enjoyed it. Pierce, or Peter, first Lord of Athenry, distinguished himself to the full, as much as did the original settler Robert, in the capacity of harrowing, hunting and slaying the natives: so did likewise Sir John de Birmingham, who struck out a new hunting ground for himself, in Louth, where he planted a branch of the family, and was treacherously murdered by the Gormans, who were colonists of Norman descent.

As time went on, we find all this savage warfare subsiding, and the old story repeating itself of the lion lying down with the lamb; in other words, the conquerors and the conquered were blended into one, the English settlers becoming, in many instances more Irish than the Irish themselves,[1] and we are not surprised to find that in the fourteenth century the Birminghams with other chiefs (of English origin) being suspected of abetting rebellion, the head of the family, William, Lord Birmingham of Athenry, was executed for high treason, and buried among the friar preachers in Dublin.

We need not now follow the varying fortunes of the twenty-two Lords of Athenry, which are set forth at length in *Lodge's Peerage*. They were men of courage, and came well to the front. They had a fine castle called Birmingham Castle,

[1] Sir John Davies observes on the general defection of the old English into the Irish customs, "for about that time," says he, "they did not only forget the English language and scorn the use thereof, but grew to be ashamed of their very English names, and took Irish surnames and nicknames.

and as they lived in troubled and stirring times, had enough to do to defend themselves against the attacks made upon them. Francis, the nineteenth lord, maintained the rights of the Stuarts until after the battle of Worcester, when the King wrote to him from France, advising him to submit to the powers in authority, who, nevertheless, excepted him from the general pardon. His son Edward, twentieth baron, was also on the Stuart side, but, after the battle of the Boyne, William III. reversed the bill of attainder and outlawry, and he received a full pardon, his grandson, the twenty-second and last Lord of Athenry, being created Earl of Louth. Another offshoot of the family was the ancient branch of Carbery, which separated from the original stock early—a younger son of the third Lord Athenry settling in Carryck in Carbery.

The family of Birmingham, to which the beautiful subjects of our present story belonged, were a branch of the Lords of Athenry, and always considered as kinsmen. They dwelt at Ross Hill, situated in perhaps the loveliest spot along the western coast. Lough Mask, one of the large tributary lakes fed by the Atlantic, lies at its feet: its clear, smiling waters are oftentimes a veil for the hidden dangers that lurk beneath a treacherous serenity, fitful and changeable as a woman's smile. The lake's smooth waters are not to be trusted, and have, rising, wooed many a trusting lover to eternal sleep, for the storm suddenly catches the unwary navigator, leaving him no chance of escape; his boat is tossed and rent asunder amid unearthly shrieks and howls, like lost souls or demons at play. The peasants, when they hear the tumult, cower in their beds, or by the fireside; none would dare to venture outside, for all know that the lake fiend is abroad and will do his will; and when his mood is past, the waters will be all smiling and inviting again.[1]

On the summit of gently sloping hills stand the ruins of Ross Abbey, once the home of the learned order of Benedictine monks. These now lend to the scene the interest of picturesque

[1] Lough Mask has a tragic record in the murder of the Huddys during the troubles of recent times.

decay. Ross Hill, too, is a dilapidated and battered remnant of what was once a commodious dwelling-house, of which only a bay window is now remaining, the house having been sacked in the rising of 1798 and only the shell left.

At this time the head of the house was William Birmingham [1] who had married Miss Jane Rutledge of Bushfield, County Mayo, a beauty in her day, a gift inherited by her two daughters, Mary and Anne, who likewise were the heiresses of their father's large property, he being the last of his line. The times were terribly out of joint, and although during the childhood of Mary and Anne there were only grumblings of the storm, wise and prudent men foresaw that the general shipwreck was at hand. Residence in a sequestered place such as Ross Hill, where help was not easily attainable, was naturally fraught with considerable danger, especially when two beautiful and wealthy girls were the prizes which might fall to a gallant abductor. In the latter part of the eighteenth century a marked feature of Irish life was the forcible abduction of women. This outrage was either actuated by love or a desire to possess the fortune of the unfortunate victim (the latter being the more general). Sometimes it was committed with the consent of the weaker party, sometimes it was the end of an unfortunate courtship, the girl being dragged away by a man she had refused. Occasionally a woman having remained, in the opinion of her neighbours, too long unmarried, her husband was selected for her, and the abduction was arranged. The process was generally the same. In the dead of the night the lonely cottage where the victim lived was surrounded by a band of ruffians with black crape over their faces, the girl was dragged from her bed and carried to some wild district amongst the bogs and mountains, where, after some days, away from all help and terrified by the most lawless threats, she consented to go through the marriage ceremony. One of the worst features of this form of outrage was the admiration it excited in the popular mind, the perpetrator being often elevated to the rank of a hero, and his crime

[1] The name of Birmingham was pronounced in Ireland *Brummagem*.

looked upon as a gallant achievement. Nor was abduction confined only to the lower orders. Gentlemen were often mixed up in such transactions, and some high-sounding names could be found amongst the members of the abduction clubs. An interesting case was that of the abduction by Willy Reilly of the beautiful Miss Folliot, whose fame for loveliness and accomplishments had earned her the sobriquet of "the Lily of Longford." Her father, Colonel Folliot (or Folliard, as it was pronounced by the country people), was a man of consideration, owning a large estate in Westmeath, where the romantic drama took place, the interest of the situation being intensified in this instance by the heroine belonging to the State religion, while the hero was of an old Catholic family. This fact accounts for the unbounded popularity Willy Reilly's story achieved, and the hold it took of the imaginative Irish, always ready to range themselves upon the side of unfortunate lovers—in truth this case cannot be counted amongst those of forcible abduction, as Helen Folliot was quite willing to trust herself to the honour of her lover rather than submit to a hateful marriage, forced upon her by her father. Nevertheless, in spite of every effort made to save him—the poor girl herself coming into Court to tell her story of their love—Willy Reilly was condemned to death, but the extreme penalty of the law was commuted to transportation. The poor Lily of Longford pined away in hopeless melancholy. Her beauty was a wreck and her mind was clouded by her misfortune—her one idea being to get news of Willy. With the hope of effecting a cure her father made Helen go into society, where she would, so long as the parental eye was on her, conduct herself quietly though sadly. So soon as she found the opportunity, she would put the question that was for ever hovering on her lips—"Can you tell me where is Willy Reilly? He is gone away and I cannot find him." For many years the love episode of Willy Reilly and the Lily of Longford remained enshrined in the hearts of the peasantry, and the ballad of Willy Reilly was popular at all village gatherings.[1]

[1] The story of Willy Reilly and the Lily of Longford is the subject of one of Carleton's popular novels. Amongst other incidents he mentions what actually

Miss Corbally's was a far less romantic abduction, the motive being the possession of her large fortune. In this instance a ruse was resorted to, a sham messenger being sent to inform her that her brother was ill and wanted her to come to him. As she was going over Essex Bridge, in Dublin three or four ruffians seized her, thrust her into a coach and drove away with her. Numbers of persons pursued the coach along the quays, but in vain. She was, however, ultimately rescued.

Mrs Delany in her autobiography relates at great length the story of the abduction of the two Miss M'Dermotts, who were heiresses to their dead father's estates in Connaught, a circumstance which excited the indignation of their cousin, Mr Flynn, who considered himself the proper heir to his uncle's property, as being the male representative of the family. He was determined to possess himself of what he considered his right, and, there being no other way, made up his mind to make Maria, the elder and richer, his wife, although she was neither young nor handsome. Mrs Delany describes her as a tall, large woman, with a sensible face, a sweet voice and great gentleness of manner. The proposed marriage found great favour with Flynn's family. Miss M'Dermott, however, decidedly rejected her cousin's proposals. The discomfited suitor behaved apparently with the utmost generosity, bearing his disappointment like a man, only requesting the old cousinly relations should not be interrupted, all this in so friendly a manner and with such apparent good faith that the ladies showed their desire to correspond by at once accepting an invitation to spend the day with their uncle's family. Having dined, they ordered their carriage to return home, when the uncle, who had been all kindness to them, now insisted they should stay the night. They, however, remained firm in their determination to leave, when they were told both servants and carriage had been sent away early in the forenoon and would come back next day. Maria at once felt a foreboding of evil;

did occur, that Reilly was accused of stealing some family jewels, which were found upon him when he was arrested. From this accusation The Lily exculpated her lover; the jewels, it appeared were taken by her.

this terror remained with her while the family sat down to cards. They were in the middle of the game when suddenly men with masks rushed into the room; the two girls rose with a horrified cry and ran into an inner room, where one hid herself under the bed, the other behind it. They were soon discovered. One of the masked villains seized upon the younger, but finding she was not the one he wanted, cursed her heartily and then laid violent hands upon Miss M'Dermott who was still under the bed. She fought *manfully*, says Mrs Delany. He was not with all his efforts able to drag her out until her clothes were nearly all torn off. The poor woman threw herself upon her knees to implore mercy, but, seizing her by her arms, he dragged her into the adjoining room where her uncle was standing before the fire, looking on with perfect indifference. Appealing to him was of no use, and when she was dragged into the hall, she found two hundred desperate-looking men ready to help her savage assailant. She was seized by a dozen hands, her hands and feet tied; she was then lifted to the saddle, upon which her cousin was already seated, and securely fastened with ropes. They tried to gag her, but she resisted so violently that, as time pressed, they desisted.

After travelling some time this spirited woman managed, by struggling violently, to free her hands, and then deftly untied the rope and slid softly from the horse; but she was soon surrounded, and although with her back to a tree she fought for some time, she was overpowered. One of the gang ran a sword up her arm from the wrist to the elbow, and, fainting with pain, she was once more strapped on the horse and they travelled on again. After some time they arrived at a cabin, where she was lifted off and consigned to the care of a woman who received orders to watch her carefully. Finding she knew this person, the unfortunate girl besought her to let her go, offering a large sum of money to tempt her. The hag was about to yield, when suddenly the door opened and her persecutor returned in company with a

[1] The marriage, even if solemnised by a Catholic priest, would have been illegal, as the penal law on this point was then in force.

E

man dressed as a priest,[1] who tried to persuade her to be married at once, assuring her that Flynn was resolved to make her his wife by force. Nothing daunted, Maria persisted in her refusal, declaring she would rather die than consent to such a marriage. The ceremony was, however, proceeded with. When they tried to force the ring upon her finger, she tore it off and, snatching up a mug of milk standing on the fire, she threw it, boiling hot, into the mock priest's face. Just then one of the party came in, and speaking in Irish, which fortunately Maria understood, told Flynn the county was in pursuit, which gave her some comfort. However, they once more seized her, and, finding she was bleeding profusely from the wound in her arm, they were afraid to go much further, but carried her to a bog close by, where they plunged her up to her shoulders, and placed a man, heavily armed, on each side to prevent her escaping. Her friends soon found her and released her, carrying her to the house of a gentleman in the neighbourhood, who received her most kindly, and where she had the best medical advice and care. She was in danger for twenty-one days, but finally recovered. The plunging in the bog really saved her life by stopping the bleeding. After this adventure the Miss M'Dermotts left the country and came to Dublin, where their story excited much interest. Their cause was taken up by Dean Delany, and Mrs Delany has immortalised their wonderful escape in her memoirs. The heroine was married at Delville Church to a young man able to protect her against abductors.

The case of Miss M'Dermott was fully forty years before our two heroines appeared on the stage of life. The taste for such outrages was, however, still keenly alive, abductions being carried on in a more organised fashion. In 1794 there were abduction clubs for the express purpose of supplying the means of carrying off *heiresses*, this last fact proving that love was not so much the motive that actuated the abductors as money.[1]

[1] The last abduction case on record in Ireland must be fresh in the memory of many still living. It was somewhere in the fifties that John Carden of Barnane a gentleman of good birth and good estate, and exceedingly popular, conceived an unfortunate attachment for Miss Arbuthnot, which, not being reciprocated, in-

Mr Birmingham was fully alive to the facilities that Ross Hall afforded for such an undertaking, and as he had no mind for a Willy Reilly as his son-in-law, he removed his daughters out of harm's way, and with a view to fitting them for the high position their beauty and wealth would probably command, he took them to Italy, where their education was completed. They moved amongst a highly intellectual circle both at Rome and Florence, their friends being chosen as much for their mental gifts as for their station.

The season of 1796 in Florence was exceptionally brilliant; the city was crowded with English visitors—Lord and Lady Cowper, Lord Holland, Lady Webster, and a host of others. Mary Birmingham, the elder sister, was the acknowledged belle, while the dawning beauty of Anne, who was not as yet "out," was duly recognised, it being pronounced by good judges that she would equal if not eclipse her sister, a prophecy which was fulfilled. Both at this time, and all through a career marked by extraordinary success, the two girls seem to have been singularly unspoilt by the admiration they excited; their unaffected simplicity appears to have added to their charm and won for them a number of friends.

"They are all bent upon being kind to us," writes Mary Birmingham to a friend. "Lady Cowper dressed me last Saturday for a ball at the Casino, where I went with Madame d'Albani. Lady Webster and Lord Holland came. I bored myself extremely at the ball, and wherever I go I am always bored since I have been at Florence." And then she confesses with adorable candour that she is always so—"when I am not quiet: it is constitutional, so do not scold me. And as for being an old maid, do not speak against that brilliant state, for certain it will be mine as the only one I deserve." In the next paragraph she goes on to describe her dress, and considering her depressed state of mind, she takes a natural and very feminine satisfaction in dwelling on such adornment.

duced Mr Carden to revive the old method of carrying off his lady-love. The number of times he essayed this feat without success, and the hairbreadth escapes of the lady would fill a small volume. Mr Carden was brought before the magistrates scores of times; he was fined and imprisoned—all to no purpose. No sooner was he let out than he began again. The lady, however, escaped his persecution.

"I must, however, tell you about my dress on Saturday, for it was almost entirely the work of Lady Cowper. On my head I had a long roll of crape turned round and round, and between my hair two feathers of half a league of height, with an *ésprit* between them; sleeves of white satin (this is the fashion with all sorts of dresses); a body of purple satin with little sleeves of the same, and a purple fringe which hung on the white satin; waist very short, and the petticoat of plain muslin; the belt a narrow white satin ribbon with a rosette behind. This is detail enough."

Madame d'Albani, mentioned in the previous letter, was the Comtesse d'Albanie, widow of the "Young Pretender," the man for whom Esmond conspired and Beatrix had a desperate quarrel with Lady Castletown, as readers of that most enthralling romance will remember. By all accounts, he was in his later days a good-for-nothing, drunken sot, a terrible incubus on the Countess, as she was called, who was many years younger than her husband. She was a genuine princess of the House of Stolberg, and a handsome, clever, capable woman, wealthy into the bargain. Everyone knows the romantic passion she excited in the heart of Alfieri, who, during the lifetime of her husband, occupied the position of *amico di casa*, dining every day with the Countess and her peevish, half-fuddled consort. In 1780 the Countess's life was, according to her statement, endangered by her husband's violence when in his drunken fits.[1] She therefore quitted his house, and, going to Rome, placed herself under the protection of his brother, Cardinal York. Alfieri followed her. The world, which has argus eyes for such little affairs, began to wag its malicious tongue, and Alfieri, finding the popular voice

[1] The general retailer of news, our ever-gossipy Horace, tells us what actually did happen :—"Last Wednesday the Count got so beastly drunk that he tore the Countess's hair and endeavoured to strangle her; her screams alarmed the family, who saved her. She contrived to take shelter in a convent, and declares she will never return to her husband." Wraxall mentions in his memoirs seeing Charles Edward, in 1779, at Florence, where he made a nightly exhibition of personal humiliation: he was carried into his box at the opera by his servants, and laid upon a sofa in the back part, while the Countess occupied the front seat, attended by Alfieri. According to this witness, she had very little pretensions to beauty. Raikes found that she had none of the ideal beauty about her which we could have imagined the object of Alfieri's love possessing.

against him, and having a chivalrous desire not to compromise "*his sovereign lady,*" quitted Rome and wandered about for some years, until in 1788 the death of her husband set the Countess free. Whether the lovers availed themselves of this liberty has remained always an uncertainty. They were both living in Florence in 1796. The Birminghams were very intimate with Madame d'Albani, who was a leader of society. She entertained a warm admiration for the two beautiful Irish girls, who fully returned her liking. "There is not a soul that interests me here but Madame Albani," writes the somewhat *blasé* young philosopher, Mary. This indifference to everything, and general distaste to society, unusual in one so young, and whose charms made her the object of general admiration, may have been caused by some attachment which was not viewed favourably by her parents, or it may have been merely a girl's whim. For the rest, Mary and her sister were decidedly superior to the ordinary run of girls of their generation. Both sisters had artistic temperaments, this tendency being developed by their residence in Italy, where alone Art was properly reverenced. Mary was a fairly good artist, while Anne had a pretty gift for rhyming. Their father, too, was a man of culture, so that probably the *précieuse* manner adopted by Miss Birmingham was no affectation but the natural outcome of her education. She speaks of herself as being an old woman at the age of nineteen, and attributes her extraordinary gravity to the tranquility of her early life in Italy. It is pleasant, however, to find that later her girlish nature asserted itself. Her letters from Germany, where they went on leaving Italy in 1796, are actually gay, and her descriptions of social life at a small German Court a hundred years ago, are delightfully written and well worth reproducing here.

"CARLSBAD,
"*9th July*, 1796.

"Wednesday we were presented at the reception. I was never more astonished than with several things that occurred. In the first place we entered—my mother and I and the Baron

Schimananski (one of our Poles). We passed quietly into another room, where the sister of the Duchess of Kurland, with a suite of twenty ladies, besieged us from behind, so we had to face round and be presented one after the other. As they were all married, I took no part, but my turn came. From the other end fifty young ladies came and made me curtseys and overpowered me with English, which they all talked. Really, at the end of a quarter-of-an-hour, with all the noise, my senses had departed, and I did not know whether I was standing on my head or my heels. In the end a young person arrived, whom everyone kissed and whom everyone hastened to present to me as one who talked English. But she was very different from the numerous crowd I had seen hitherto. She was as beautiful as an angel, and really spoke English well. We began talking to each other, and the evening passed very agreeably. But this was not all. We were in the midst of a circle of one hundred people, young men and young women, when all of a sudden a signal was given, and everyone ran to the other side of the *salle* with all their strength. You may judge how this ruse seized me with astonishment, and I remained quite stupefied. I thought the house had taken fire. It was only a few cups of chocolate that had caused all this *fracas*. Only for my charming Countess Clare, I should have remained standing in the middle of this enormous *salon* without a living being within a hundred steps of me. I assure you, my knees ache with all the curtseys I had to make that night. Amongst the people there were some very nice and very elegant. Madame de Rodenham, her daughters and Countess Clare, and, above all, the Prince of Saxe-Gotha was very agreeable. The Duchess of Kurland was so amiable as to ask that my mother should be introduced to her. The eldest of the princesses, who is beautiful, is in love, they say, with the Prince of Saxe-Gotha. His father sent him here expressly to make up to her; but he doesn't care for her, and she is so used to be sought out and almost adored (for she is very rich) by many princes, that she is quite piqued with the coldness of this one. She is very beautiful. We are to be presented to them at the ball on Sunday or Monday, and my mother is to go to the Duchess. You know, or you do not know, that the Duke of Kurland is no longer a sovereign prince; for, seeing the ability of the Empress of Russia, seeing the fate of the King of Poland, trembling for himself, he sold his estates a year ago to the Empress: he is now enormously rich, but no longer a sovereign. He has no son, therefore it is just as well. The gaiety of the Germans is astonishing. You can imagine how it strikes a person who has lived so long in quiet Italy, and who at the age of nineteen is almost an old woman. I am quite delighted to do my apprenticeship before returning to Ireland, where the young ladies are almost as youthful as here."

Before closing this letter, she gives her correspondent an account of the ball given by the Duchess of Kurland, and from the tone of unconscious elation in the letter, it is evident that she had been much admired—especially by the Prince of Saxe-Gotha—and enjoyed her triumph as much as so sensible a young person could.

"I have just returned from the ball, my dear. I danced all the possible dances, except waltzes, which are not in the least *bon ton* or *comme il faut.* I have had more partners than I wanted, and am engaged to-night till the fourth with excellent partners, the Prince of Saxe-Gotha amongst others. He is devoted to dancing, and resembles in that, and in his manner generally, Prince Auguste. Of the Duchess and the Princesses, the mother is the most beautiful. I will tell you what the Prince of Saxe-Gotha said to me:—'The mother is a thousand times more beautiful; the eldest is pretty, but knows it too well, and is full of pretension: the second is not at all so pretty, but more amiable. The little one begins already to know the attractions of her person.' Ah! by-the-bye, I want to tell you a little story that the young Count Slam told me yesterday. His father was great friends with Lord Gilford, just when this one left Ireland; they were at Milan, where Lord Gilford bored himself to death. Count

Slam said to him,—'But, my friend, let us try Vienna; perhaps that'll please you better.' 'Oh, no,' said the other, 'I have a horror of Vienna; I'll never go there.' After repeating very often this thing, he said,—'To satisfy you, I'll go there for ten days. I leave everything behind me here.' He went to Vienna, spent three months there without leaving it, and married Mdlle. de ———. Predestination, my dear! It will be for you one day. I am going to the ball, but I should almost prefer to die than to be always in society; there is nothing which so tires the heart, the spirit and the soul.

"The French are two leagues from Frankfort. What do you think of that?"

In October 1797, Mr Birmingham and his family returned to Ireland. It was hardly a felicitous moment for the introduction of the young beauties into society. Already the mutterings of the storm were heard that broke over the whole country a few months later, while the danger of foreign help supporting the disaffected had become a possibility.

The attempt made by the French fleet at Bantry Bay (which is one of the most dramatic incidents of this sad page of Irish history) was of recent occurrence. Men's minds were still full of the danger of a foreign invasion, which had been averted mainly through the unexpected loyalty shown by the militia and the Catholics. The "United Irishmen" indeed urged that the French had attempted to land in one of the parts of Ireland where the organisation was least extended, and that if they had appeared in the north or north-west, the result would have been very different. There was no doubt that a disaffected spirit in Ireland was widespread, but so also was the intimidation used by the leaders to enrol members in the association of "United Irishmen." This intimidation was carried on by small bands of conspirators, who exacted *vi et armis* the oath which the new member took without, in many cases, any intention of observance. In addition to this, as Mr Lecky points out with an insight into the Irish character which will be endorsed by everyone who has any real knowledge of the people, disloyalty was and still is often "a fashion, a sentiment, often an amusement which has abundantly coloured the popular imagination, but which has never been strong or substantial enough to induce any genuine sacrifice in its cause."

These remarks, however, would not apply to a certain section of the "United Irishmen," who were desperately in earnest in their resolve to plunge their unfortunate country in all the horrors of civil war. These men had determined on a rising so soon as a landing for their allies from France could be effected, and there was every probability that if the attempt was made again it would be successful. The drilling, marching and training of large bodies of men went on by day and night, while republican ideas were inculcated and rewards lavishly promised. French assistance was guaranteed by Bonaparte to the leaders of the rebellion of 1798, and even serious preparations were made. The French fleet was to sail from Boulogne: whether it would have reached the Irish coast, it is impossible to say, but no one can question that, if it had, the effect would have been most serious. Napoleon always repented that he had abandoned this undertaking, and considered his vacillation as one of the errors of his life. It is, however, doubtful whether any large expedition could have succeeded in reaching the Irish coast. If it had done so, no one could have seriously questioned the gravity of the situation. Humbert's expedition cannot be regarded in any light but as a comedy, a comedy that ended tragically for the actors therein. It seems hardly credible that, after the fiasco of "La Hoche," another such invasion should have been attempted; yet it actually happened, the scene being on this occasion Killala instead of Bantry Bay: here, on August 22, 1798, a small flotilla of three frigates made its appearance, the English flag flying from their masts. Its commander, Humbert, had a small force of 1000 men and a large cargo of uniforms wherein to clothe the natives as good French (Republican) soldiers. The result of the expedition is well known, the last scenes presenting the usual savage and revolting features which marked the course of this bloody rising. The loss of property was enormous. The claims sent in by those who had suffered in the cause of loyalty amounted to £823,517. "But who," writes Gordon, "could estimate the damages of the croppies,[1] whose houses were burned and effects pillaged and destroyed, and who, barred from compensation, sent in no estimate to the Commissioners?" The moral scars left upon the country were, however, far worse than any loss of property which, as a matter of fact, was only a temporary evil. The spring of national prosperity, being agriculture, was bound to recover itself, given certain conditions. In the very height of the struggle, Beresford wrote that it was "most strange and extraordinary that the revenue every week was rising in a degree that had been hitherto unknown." The harvest of 1798,[2] fortunately, was exceptionally good, and this fact did more than any measure that Government could bring forward to alleviate the general panic.

Society likewise recovered (especially in the capital) with wonderful elasticity. In reading of the upheavals that have taken place from time to time in this part of the world, nothing is more surprising than the recuperative power evinced by those who have passed over the fiery ploughshares of life, which, we imagine, would have hopelessly crushed more refined and sensitive organisations. Had we lived through some national crisis, and been deprived of friends, home and fortune as these were, we imagine we could never have built up the foundation of fresh happiness. We should have done so, for the human mind is always the same in its elasticity. And so we come to understand that in an incredibly short space of time the actors who played their parts (either for good or evil) in the most harrowing scenes of the Rebellion of 1798 resumed their places on the stage of society, and having buried the hatchet shook hands with their opponents.[3]

[1] Croppies, a term of contempt from the song, "*Croppies*" or "*Cropped heads* lie down."

[2] In the month of August, Lord Clare noticed the rich corn crops that were ripening over the districts through which he passed. He also observed that the peasants were everywhere returning to their ordinary occupations.

[3] The moral effect of the Rebellion made a more lasting impression than did

The season of 1799 was a brilliant one in the little Irish capital, which was full to overflowing with the nobility and country gentlemen, with their wives and daughters, who had come to town to spend their last halfpenny in a gentlemanly manner, and do honour to the King's representative, Lord Cornwallis, who had, for he was a soldier as well as a politician, taken the field against the rebels, and saved the country from the French invaders. The Viceroy was surrounded with a brilliant staff; so, too, was Lord Carhampton, the Commander-in-chief; the Chief Secretary was Lord Castlereagh,[1] the first Irishman who had held the post. Castlereagh was exceptionally clever, and his busy brain was now working out the intricate problem how to force his great scheme of uniting Ireland to England upon the people and the country. This scheme, as everyone knows, he carried into effect by the most outrageous bribery the following year. It would be quite unnecessary to enter here upon the story of this historical event, which changed the whole social condition of Ireland, and gave a blow to the Protestant nobility and gentry from which they have never since recovered.[2]

the ruin which it undoubtedly brought upon the upper classes. A lady who visited Ireland in 1801 found that the Rebellion was the prominent object in the minds of most of those who passed through it. "It is their principal epoch, and seems to have divided time into two grand divisions, unmarked by any lesser periods, before and after the Rebellion; the first of these seems to resemble Paradise before the Fall. They had then good servants, fine flowers, fine fruit, fine horses, good beer and plenty of farm, that indispensable requisite in rural economy. Since that period of perfect felicity, the servants have been unmanageable, the horses restive, the beer sour, the farm uncome-at-able, and all things scarce and dear. Great part of the evils complained of are undoubtedly felt; some are imaginary, and some arise from causes which are not so important or so pleasant to put forward as the word rebellion." Mrs Trench's remarks on the truth of this last observation were exemplified in the recent troubles in Ireland,—"The cry of the ruined landlord was often raised not so much by those who actually suffered from the times as by these who were ruined by other causes, but found it more pleasant to put forward the land agitation."

[1] Robert Stewart, Lord Castlereagh, son of Robert Stewart of Ballylawn, Co. Donegal, and Mount Stewart, Co. Down, who was created a viscount in 1795, an earl in 1796, and Marquis of Londonderry in 1816. Lord Castlereagh was a distinguished politician, and stood out as a central figure in Irish history, and to him was due the Act of Union. He is constantly mentioned in Lord Charlemont's letters as "Our dear friend Robert, a very able young man, who unfortunately was Pittised with a vengeance."

[2] A singular proof of the effect produced by the Act of Union is afforded by one fact alone. In 1799 there were in Dublin fifty-seven resident peers, with fine mansions and large retinues of servants. At the present moment there is not one resident nobleman. The last who had a house in Dublin being the late Lord James Butler, but this solitary relic of a bygone nobility sold his mansion in Rutland

The opposition to the Act came altogether from men of this class, who, under the leadership of Oriel Foster, the Speaker of the House of Commons, made a magnificent fight for their rights throughout the winter of 1799-1800. The fight went on, the most splendid display of eloquence being made by Grattan, Foster and Sir John Parnell; it was a death struggle, but the result was easy to prophesy. Everyone is familiar with the saying of the gentleman who wished he had

THE LAST SITTING OF THE IRISH HOUSE OF COMMONS.

a country to sell, and even the most ardent patriot must own that Irishmen who possessed this treasure were willing to part with it[1] for a consideration. The most fervid eloquence

Square some years before his death. We cannot, however, shut our eyes to the fact that a similar depletion of the titled class would in all probability have taken place under any circumstances. The story of the Encumbered Estates Court throws considerable light upon the causes (other than political) of the decay of the Irish nobility.

[1] The revelations made by the publication of the Secret Service Records unfold a curious chapter in Irish history.

could not make head against the bribes offered by Castlereagh, who drew from the English Exchequer over a million, while peerages were scattered broadcast.

Meanwhile, society profited by the general stir and commotion. Dublin was crowded to excess, and upheld its reputation as the gayest of capitals. Lord Cornwallis and Lord Castlereagh[1] were diffuse in their hospitalities, the latter and his young wife, daughter to the somewhile Viceroy of Ireland, the Earl of Buckingham, surrounding themselves with a group of the most attractive women and the most distinguished men. The Miss Birminghams were special favourites with both Lord and Lady Castlereagh. Mr Birmingham had suffered considerably for his loyalty during the recent troubles. Ross Hill had been surrounded by the rebels, and hardly a stone of it was left standing. This alone would have given a claim on Lord Castlereagh's friendship, without the addition of having two lovely daughters. The Miss Birminghams, for Anne was now a fully-fledged young lady, were the belles of the Dublin season of 1799. Since the days of the Gunnings, no greater beauties had appeared, and, as Horace Walpole had said of the first-named, the fact that they were two equally handsome increased the effect, for, taken singly, there were many women quite as beautiful.

"I never saw two such beautiful creatures as the Birminghams," writes Lady Morgan; "the youngest the loveliest of the two." This would appear to have been the universal opinion. Mary, however, had special charms of her own. She was full of *esprit*, as we have seen by her correspondence, with a true artistic nature, as was evidenced by her fitful moods. She was engaged, before the end of this season of 1799, to the eldest son of Lord Leitrim, and was married to him early in 1800. There is little heard of her after this. We have glimpses of her occasionally, but her name was not so well known in the world of fashion, both at

[1] Until within the last twenty years, "Union Lord" was a term of reproach, as revealing the fact that the recipient of this honour had sold his country. In person Lord Castlereagh was calm, engaging, mild and dignified. His enemies have often ascribed his unfortunate end to remorse for having, as the saying goes, *sold his country.* A politician's conscience is hardly so tender, and, as a matter of fact, Lord Castlereagh, who had then become Londonderry survived the Act of Union nineteen years.

home and abroad, as that of Anne, who, in 1802, when she was barely twenty, became the wife of Francis William, second Earl of Charlemont, who had succeeded his father in 1799.

No two men could be more unlike than this father and son. The character of the great Earl, as he is called, has been admirably sketched by Mr Lecky, who says: "In him Ireland lost a true patriot, who had for a short time played a leading and very honourable part in her history, and the transparent disinterestedness of his public life, the soundness and moderation of his judgment, and the readiness with which he was always prepared to devote time, labour and money to the public good, established his position. In one critical moment," Mr Lecky adds, "Charlemont's services to his country had been transcendently great." This moment was the formation of the Volunteer Corps, the finest body of men ever brought together. "The brief career of the Volunteers," writes Mr Wingfield, "stands as a unique example in Irish history. Urged by a strange series of events, Ireland rose up from her dust-heap and was clad for the nonce in glorious raiment." It was in February 1782 that the delegates of one hundred and forty-three corps of Ulster Volunteers met in the great church of Dungannon in full uniform. Many of them were men of high rank, large property, excellent character, and they conducted their debates with a gravity, decorum and moderation which no assembly could surpass. The result of the

AN IRISH VOLUNTEER.

meeting was the victory of the Bill of Rights, which was wrested from the then Minister, Lord North, and gave to the Catholics of Ireland a larger measure of freedom than they had hitherto enjoyed. It was mainly due to Grattan that this great victory was achieved. Mr Lecky tells us how this great and eloquent man moved the amendment in the Irish House of Commons:—"he was still weak and pale from recent illness, and his appearance denoted the evident anxiety of his mind, but as he proceeded his voice gathered strength, and the fire of a great orator, acting on the highly-excited and sympathetic audience, soon produced even more than its wonted effect." The strange, swaying gestures which were habitual to him were compared by one observer to the action of the mower as his scythe sweeps through the long grass, and by another to the rolling of a ship in a heavy swell.

Another name which must be for ever associated with the Volunteers is that of the first Lord Charlemont. He, more than any other man, devoted himself to the development of a movement which he conceived was for the good of the country he loved so well. To it he gave his best energies, his influence, his money, his time, his whole heart—and for some years there seemed every prospect that his hopes would be realised, and that a permanent benefit had been secured to Ireland. The Volunteers grew more and more into a national militia—self-constituted, self-governed, and, for the most part, self-armed; they had attained a degree of discipline little inferior to the regular army, and were doing excellent work in guarding jails, keeping order at public meetings, and other services usually performed by the military or police. Their reviews, which were generally held in College Green, were on a scale of great splendour, as is seen in Wheatley's picture. *See* p. 81.

Unfortunately, the serpent of distrust began to creep into the hitherto united body of Volunteers. Some of the members grew to look upon the development of the movement with alarm, and to doubt that so large a force could be kept under proper control. The Duke of Leinster was one of these. Napper Tandy, who was tainted with the doctrine of revolution which was in the air, moved that the

Duke should be expelled from the division, and was at once expelled himself. This was the beginning of the downfall of this splendid body of men who had been actuated by a truly patriotic spirit. As Lord John Russell says, there is no sadder chapter in the sad chronicle of Ireland than their fall ; but, he adds, the characters of Lord Charlemont and Mr Grattan deserve to be drawn with a pencil of light. Purer and more upright statesmen have never adorned the annals of any country. To a man of Lord Charlemont's elevated mind,

EARL OF CHARLEMONT.

the falling away of the Volunteers from their original standard and their lapsing into disaffection, was a sore trial, which darkened the closing years of his life. A lesser one was the knowledge that his son and successor inherited no spark of the spirit of patriotism which had burned so ardently in his own breast. Francis Caulfeild, second Earl of Charlemont, does not stand out as a central figure in the history of his country. It is often the case that Nature seems to exhaust her gifts, either personal or mental, in one generation, and does not repeat them in the next. There is not much to record of the second earl. In his youth his somewhat dissipated habits had caused considerable anxiety to his father, and in the correspondence published by the Historical Commission we find one or two beautiful letters from him to his son. Later on, Mr Caulfeild represented Charlemont (a pocket borough) and on his first night in Parliament made a commendable *début;* but here his political career ended. Neither did the second earl inherit the artistic tastes of the first or Great

THE VOLUNTEERS IN COLLEGE GREEN, FROM THE PICTURE BY WHEATLEY, R.A.

Earl, who was a nobleman "after the pattern of Chesterfield or Rockingham." The latter was his intimate friend, and they vied with one another in collecting the finest pieces of sculpture, the best paintings, the most elegant ornaments. The letters of Lord Charlemont to his friend Malone, which have been lately published by the Historical Commission, testify that the sums of money he spent upon statues books, paintings, intaglios, vases were enormous for the time in which he lived, but would not be thought much in our own day, when a volume of scarce, old printing will fetch two or three hundred pounds. We find that the price given by Lord Charlemont to Hogarth's widow for "The Lady's Last Stake" was only one hundred pounds, and for the "Gate of Calais" the same; the bust of Rockingham, by Nollekens, only cost fifty pounds. Still, although the cost of each article taken separately was, according to our views, small, the aggregate amounted to thousands, and the collection of articles of virtu was unrivalled. Charlemont House was built, in 1763, from the design of Sir William Chambers, who, in March of that year, wrote to the Earl:—"I have sent herewith a plan of the manner in which I think The Sweepstakes should be ornamented. As you cannot have a court deep enough to turn carriages in without throwing the house too far back to be an ornament to the street, I have designed the entrances with piers at the two extremities of the court, and the space between them may be closed with iron grilles, which will look well." The fact that the Great Earl had chosen Rutland Square for his town residence made the locality at once fashionable, every house being occupied by noblemen or gentlemen of the highest position. On the parade day of the Volunteers a guard of honour would be detailed to wait upon the Colonel, Lord Charlemont, and accompany him and a brilliant staff to College Green, where the reviews were held. In addition to these advantages, the Rotunda Gardens were at that time a fashionable resort, and nightly crowded with the beaux and belles of Dublin. *Sic transit gloria mundi*, the ominous flag of the house-agent now decorates most of the deserted tenements in Rutland Square, and a few nursery-maids are the only tenants of the Rotunda Gardens.[1]

Charlemont House, large as it was, could not contain

[1] During the lifetime of James Molyneux, the late and last Earl of Charlemont, Charlemont House and Marino were the scene of many a pleasant revel. On one occasion a fancy ball took place, when Lord Charlemont appeared in the uniform worn by his famous ancestor as Colonel of the Volunteers. The historic house in Rutland Square lent itself to such revels. Like a *ci-devant* beauty, anxious to live up to her former reputation, it resumed for the night a touch of its old magnificence; it was, however, only a flash before final darkness. Charlemont House has been for many years a Government office. Its fine rooms and spacious library are partitioned off to suit the different requirements of red-tapeism. On the last occasion upon which I visited Charlemont House I was painfully impressed by its desolate aspect. There was the silent coldness of official life, the only interrup-

all the treasures amassed by the artistic Earl: and in 1789 Chambers was again called upon to send over plans for a country residence. Marino lies in a prettily-wooded country not more than half-an-hour's drive from Dublin: it unites the charm of a fine dashing seaboard to its inland advantages, and it was not surprising that the quiet of the sequestered retreat, upon which he had lavished care and money, appealed strongly to one of the Earl's temperament. By degrees he withdrew there almost altogether. In the grounds he caused to be erected a delightful casino, from a design of Sir William Chambers. "It was the very perfection of architectural elegance, being of the Sicilian Doric order, constructed of stone of dazzling whiteness and raised upon a square base." The entrance was ornamented by a series of chiaroscuros of classical subjects: the designs by Cipriani, executed under the superintendence of Verpyle. Marino[1] was very dear to Lord Charlemont's heart, especially after the disappointments which attended the breaking up of his cherished hopes in regard to the situation of Ireland. Like many another, what he loved most was a matter of indifference to his heir. Neither Lord nor Lady Charlemont had any affection for Marino. Her early education made her care more for foreign life, and the first years of her marriage were spent abroad.

At Florence she found her former friend, the Comtesse d' Albanie grown older and fatter, but kind as ever. Lady Mansfield described to Moore the effect Lady Charlemont's beauty produced upon the enthusiastic Italians. "Last night, at the Comtesse d'Albanie's, they were ready to fall down on their knees and worship her." Her portrait undoubtedly presents a lovely face, contour perfect, the eyes large and starlike, the mouth irresistible. "Thoroughly unspoilt by

tion the footfall of a chance visitor echoing on the marble hall. As I stood there. I peopled the silent house with the forms of the brilliant throng who had been wont to assemble there—the beauties, the wits, the statesmen, the politicians. Grattan, Burke, Flood, Ireland's loved Kildare, Lord Edward Fitzgerald, and his lovely Pamela. What a shifting scene; what a rustle of silken skirts up and down the grand staircase; what laughter and chatter from those rosy lips, with now and then an occasional oath or doubtful story.

[1] Marino, like Charlemont House, is sold. It is now the property of the Christian Brothers.

all the homage paid to her, that beautiful creature, Lady Charlemont," writes Moore, "has not yet seen Lord Byron's tribute to her beauty." The lines he alludes to appeared in the first edition of "Don Juan," but were later expunged, probably by the wish of Lord Charlemont, who may not have liked his wife's name to be associated with a poem so universally condemned. Here are the lines as they originally stood:—

> "There was an Irish lady, to whose bust
> I ne'er saw justice done, and yet she was
> A frequent model; and if e'er she must
> Yield to stern Time and Nature's wrinkling laws,
> They will destroy a face which mortal thought
> Ne'er compassed, nor less mortal chisel wrought."

And nine years later, writing to Bowles, he says: "The head of Lady Charlemont, when I first saw her, seemed to possess all that sculpture could require for the Ideal."

There is constant mention in Moore's diary of Lady Charlemont. The poet was on terms of intimacy with both husband and wife; the latter's love of rhyming, however, made a special bond of union. "Lady Charlemont is again on the wing to Dublin," writes Rogers, "as beautiful as ever. She talks of your songs with the same enthusiasm she used to do."

Lady Charlemont's own verse was like that of many amateurs—graceful but feeble. Two or three of her poems are now lying before me: they are very much of the character that we find in some of the inferior annuals or books of beauty of the period. The first of these is an epitaph on poor Braham, whose tomb is erected on the top of three pollards at Beechgrove, Killadoon. Braham was a pet canary bird evidently much cherished by his mistress. The verses to his memory are not, however, so remarkable as the lines on the singular death of poor Cob, a favourite swan who committed *felo-de-se*:—

> "To terminate his mortal span,
> Impatient of Time's dull delay,
> He flew upon the scythe of man."

These lines someway convey a reminiscence of Mrs Leo-

Hunter's "Frog," and we turn with more pleasure to the following, which have a certain go in them :—

"Away with melancholy,
  Nor doleful dirges bring
On life and human folly,
  But merrily, merrily sing.

Oh, what's the use of sighing,
  When life is on the wing!
Can we prevent its flying?
  Then merrily, merrily sing."

Lady Charlemont might have been satisfied with her gift of divine beauty, and have let alone meddling with the Muses, her gifts not lying in that direction. Her ambition, however, was to be not only a poetess but a blue of the first order, a fact which her devoted admirer, Byron, acknowledges with much sorrow. But so potent was the spell of her beauty that even this lapse into what he held in especial aversion was forgiven by him. In a long diatribe against the hated blue, he says, alluding to Lady Charlemont: "I say nothing of her . . . look in her face and you forget all—everything else . . . . Ah, that face!—to be beloved by that woman, I would build and burn another Troy." Lady Charlemont's blueism need not have alarmed Byron, she being in reality quite as silly as any woman should be. The family traditions are full of the poor beauty's sprospositos, which equal, if they do not surpass, Lady Coventry's, as when she heard someone talking in praise of Lord Bacon's works, she said, "*Oh, Charlemont, do let us have a bacon.*" And on another occasion, when stagheaded trees were under discussion, she proffered the request to have an avenue of stagheaded trees. On one occasion when she dined with Lady —— her hostess sent her down to dinner with the American minister whose name began with Van. To his surprise, his beautiful neighbour questioned him closely as to the habits of lions and tigers, and when he professed ignorance she said earnestly, "Ah, you must tell me, Mr Van Hamburg, what you feel when you have your head in the lion's mouth." [1]

[1] Van Hamburg, a famous lion tamer.

Beauty is a perishable gift, as we all know, but somehow it gives one a shock when later this passage occurs in Moore's diary: "I think Bessy (his wife) looked even prettier than Lady Charlemont: but then she is younger." Alas! for the flight of years that dims even such glorious eyes as hers. Tears had, perhaps, some share in dimming their brilliance—Rachel mourning for her children. Once more we quote from the ever-garrulous Moore. "1827. Went down to the Charlemonts' to pass the day at a very pretty place near Teddington. They were just recovering the loss of one of their daughters, who died of a long illness. The other girl, a very lovely person, felt it so much that they have great fears for her." Those fears were realised—the Honourable Emily Caulfeild died that year, 1829—her death being preceded by that of the only surviving son, James, Lord Caulfeild, a young man of much promise.

These sad bereavements (which always seem to fall at the moment when advancing years make the trial all the harder to bear) changed the bright aspect of Lady Charlemont's life. She was just preparing to live again in the triumphs of her beautiful daughters, but from this period we hear little more of her. In 1837 she lost her husband, and three years later her sister, Lady Leitrim. To the children of this last she was much attached, extending her affection to the second generation, by whom "Aunt Charlemont," in spite of her fidgety ways, was much loved. In her old age there was no trace of the beauty which had charmed Byron and Moore. She was a tiny, shrivelled old lady. She drove about Dublin in an old-fashioned chariot, with a hammercloth, upon which were emblazoned the Charlemont arms, a fashion which has passed away with the chariot. To the last, Lady Charlemont kept up her *blue* tendencies, attending lectures at the Dublin Society House, and patronising all artistic gatherings. She was lady of the bed-chamber to the Queen up to 1854. She died at her residence, 14 Upper Grosvenor Street, on December 23, 1876, at the advanced age of ninety-five.

SARAH CURRAN.

*From the Original Picture by Romney, in the possession of the Hon. Gerald Ponsonby.*

## SARAH CURRAN (1780-1808)

NOT far from Cork there is a small town called Newmarket, which in olden days was peopled by vassals or kerns of the great Desmond family, by name M'Auliffe. The M'Auliffes were a resolute clan; they shared the opinions and they suffered the same fate as did their chief, the Desmond of Queen Elizabeth's day. The M'Auliffes, being, so to speak, cleared out of the way, were succeeded by the Aldworths, a planting of James the First. The Aldworths did not care to inhabit M'Auliffe Castle, which was picturesque but uncomfortable, requiring a host of retainers to defend it against the attacks of wandering marauders. So it was let go to ruin in a most picturesque manner, while the new-comers built themselves a plain, substantial dwelling called Newmarket House, with a long, straight avenue, thickly planted with elm, sycamore and beech trees, which we are told "grew into *giants*, for the Aldworths, although *good* and *hospitable* were not extravagant." There is an unconscious irony in this remark most diverting.

Amongst the inhabitants of the small town of Newmarket there was one family whom the Aldworths distinguished by especial acts of patronage. The Currans were of English origin, and had followed the Aldworths when they had been transplanted to Ireland. The first of the family had been (in view of his fidelity) appointed to the post of seneschal of the town; his son married Sarah Philpot, a thorough gentlewoman, "with a woman's deep, fresh but irregular moods." Sarah's mind was like the clear river of her native town, that came gushing from the lonely mountains down to the village. She hid under a somewhat cold and severe exterior a waste of passions, traditions and aspirations, all lying in a tumultuous jumble in her soul, and in their turn being overpowered by intense love for her son, John Philpot. The affection between the mother and son was deep and strong, and to her influence may be traced that love of his country for which he was remarkable. In his boyhood she flooded his mind with stories and memories of the bygone glories of Ireland, and filled his young heart with soft lullabies that permeated his very being.

It was Mrs Curran's wish that her son should enter the Church. He was therefore sent in 1767 to Trinity College, where he was entered as a sizar: but in 1770 he got a scholarship, and, abandoning the Church, turned his attention to the Bar. The College boys were a most unruly set; they mixed up in every fight and frolic of the city. An internecine warfare waged continually between them and the townsmen, and on these occasions the college gown became a weapon, for in its folds was concealed a heavy key. In every scrape John Philpot Curran was the foremost rioter. It was said of him that he was the wittiest, the dreamiest, the most classical and ambitious, the wildest and the most mischievous scamp in Trinity College.

The youth is father to the man, and all through his life Curran retained these characteristics. His character has been somewhat misrepresented by his biographers, who, while they talk of his witty sayings and quote his puns, take little note of the fervid nature, the passion of which shines through those luminous eyes which look at us from his well-known portrait by Lawrence, and which light up his face like coals of fire—a face, by the way, by some called ugly, but which, nevertheless, possessed, as some ugly faces do, a most extraordinary attraction, especially for women. His unprepossessing appearance and his great success with the fair sex was commemorated in a small compass by his friend, Mrs Battier, (one of the Dublin blue-stockings), who wrote the following couplet:—

> "For though his monkey face might fail to woo her,
> Yet, ah, his monkey tricks would fain undo her."

His nature was intensely sensitive. His love for his mother continued all through his life, and did not cease with her death.[1] He married his cousin, Miss Creagh of Newmarket, who was eminently unsuitable as a wife. He was, however, passionately attached to her, in spite of her affectations, her laziness and her inordinate conceit. Curran had no means save what his intellectual qualities would gain for him, but these were of such a striking order that, instead of being surprised at his eminent success, the wonder would have been had such a man failed. He rose rapidly at the Bar, his reputation being greater amongst his friends than with the public—a sure sign, his biographer says, of a genuine man. His first great case was against Lord Doneraile, and, in consequence, he was challenged by Captain St Leger and fought a duel—not by any means the only encounter in which Curran took part.[2] A lawyer in those days had need to be a good shot, for a duel often followed a day's work in the Courts, and such affairs rather increased than diminished a man's reputation. The Irish Bar at this time presented a scintillation of brilliant men—Burke, Plunkett, Wolfe (Lord Kilwarden), Toler, (Lord Norbury) Yelverton, O'Grady, all men of remarkable talent and keen wit.[3] Curran took his place in the foremost rank, being counted one of the ablest men in certain cases. Unfortunately, as his business increased, he had less time to give to family

[1] The epitaph he placed on her tomb is a touching record of his filial affection—

Here lies the body of Sarah Curran.
She was marked by many years, many talents,
Many virtues, few failings,
No crime.
This memorial was placed here by
a son—whom she loved.

[2] He fought a duel with Lord Clare, the Chancellor, when he was Mr Fitzgibbon.

[3] They were all Monks of the Screw, a society under the care of the Patron Saint of Ireland—St Patrick. Their convent was in Kevin Street, where their somewhat noisy meetings took place. Curran wrote the charter, which ran:—

"When St Patrick our order invented,
And called us the Monks of the Screw,
Good rules he revealed to our abbot,
To guide us in what we should do.
But first he replenished his fountain
With liquor, the best in the sky,
And we swore by the word of his saintship
That fountain should never run dry."

life, and the happiness which had marked the earlier years of his married life suffered a total eclipse. Mrs Curran complained of the dulness of The Priory, a place Curran had bought near Dublin. "An ugly villa," says one who knew it, "built in the usual style of the suburban architecture of the day." Mrs Curran's solitude (for Curran was undoubtedly not domestic) was cheered by the constant visits of an intimate friend of her husband—the vicar of the adjoining church—who took a kindly interest in the lady's welfare. The usual result followed—the Rev. Mr Sandys eloped with Mrs Curran, leaving four children of different ages without a mother's care.

This blow was keenly felt by Curran, and it may be said that he never recovered from it, his genial nature being tinged from this time with a certain bitterness, his affections growing colder. It was noted that from the time of his wife's desertion, Curran, when he pleaded in a divorce suit, was remarkable for his scathing denunciations of the male offender. On one occasion, the eloquence with which he described the consequences of the fault, and the touching picture he drew of the deserted husband and neglected children, affected the listeners deeply. There was not a dry eye, we are told, in the Court, and the jury assessed the damages at the unprecedented sum of £10,000.

Unfortunately, in his own family, Curran made the mistake of punishing the children (who had suffered as much, if not more, than he had, from losing their mother's care) for their mother's fault—not that he treated them with either severity or unkindness, but he set up a barrier between himself and them that they could not pass. He encouraged no demonstrations of affection, and although willing that they should have all the advantages of his wealth and position, he neither sought their intimate friendship nor invited them to repose confidence in him.[2] If he had done so, Sarah Curran's pitiful story might never have been written. She,

[1] Richard, Henry, Amelia and Sarah.

[2] It must be remembered, however (when judging Curran's conduct as a father), that in the last century and beginning of this, parents and children were on a totally different footing from what they are in our day. The formal respect, the unquestioning obedience, the abject fear have given place to an equality and independence of thought and opinion which, although it may be more healthy, is

it was said, stood especially in awe of her father, being of a delicate and timorous nature, carefully concealing the depth of her nature and its capabilities of loving. Had she lived in less stirring times her path might have been peaceful and happy, but the history of her country was bound up in the sad tragedy of her life, and I must again ask the indulgence of my readers while we take a glance at what brought about her misfortunes.

The short, wild rising of 1798, which had choked every prison in Ireland with prisoners, was over, and the new panacea of a union between the countries—Pitt's pet scheme—had been forced upon an unwilling country. We have seen that it was more unpopular with the northern and Protestant section than with the Catholics of the west and south. The Presbyterians and Dissenters were filled with distrust of the measure. Castlereagh, however, was bent on carrying it through, and did so at the expense of his own credit, which was considerably lowered by the bribes he distributed to the *patriotic* members of the Irish Parliament. The moment, moreover, was ill-chosen, and the result was at first not commensurate with the outlay. In 1803 the country was still seething with agitation, when Robert Emmet stood forward as the new champion of Ireland's wrongs. Amongst many enthusiastic patriots, few were so sincere in their enthusiasm as this youth, round whose story a halo of romance has been cast which enlists the sympathy even of the most earnest enemy of such sentimental vapouring as he indulged in.[1]

nevertheless liable to the danger hinted at in the old proverb, *Too much familiarity begets contempt.* Curran's coldness was principally displayed towards his younger children. To Henry, his youngest son, he showed a marked dislike. Cyrus Redding, who was on intimate terms with Henry Curran, describes him as a most interesting and amiable man whose life was darkened by this shadow—to which he occasionally alluded—attributing it to a very obvious reason.

[1] One of the foremost opposers of the Union was Plunket. "For my part," he said, "I will resist it (the Union) to the last gasp of my existence and with the last drop of my blood, and when I feel the hour of my dissolution approaching. I will, like the father of Hannibal, take my children to the altar and swear them to eternal hostility against the invaders of their country's freedom." Often enough did the disturbers of Ireland's peace found their justification on these impassioned words. A little reflection, however, shows how wiser counsels prevailed over genuine patriotism. Had Mr Plunket persevered in his wild vow, the scaffold would have intercepted its performance, and Ireland would have lost an able Chancellor, as well as a bishop and archbishop.

Robert Emmet had from his childhood been bred up in an atmosphere of hatred to the yoke of England. This hatred was by no means confined to the poorer and more oppressed Catholics, but was fully shared by the Dissenters, Presbyterians, and, strange to say, by a large section of the dominant Protestant Church. To this last Emmet's father belonged.[1] He was a well-known and distinguished physician, his political opinions were of the most advanced description. Grattan, who was his intimate friend, describes the principles he inculcated at his breakfast-table. He had a sort of catechism for his sons.

"Well, Temple,[2] what would you do for your country? Kill your sister? Addis, would you kill your brother? Would you kill me?"

One can imagine how such a training was likely to excite young and ardent minds. Temple Emmet died early, but Thomas Addis, the second brother, threw himself warmly into the rising of '98. He was the intimate friend of Wolfe Tone, who describes him in his journal as a man after his own heart. He belonged to the executive committee, and, for publishing a most seditious newspaper, was expatriated for life. Robert at this time was a mere boy. He soon, however, began to walk in his brother's footsteps. Handsome, winning, eloquent, Robert had exceptional gifts. Moore, who was his fellow collegian and knew him well, has left a portrait of his friend, for whose memory he always retained a sincere respect and affection. "Were I to number among all the men I have ever known who seemed to me to combine in the greatest degree moral worth with intellectual power, I should amongst the highest of the class place Robert Emmet. Wholly free from the follies and frailties of youth, though how capable he was of the most devoted passion events afterwards proved,

[1] It is somewhat singular that in every struggle for independence made by the Irish nation, the leader of such attempts (with the one exception of Daniel O'Connell) has been a Protestant.

[2] Of the three sons of Dr Emmet, Temple, the eldest, was perhaps the most gifted. He passed through Trinity College with such success that the examiners changed the usual "*Valde bene*" into the more laudatory "*O quam bene.*" He was called to the Irish Bar, and was rising to possible eminence, when, at the early age of thirty, he died.

simple in all his habits, and with a repose of look and manner indicating but little movement within, it was only when the string was touched that set his feelings, and through them his intellect in motion, that he at all rose above the level of ordinary men. On no occasion was this more striking than in those displays of oratory with which both in the Debating and Historical Society he so often enchained the sympathy and attention of his young audience. No two individuals, indeed, could be more unlike to each other than was the same youth to himself before rising to speak and after. The brow, that had appeared inanimate and almost drooping, at once elevated itself in all the consciousness of power, and the whole countenance and figure of the speaker assumed a change as of one suddenly inspired. Of his oratory it must be recollected I speak from youthful impressions, but I have heard little since that appeared to me of a loftier, or what is far more rare in Irish eloquence, purer character, and the effect it produced, as well from its own exciting power as from the susceptibility with which the audience caught up every allusion to passing events, was such as to attract seriously the attention of the heads of the College: and by their desire a man of advanced standing in the University and with a reputation for oratory, came to attend our debates expressly for the purpose of answering Emmet and endeavouring to neutralise the fervour of his impassioned eloquence."

Later on a formidable inquisition was held within the walls of Trinity College by the Chancellor (afterwards Lord Clare), the students being all examined on oath in his presence. To many of them the startling disclosures made were revelations of plans and conspiracy of which they knew absolutely nothing. "There were a few—amongst the number was poor Robert Emmet—whose total absence from the scene, as well as the silence that followed the calling out of his name, proclaimed how deep had been his share in the transactions now about to be inquired into."

Nothing daunted by this beginning, nor by the failure of the rising of '98, Emmet, with all a young man's optimism, imagined that he would succeed where others had failed. He fully believed that Wolfe Tone's mantle had fallen upon his shoulders, with the additional conviction that his, Emmet's, star was certain to be in the ascendant. Those vain dreams became more definite after his meeting with Sarah Curran, his love giving an uncontrollable impetus to his patriotism. They met for the first time (one year before the disastrous termination of the love idyll) at the house of Mr Lambart of Rath Castle, Wicklow. The occasion was a ball where Sarah made her *début* in society. She was barely seventeen, with a sweet pale face surrounded by an aureole of golden hair.[1] Her refined, delicate beauty, her soft, gentle voice and manner completely captivated the young patriot: he fell fathoms deep in love. "She is kind, she is lovely, "he writes to Miss Lambart, "and heaven only knows how good."

Soon after the meeting at Rath Castle, Emmet became on terms of intimacy with the family of Sarah. This was only natural. Doctor Emmet had been a friend of Curran's, and the son was made welcome for the father's sake. Moreover, Curran, who was accustomed to be the centre of a group of admiring friends who listened to his brilliant, sparkling conversation, never for one moment imagined that his daughter was the attraction that made Robert so constant a visitor. That he should be unobservant of the growing attachment between the young people was only natural, fathers, and mothers sometimes, being proverbially blind. That the brothers and sister of Sarah should have been kept also in ignorance seems hardly credible, and a passage in Emmet's last letter to Richard Curran points to the fact that he, at all events, was to a certain extent in the secret. For the rest, Robert was not a suitor likely to find favour in the eyes of a prudent father; his youth, his want of fortune, and his well-known political opinions made him an unsuitable husband, as no one realised better than Emmet himself. "I must make myself worthy of the woman of my choice," he

[1] Another writer describes Sarah as having black hair and dark eyes, the latter being "large, soft and brilliant," capable likewise of a great variety of expressions; her aspect, says this authority, indicated reflection and *personal* abstraction, her wit was keen and playful, her musical talents of the first order. This last was undoubtedly the fact, but her mental gifts are exaggerated by this friendly critic.

tells the faithful confidante of his passion, "and the glory which sheds its lustre on the husband, shall reflect its splendour on the wife." Only that a deep tragedy underlies those word (the tragedy of his own life sacrificed and her youth blighted), one could laugh at this high-flown language. Like all lovers, Emmet imagined that the woman he loved was all his fancy painted her. As a matter of fact, Sarah was thoroughly unfit for the position he wished her to occupy. Gentle, sensitive, lovable, and weak in body and mind, she would in all probability have led (had Emmet never crossed her path), a peaceful life as the wife of some country gentleman, far from the struggle and excitement of passion, and content with her home and her children. That in the first chapter of the romance she did not respond to Emmet's violent passion, but rather shrank from it, we hear from his own account, written before his death:—

"I received no encouragement whatever," and, later on, "She told me she had no attachment for any person, nor did she seem likely to have any that might make her wish to quit her father."

After this rejection Emmet went to Paris, and there sought to distract his mind from love and politics. Both passions were, however, too strong for him, and, against the advice of his friend Lord Cloncurry, who made the most strenuous efforts to detain him, he returned to Ireland instead of sailing to America to join his brother, Thomas Addis.

A sort of infatuation led him at once to the Lambarts, where he found Sarah, sweet and lovely as before. His confidante, Miss Lambart (whose share in the miserable story was culpable in the extreme) gave him hopes. The lover however, confesses *he* "saw no progress of attachment on Sarah's part, nor anything in her conduct to distinguish *me* from a common acquaintance."

It was only when the clouds began to gather round her lover, and that he stood in need of sympathy, that the girl's gentle nature seems to have been touched with pity. "I had reason to suppose," writes Emmet, "that discoveries had been made, and that I should be obliged to quit the kingdom immediately. I came to make a renunciation of any approach to friendship that might have been formed. I then for the first time found when I was unfortunate, by the manner in which she was affected, that there was a return of affection, and that it was too late to retreat."

These simple words are touching, and condone, in a measure, Emmet's culpability in entangling so young a creature in his miserable fate. Still, he cannot be justified in his subsequent conduct. The danger of discovery (if it ever existed) blew over, and Emmet remained to rivet with still stronger chains the heart of the poor girl to his. With the assistance of Miss Lambart, he carried on a constant correspondence, and the same help contrived secret meetings for the lovers. Sarah in the hands of those stronger minds was malleable as wax, and the affection, which at first was only a spark of compassion, developed by degrees, until it quite equalled the passion he felt for her. Still not a word was said of the attachment either to her father, of whom Sarah stood terribly in awe, or to any member of the family, Miss Lambart remaining the sole confidante and means of communication between the lovers. In his letter to Curran, previous to his execution, Emmet excuses this dishonourable secrecy by the conviction he had that he would succeed :--

"I knew that in case of success many others might look on me *differently* from what they did at that moment, but I speak with sincerity when I say that I never was anxious for situation or distinction *myself*."

Meantime the young lover was busily engaged in organising the new insurrection. At first it seemed as if his star was about to rise. His schemes were all prepared, promises of help came from all sides, Keogh assured him that he would have the support of five counties. These promises, however, dwindled down to one. Still Emmet, with an almost insane obstinacy, refused to listen to the safer advice of older heads. The remains of his little fortune were spent in manufacturing arms, a business he carried on stealthily in Patrick Street. His deluded fancy made him see no difficulties in his path, and he convinced himself that, with the aid of a few desperate,

ROBERT EMMET ON HIS TRIAL.

(*From the Picture by George Petrie, R.A.*

undisciplined followers, he could make himself master of the Castle, and when this post of vantage was in his hands, Dublin would surrender without striking a blow. His scheme was all prepared. The Wicklow contingent, joined to the scum of the Liberties, were his forces, and this lawless horde had instructions to creep to their posts at nightfall and await the signal, a rocket. The duty of sending it up was to be Emmet's. They were then to rush from different points upon the Castle, choosing the narrowest streets in order that, if attacked, their peculiar style of warfare might prove more effective in a narrow passage: where, argued the young general of the banditti, a weapon such as a pike nine feet long would prove more telling than a musket or bayonet. He further convinced his hearers and himself that the inhabitants of the neighbourhood adjoining the Castle might be reckoned upon to take part against the military, and to give them a fine accolade of saucepans, boiling water, coping stones, slates, and anything else that came to hand. Emmet's own position was to be the watch house [1] on the old bridge, which commanded the narrow entry by which troops could come from Chapelizod. Once his rocket had ascended, he would wait a certain time to allow of the marching of the different divisions, and then rush to the Castle to tear down the hateful flag of England.

In theory his plans were absolutely perfect, and had Emmet and his wild mob been possessed of common sense, success would undoubtedly have crowned their efforts. As a matter of fact, the Government was totally off its guard; the usual battalion of spies and informers seem to have been off the scent, and, knowing nothing, had nothing to sell. It is clear that if Emmet had followed his original plan and attacked the Castle, he would have captured it. Nothing succeeds like success. At the first evidence that the tide was turning in favour of the rebels, hundreds who were undecided would have joined the movement. As it was, the whole face of the undertaking was changed by the tragic incident of Lord Kilwarden's murder. Up to this point all had gone well. The night of the 23d July was clear and

[1] Formerly the Custom House.

starry, the rocket had gone up unperceived by the authorities, but marked by those in the secret. At the signal, out poured the rebels from their hiding places, rushing through the narrow streets on their way to the Castle. As the disorderly mob debouched into Meath Street, they saw coming in the opposite direction a handsome carriage and horses. Mob instinct for plunder was at once aroused, the carriage was stopped, surrounded by an excited, howling and armed crowd; eager hands seized the horses' heads, others equally zealous tore the door with its elegantly-painted panels from its hinges, and rent the silken curtains into ribands. The occupants were dragged out—one a fine-looking man of middle age, the other a mere girl, his daughter, both in evening dress, for they had been dining with Lord Castlereagh at the Castle, where no hint of insurrection had been dropped. Holding on by the carriage wheel, Lord Kilwarden held up his hand to obain a hearing.

"My good people," he said, "I have never done you harm. I am Kilwarden, Chief Justice of the King's Bench."

"Justice!" yelled the man nearest to him. "Much justice you gave my boy! Justice! You shall have the same justice as he had. I have waited all these years for my revenge. I shall have it now!"[1] and he thrust his pike through Lord Kilwarden's heart.

For this foul deed Emmet was in no way accountable; in fact, he only appeared on the scene when the murder was an accomplished fact. His horror at the act, a horror which was intensified by his morbid dread of the sight of blood, together with his total incapacity to control the lawless mob he had called into existence, seemed to paralyse him. He could rouse himself to make no effort, and fled precipitately

[1] In the year 1795, when Lord Kilwarden, then Mr Wolfe, was Attorney-General, a number of rebels, most of them lads of fifteen and twenty, were indicted for high treason. The judge, who was trying the prisoners, made a heartless joke about those "truckered traitors," which so disgusted Wolfe, who was a most humane man, that he used all his best efforts to get these boys the king's pardon. He succeeded on the condition of expatriation for life. One of them, however, obstinately refused to accept this condition, and was accordingly tried and executed. His relatives conceived the idea that the Attorney-General had selected James Shannon, as he was named, as a scapegoat to satisfy the Government, and vengeance was sworn against Wolfe. It was said that the man who stabbed Lord Kilwarden was Shannon's father.

from a scene abhorrent to his nature, leaving his "banditti" to their own devices; and, with no leader to guide them, his disorganised forces soon fell into the hands of a detachment of regular troops.

The insurrection so carefully planned was over in three hours. So ended this miniature rebellion, which, apart from its disastrous issues, reads somewhat like a schoolboy's barring-out, its visionary leader flying precipitately when he saw the day was lost. This, the last attempt at an armed rising, has been designated as "the vulgarest of riots." It had not one redeeming feature, and was stained with the base murder of an unoffending gentleman before his daughter's eyes. A parallel to such a deed can only be found in the days of the French Revolution.

But although all danger to the peaceful citizens of Dublin was over, the train of misfortune following on Emmet's ill-omened attempt was yet to come. The first shadow fell on "The Priory" on the morning succeeding the rising. Curran, as he was riding down the avenue on his way to Dublin to attend the Four Courts, saw through the trees the gleam of weapons glistening in the summer sunshine. He had heard nothing of last night's riot, and his astonishment and indignation may be imagined when Major Sirr, the officer in command of the detachment, informed him that, in consequence of information found amongst Mr Emmet's papers, he had a warrant to carry into effect, that of searching "The Priory."

"Almost thunderstruck," says Curran, "I at once proffered every facility in my power. To my utter amazement, a correspondence of which I had not even a suspicion was discovered."

One can imagine with what feelings, both as a father and a public man, Curran received this sudden blow. That the daughter he had so carefully trained should have lived in the house with him day by day, with a secret in her heart concealed from him, was a deception little inferior to that of her mother; while for herself the blow was a crushing one. It was not alone, however, the present calamity which overwhelmed Curran. He was a prominent public character, and his intrepidity of resistance to all unconstitutional measures exposed him to the political hatred of many who would have gloried in his ruin. One of these was the Chancellor Fitzgibbon, afterwards Lord Clare, who had long hated his successful rival, and now sought to fix the odium of complicity in the rising upon Curran. In this he did not succeed. The rest of the Bar, with one accord, sided with Curran. The Attorney-General, Standish O'Grady, showed him the utmost sympathy, and, by his orders, at the trial only a few extracts from Emmet's letters to Sarah were read in court. Previous to the trial it was necessary for him to examine the poor girl as to how much she knew of her lover's intentions. He executed this task with so much kindness, that he converted an official interview into a visit of consolation, Sarah acknowledging that she had never more sensibly experienced the affection of a father.

Meantime, the unfortunate author of all this misery was still at large. He had taken refuge in the village of Harold's Cross, half-way between Dublin and "The Priory." There he lay, concealed in a house which had belonged to his father, and which was tenanted by an old and faithful servant of the family. There is every reason to believe that if, in the first instance, he had attended to his own safety, he could easily have effected his escape.

"But in the same spirit of romantic enthusiasm which distinguished his short career, he could not submit to leave the country without making an effort to have one final interview with the object of his unfortunate attachment, in order to receive her personal forgiveness for what he now considered the deepest injury."

Mr Richard Curran, who gives this account, does not say whether this interview ever took place. Others, however, less well-informed, have given a description of the meeting between the lovers, which, it is stated, was interrupted by Curran himself, who (according to these self-constituted authorities) overwhelmed the lovers with reproaches for their dishonourable conduct. This story, although sufficiently dramatic for introduction into a melodrama, has no actual foundation.

There is more truth in the story that after his arrest Emmet confided a sum of money he had about him, together with a letter to be delivered to Miss Curran, to a friend he thought he could trust. The person, whose name does not transpire, pocketed the money, and carried the letter to the Government, on hearing which, Emmet, in despair at having committed Sarah by anything he might have said in the letter, addressed, through some channel, the most earnest entreaties to the Government that they should suppress the letter, engaging himself, if they would do this, not to say a word in his own defence, but to go to his death in silence. This offer he made, knowing how much it was an object with the authorities that he should not address the people. In Emmet's last letters to both Curran and his son Richard, he alludes to this unfortunate occurrence, and to the reparation he had tried to make.

"That I have written to your daughter since an unfortunate event has taken place was an additional breach of propriety, for which I have suffered well. But I will candidly confess that I not only do not feel it to have been of the same extent, but that I consider it to have been unavoidable after what had passed; for though I will not attempt to justify in the smallest degree my former conduct, yet when an attachment was once formed between us (and a sincerer one never did exist), I feel that, peculiarly circumstanced as I then was, to have left *her* uncertain of my situation would neither have weaned her affection nor lessened her anxiety; and, looking upon her as one whom, if I had lived, I hoped to have as my partner for life, I did hold the removing her anxiety above every other consideration."

That Curran should have defended Oliver Kirwan on his trial for treason, while he refused his help to Emmet, has always been cited as a proof of his implacable disposition. To use Emmet's own words, "A man with the coldness of death upon him need not be made to feel any other coldness, and should be spared any addition to the misery he feels, not for himself, but for those to whom he has left nothing but sorrow."

It was this very legacy of sorrow that steeled Curran's heart against the man who had so treacherously linked his daughter's fate to his own unhappy destiny. The wonder would have been to see a father defending the cause of one who had so deeply injured his child. Such Godlike virtue is beyond human nature. That, under the circumstances, Emmet should have asked such a favour, showed not only a lack of delicacy, but also that all his talk as to the injury he had inflicted and the sacrifices he had offered to make, "did not come from his heart." His acts of contrition are indeed mingled with a good deal of bitterness. "I did not expect you to be my counsel. I nominated you because not to have done so might have appeared *remarkable*. Had Mr Burrowes been in town, I did not even wish to see you, but as he was not, I wrote to you to come to me. I know that I have done you a severe injury—much greater than I can atone for with my life. That atonement I did offer to make before the Privy Council, by pleading guilty if those documents were suppressed. I offered more. I offered, if I was permitted to consult some persons, and if they would consent to an accommodation in saving the lives of others, that I would only require, on my part of it, the suppression of these documents, and that I would abide the event of my own trial. This also was rejected, and nothing but individual information would be taken. I own there has been much culpability on my part, but there has been also a great deal of that misfortune which seems uniformly to have accompanied me."

As a matter of fact whether from delicacy towards the young lady, or in consequence of Emmet's offer, his letter to Miss Curran was not read and we must suppose that it was in consequence of this forbearance on the part of the prosecution that Emmet made no effort at speechmaking.[1] He was defended at his trial by a well-known lawyer, Peter Burrowes, who did all he could for his unfortunate client. The result, however, was a foregone conclusion, as Emmet

[1] This matter is differently stated; some sources of information putting a long and inflammatory speech into Emmet's mouth.—*Vide* "Walker's Hibernian Magazine," etc.

was well aware. Whenever his counsel was cross-examining or brow-beating a witness with unnecessary severity, the prisoner would interfere, saying, "No, no: the man is speaking truth." This, however, was only when the points were bearing against himself. Likewise, when Burrowes, about to avail himself of the privilege of reply, was wearied to death with anxiety, and feeling both the painfulness and futility of what he was about to say, Emmet again interfered. "Pray do not attempt to defend me," he said, "it is all in vain." Burrowes accordingly desisted. In his later years, nothing could be warmer and more unqualified than his praise of Emmet's conduct all through the trial.

Emmet's farewell letter to the brother of Sarah, and his own intimate friend, is most touching. It was written just before he left his cell for the place of execution, and shows not a trace of the vapouring talk he was wont to indulge in. A tender sadness is mingled with manly resignation to the inevitable, and it must be a cold heart that would not feel touched at the outburst of grief for "my love Sarah."

"MY DEAREST RICHARD,—I find I have but a few hours to live; but if it was the last moment, and that the power of utterance was leaving me, I would thank you for your generous expressions of affection and forgiveness to me. If there was anyone in the world in whose breast my fate may be expected to stifle every spark of resentment, it would be you. I have deeply injured you; I have injured the happiness of a sister that you love, and who was formed to give happiness to everyone around her, instead of having her own mind a prey to affliction. Oh, Richard, I have no excuse to offer, but that I meant the reverse. I intended as much happiness for Sarah as the most ardent lover could have given her. I never did *tell you how much* I idolised her.[1] It was not with a wild, unfounded passion; it was an attachment increasing every hour from an admiration of the purity of her mind and respect for her talents. I did dwell in secret upon the prospect of our union. I did hope that success, while it

[1] These words give the idea that Richard had been, to a certain extent, the confidant of the attachment between his sister and Emmet.

afforded the opportunity of our union, might be the means of confirming an attachment which misfortune had called forth. I did not look for honour for myself—praise I would have asked from the lips of no man—but I would have wished to read, in the glow of Sarah's countenance, that her husband was respected. My love Sarah, it was not thus I thought to have requited your affection. I did hope to be a prop round which your affections might have clung, and which would never have been shaken; but a rude blast has snapped it, and they have fallen over a grave. This is no moment for affliction. I have had public motives to sustain my mind, and I have not suffered it to sink; but there have been moments in my imprisonment when my mind was so sunk by grief on her account, that death would have been a refuge. God bless you, my dearest Richard."[1]

This letter, and a long tress of Sarah's beautiful hair, which after his death, was found next Emmet's heart, were brought, the same evening, to Miss Lambart by a man whose face was carefully concealed, but who was said to have been the jail warder, who kept constant watch over Emmet for fear that, like Wolfe Tone, he might defeat the ends of justice by taking his own life. Like all who came in contact with Emmet, this rough jail-bird had grown to love this prisoner.[2]

The packet must have been a painful reminder (if such were needed) to the indiscreet lady who played so prominent a part in this tragedy. Her act, however, brought its own punishment, the unavailing regret she suffered at the consequences of her imprudence.

[1] Emmet went to the scaffold with singular composure. He made two requests of the sheriff—one, that his arms might be left as loose as possible, which was complied with; the other, that he might wear his uniform, was naturally refused. On the table of his cell was found, sketched by his own hand in pen and ink, an admirable likeness of himself, his head severed from the body, which lay near it, surrounded by all the frightful paraphernalia of a high treason execution.

[2] This personal attraction, together with his love story, has caused Emmet's memory to linger in the minds of the Irish people longer that some of their popular idols. Men who have done far more for their country than Emmet's visionary schemes would (if brought to fruition) have accomplished, are consigned to undeserved oblivion, while a tender interest still centres in Emmet, whose story has been handed down from generation to generation, and is still told by the fireside of a winter's evening. Had Emmet's sentence been commuted to expatriation, and had he married Sarah Curran, his place as a hero would have been beneath that of even Smith O'Brien.

Sarah Curran was not made of the coarser stuff that can breast misfortune. She was constituted like a delicate plant which basks in the sunshine, opening its flowers to the radiance and giving joy alike to itself and to those around; but at the first touch of winter hangs its head and withers before our eyes. So it was with Sarah. Love to her gentle nature was like the sun to the plant; she had basked in its plenitude, and all at once winter had come and all was desolate. She had not alone lost her handsome, loving worshipper, but old ties were broken. After such a terrible uprooting, home life at The Priory could not be the same. A shadow stood between father and child, sisters and brother. It has been said that Curran showed considerable harshness towards his stricken daughter, and that, weary of her sad lamentings and face of woe, he ordered her to quit his house.[1] All this is mere gossip, Curran's biographers maintaining a discreet silence as to his domestic relations. A story, however, seldom gains universal belief without some foundation of truth, and we may assume that the situation between father and child was strained, and that to relieve the tension, both caught at the idea of temporary separation. The doctors, moreover, advising change of air as the best remedy for a mind diseased, Sarah, accompanied by her sister Amelia,[2] went to visit some old friends at Cork, of the name of Penrose. They were Quakers—quiet, kindly people—who did all in their power to minister to the stricken girl who had ever before her eyes the horror of the awful death

[1] It has been often insisted upon that Curran, from the time of his wife's infidelity, had become a harsh father, and that to his tyrannical disposition, and the fear Sarah entertained of rousing his anger, was due the unfortunate secrecy as to her relations with Emmet, which ended so disastrously. In all this there is probably gross exaggeration. The portrait of his father, by Richard Curran, represents an amiable, domestic man, fond of his home and his children. When absent, his letters are full of those minute details and inquiries which are only made by one who lives with and for his children. Sarah's bird, Amelia's music, are matters of interest even when in the enjoyment of a well-earned holiday. Few men, however, were more strict as to a woman's behaviour, and it was only natural that, with his wife's lapse from virtue before him, he should have been specially mindful of his daughter's conduct. It was likewise in accordance with his character, that he should have found it hard to forgive his daughter's fault.

[2] Amelia Curran was a well-known artist. She resided in Rome, and is often mentioned in Moore's Diary.

scene and unhallowed, nameless grave of her lover, so young, so handsome, so devoted.

But could the sympathy and kind offices of friends have reached a spirit so shocked and driven in by horror, she would have experienced no want of consolation, for the Irish are a people of quick and generous sensibilities. The most delicate and kindly attentions were paid to her by families of wealth and distinction. She was led into society, and all kinds of occupation and amusement were tried to dissipate her grief and wean her from the tragic story of her love. But it was all in vain. There are some strokes of calamity that scathe and scorch the soul, that penetrate to the vital seat of happiness, and blast it, never again to put forth bud or blossom.

Washington Irving, who tells her story in poetic prose, says, "She did not object to frequent the haunts of pleasure, but she was as much alone there as in the depths of solitude. She walked about in a sad reverie, apparently unconscious of the world around her. She carried with her an inward woe that mocked at all the blandishments of friendship, and heeded not the song of the charmer, charm he never so wisely. The person who told me her story had seen her at the Masquerade. There can be no exhibition of far-gone wretchedness more striking and painful than to meet it in such a scene. To find it wandering like a spectre, lonely and joyless, where all around is gay—to see it dressed out in the trappings of mirth, and looking so wan and woebegone, as if it had tried in vain to cheat the poor heart into a momentary forgetfulness of sorrow. After strolling through the splendid rooms and giddy crowd, with an air of utter abstraction, she sat herself down upon the steps of an orchestra, and, looking about for some time with a vacant air that showed her insensibility to the garish scene, she began, with the capriciousness of a sickly heart, to warble a plaintive air. She had an exquisite voice, but on this occasion it was so simple, so touching, it breathed forth such a soul of wretchedness, that she drew a crowd, mute and silent, around her, and melted everyone into tears. The story of one so true and tender could not but excite interest in a country remarkable for enthusiasm. It completely won the heart of a brave officer, who paid his addresses to her, and thought that one so true to the dead could not but prove affectionate to the living. She declined his attentions, for her thoughts were irrevocably engrossed by the memory of her former lover. He, however, persisted in his suit. He solicited not her tenderness but her esteem. He was assisted by her conviction of his worth, and her sense of her own destitute and dependent situation, for she was existing on the kindness of friends. In a word, he at length succeeded in gaining her hand, though with a solemn assurance that her heart was unalterably another's."

The gentleman to whom Washington Irving alludes was Captain Sturgeon, and the *Hibernian Magazine* duly records:—

"February 1806, at Cork, Captain R. H. Sturgeon of the Royal Staff Corps, and nephew to the late Marquis of Rockingham, to Miss Sarah Curran, daughter to John P. Curran."

The fact that the marriage did not take place at her father's house gives colour to the supposition that Curran still refused to see his daughter. In all ways, Captain Sturgeon was an acceptable son-in-law, being of good family, having independent means and high, personal character. On the other hand, the marriage, from a domestic point of view, was a mistake. It was a regretable error that an honest, loyal-hearted gentleman should have linked his life to a woman who "tried to be an exemplary and amiable wife, but was never a happy one." The shadow of her murdered hero, lying in his far-away grave, was standing ever between her and her living husband, and Sarah thought it an act of treachery towards his memory to make any effort to forget him. What chance of happiness had Captain Sturgeon under such circumstances? A scene described by an eye-witness of Sarah's uncontrolled sorrow shows how freshly the wound bled, although she had been, at the time of the incident, married some months.

George Petrie, the artist, had been a friend both of Curran

and Emmet, especially of the latter, and, after his execution, he proceeded to paint, from sketches he had taken at the time, a portrait of the patriot as he appeared at the trial.

One day, just as the picture was finished, the artist's little son was alone in the painting-room when the door opened, and a lady, closely veiled, came in and walked up to the easel on which the work rested. She did not notice the child, and deemed herself to be alone. She lifted her veil and stood long in unbroken silence, gazing at the face before her; then, suddenly turning, she moved with an unsteady step to another corner of the room, and, bending forward, pressed her head against the wall, heaving deep sobs, her whole form shaking with a storm of passionate grief. How long that agony lasted the boy could not tell; it appeared to him to be an hour. Then, with a supreme effort, she controlled herself, pulled down her veil and quickly and silently left the room. Years after, the boy learned from his father that this was Sarah Curran, who had come, by appointment, to see her dead lover's portrait, on the understanding that she should meet no one of the family.

Captain Sturgeon took his wife to Italy, thinking that a total change of scene might wear out the remembrance of her early sorrows. She was an amiable and exemplary woman, and made an effort to be a happy wife, but nothing could cure the silent and devouring melancholy which had entered her very soul. She wasted away in a decline, and died, it was said of a broken heart, at Hythe, in Kent, May 1808.

In the life of Sir Charles Napier, in one of his letters to his mother he mentions Captain Sturgeon and Sarah.

"I rode over to Hythe this morning to see poor Sturgeon, who has lost his little wife at last, the betrothed of Emmet. Young Curran is here. His sister was gone before his arrival. They are going to take the body to Ireland."

She was buried at Newmarket, in the same tomb as Curran's dearly - loved mother, Sarah Philpot. Captain Sturgeon survived his wife six years. He met his death in a skirmish during the war of 1814.

Moore, in his melodies, has immortalised Sarah Curran's sad story:—[1]

"She is far from the land where her young hero sleeps,
  And lovers around her are sighing;
But coldly she turns from their gaze and weeps,
  For her heart in his grave is lying.

She sings the wild songs of her dear native plains,
  Every note which he loved awaking,
Ah, little they think who delight in her strains,
  How the heart of the minstrel is breaking.

He had lived for his love—for his country he died,
  They were all that to life had endeared him;
Nor soon shall the tears of his country be dried,
  Nor long shall his love stay behind him.

Oh, make her a grave where the sunbeams rest,
  Where they promise a golden morrow.
They'll shine o'er her sleep like a smile from the west,
  From her own loved island of sorrow."

In conclusion, I must say a word as to the portrait of Sarah Curran here given, which is reproduced from the original painting by Romney, in the possession of the Honourable Gerald Ponsonby.

A lady on intimate terms of friendship with the late Henry Curran (Curran's youngest son), who held a good appointment in Dublin, saw the picture lying in a garret. "My sister Sarah," by Romney, Henry Curran told her. What became of the picture she did not know. (She added that during the many years she had known Henry Curran, he never but on this occasion alluded to his sister Sarah. This fact is very significant, as showing how deeply the family pride had been hurt by the publicity attached to poor Sarah's unfortunate love episode.)

Some thirty years ago this portrait and a water-colour sketch by Boreas, a Dubin artist, were sold at the auction of

[1] Moore takes poetical licence. Sarah was at this time married, and we can hardly suppose she had other lovers beside her amiable, much-enduring husband. It is not well known that Hector Berlioz arranged this melody as well as some others. They are included in an edition of the musician's works now in the possession of Sir Francis Brady, Dublin.

Mr Henry Curran's effects, and both were bought by Featherstone, a well-known and eccentric dealer, who likewise possessed a lock of Emmet's hair, and an original letter written by Sarah. The fact that it was from Featherstone that Mr Ponsonby bought the portrait is conclusive evidence that it is the Romney, and all good judges (including the late Mr Henry Doyle) are convinced of its authenticity.

MRS CHEVENIX TRENCH.

*(After the Original Picture by Romney.*

# MELESINA CHENEVIX TRENCH

(1768-1827)

More than thirty years have passed since the then Dean of Westminster, Dr Chenevix Trench, later appointed Archbishop of Dublin, gave to the reading public his interesting record of the literary remains of his mother, Mrs Richard Trench. Apart from the literary value of the book, it possesses a rare charm in the glimpses it gives of the life of a woman whose beauty and intellectual gifts gained her the admiration and esteem of those of her contemporaries best worth knowing. Not that her son, whose love for his mother is one of the most touching characteristics of the book, had any desire to make capital of either her successes or her popularity. He evidently had a morbid shrinking from exposing to public comment incidents dear to his own heart; he considered the adage, whether true or not in its first application, to be certainly correct as regarded the English matron—"*Bene vixit, quæ bene latuit.*" It was therefore no part of his plan to disturb the sacred obscurity that in his opinion should veil domestic life, or to lay bare incidents which, however interesting to the relatives and connections, can have no possible interest to anyone beyond. It is needless to remark that this sacred obscurity is not a feature of the present generation. We have, so to speak, taken down our shutters and let in a flood of daylight, so that all who pass by may look in at our inner sanctum. No one nowadays would be so quixotic as to throw Byron's Journal into Mr Murray's fireplace—*pas si bête*—"Print it, publish it," would be the cry; "who cares for a dead man's secret or a woman's good name?"

Melesina Chenevix Trench can hardly be counted as

belonging to the category of Irish beauties. In all fairness we must allow that it is a slender thread that unites her to the land of her adoption, and to which she gave her warmest affections. Her ancestors on both sides were undoubtedly of French descent, the family of Chenevix having been expatriated from Lorraine under the Edict of Nantes in 1598, when they came to England, where they found a new home and warm friends. Her grandfather, who was in the Church, owed his advancement to the friendship of Lord Chesterfield, in whose letters we find frequent mention of the "young bishop," as he was called. On Chesterfield's appointment to the Lord-Lieutenancy of Ireland he recommended Dr Chenevix, who had been previously his chaplain at the Hague, for an Irish bishopric, and "enforced his recommendation, when he was answered that 'the King wished he would look out for another bishop,' by replying, 'he wished the King would look for another Lord-Lieutenant.'" This threat had the desired effect, and Dr Chenevix was at once appointed Bishop of Killaloe, and in a few months translated to Waterford, a See he filled for thirty-three years. His only surviving son, Philip Chenevix, married Mademoiselle Gervaise, daughter to Archdeacon Gervaise, the descendant of another Huguenot refugee family who had settled in Ireland, where their only child, Melesina, was born in 1768.

She comes before us for the first time as a very small child, her entrance on the scene being marked by a peculiar tinge of romantic interest. An orphan at the early age of four years we find her growing up under the care of an aged and broken-hearted man who had lost all those he loved—wife, children, friends—and had only this one tie to life—a little, golden-haired child. One makes in imagination a picture of the little girl in her black frock, standing by her grandfather's chair, while his trembling hand rests upon her head as he gives her the morning blessing. Still, it was a sad and unwholesome surrounding for a child of Melesina's age and joyous nature, and, like all children brought up under such circumstances, she was preternaturally wise. She says of herself, "I was the best little child possible. Happy had

I been if such dispositions as I then possessed had been cherished, and the faults which afterwards sprang up eradicated. I was obedient and loving, docile and lively, although timid. I do not remember the smallest disposition to falsehood or mischief, and I sympathised with every being that felt."

It was, however, not an age when children were much considered, and although the good bishop adored this last remaining tie to life, he does not seem to have understood how to make the solitary child happy. Children in the last century were not the important personages they are now: their fancies were not consulted, their pleasures were restricted; they had to yield strict obedience to their superiors, and any infringement of rules was severely punished. That such harsh discipline was good in the main, there can be little doubt; still, an orphan like Melesina might have met with some leniency, and the reader feels indignant at the relation of her childish trials. Her faithful nurse, Alice, was sent away and replaced by a stiff, severe governess with a very long face, a very long waist, and a stocking in her hand, which she knitted so perseveringly, it seemed a part of herself. This woman, who was unfit for the care of the young, appears to have exercised much cruelty towards Melesina, whose spirits and health gave way under such a pernicious system of education. She grew pale, thin, and pined away so rapidly that it became necessary to call in a physician and to recall the faithful nurse. Under her care, Melesina recovered somewhat of her former strength, but her delicate appearance remained for many years.

The good old bishop died while she was still a child. Although he had not made her happy, she grieved for his loss with all the strength of her affectionate nature. He had not made her happy, though he had tried to do so, but she felt that he loved her more than all the world, and without knowing the value of such deep and exclusive love, the solitary child regretted the old man both from gratitude and affection.

After her grandfather's death, Melesina resided with Lady Lifford for a year, which was one of complete happiness. She describes Lady Lifford as the realisation of feminine gentleness and sensibility. She was the lovely mother of three children—Ambrosia, George, and Elizabeth—round whom Melesina's affections entwined. Being a year older than the eldest, she acquired considerable influence over them, was the leader in their sports, and each sought with eager competition for the largest share of her love. One cannot forbear a smile at her frank acknowledgment that George possessed the largest share. "I sometimes, from instinct, I suppose, teased *him*, though never his sisters. I would say, 'George, you do not love me,' and express doubts of his affection, till the large, bright drops forced themselves from his mild, hazel eyes, and then I would console him with the softest kindness, till I drew him from under the sofa, the place where he usually flung himself to hide his young sorrows. This strange exertion of feminine power over a child of nine by one three years older—was it instinct, or a species of coquetry awakened by having read, in my grandfather's study, Shakespeare, Ovid's *Metamorphoses*, Sterne, *The Arabian Nights*, an abundance of plays, and several works of imagination, which, describing the influence of female charms as invincible, excited an early desire to try their force? This childish exercise of power stands alone. I do not recollect any other instance of the slightest propensity to tyrannise; on the contrary, I did all I could to promote the pleasure of my companions, and, even in points where I had any advantages over them, to be careful they should never feel it. I was their surest *confidante*, their most disinterested adviser, and in sickness their tenderest and most unwearied nurse. This looks too much like praising of myself, yet what can I do? The kindly qualities I have mentioned are compatible with a thousand faults, of which the germs were but slightly developed in these youthful days."

After a year's residence in this happy family, Melesina went to live with her maternal grandfather, Archdeacon Gervaise. It was a curious destiny for a young and beautiful girl to be brought up under the care of *two* grave and reverend clergymen, both stricken in years, and to this may, perhaps, be attributed the thoughtfulness that was a salient feature of Melesina's character. Her gravity was, however, blended with the gaiety natural to her age, while the extreme simplicity of her manner added much to the attraction of her beauty, which was of the most captivating order. From Romney's portrait we can judge how lovely she must have been, with those sweetly seductive eyes, smiling, sensitive mouth, and mobile expression, showing every thought that passed through her mind, quickly moved to mirth and equally ready to sympathise with sorrow. Her sensibility was almost excessive, her friendship generous, her affections strong, and although she was keenly alive to the power of her own attractions, and by nature fond of admiration, she never overstepped in any way, either as wife or widow, the proper limit of all female fascinations. Reading between the lines of her simple and well-told journal, we can gather how much incense was offered at the shrine of her beauty, while here and there her natural turn for satire breaks out, and shows what a fund of observation she possessed.

Perhaps the leading feature of her character was her strong desire to do what was right. This principle seems to have guided her through every incident of her by no means uneventful life. At an age when most girls amuse themselves, she entered upon the "arduous duties of a wife," marrying Mr St George of Carrick-on-Shannon, Ireland, and of Hatley St George, Cambridgeshire. Her husband was not many years older than she was, and his "excessive fondness" made her very happy. After their marriage, they resided for some time at *Dangan*, lent to Mr St George by Lord Mornington, and here the young bride found herself the centre of a gay circle.

In the last century country life differed largely, both in England and Ireland, in its social aspects from what it is in our day. Being cut off by lengthy journeys from centres like London, Edinburgh and Dublin, society had to fall back upon the resources to be found near at hand. From the glimpses we get in the memoirs of the time, one would feel disposed to think that increased civilisation has not brought increased sociability: yet, after all, human nature repeats itself, and the accompanying account of a house-party given by Mr and Mrs St George at Dangan, reads like a society gathering of to-day, letter incident included.

"About two months after our marriage, we invited, for a Christmas party, the Duke and Duchess of Rutland, with the suite that attend him as Lord-Lieutenant; Lord Westmeath, Lord Fitzgibbon, General Pitt, General Conynghame, some of the prettiest women, and a group of the gayest young men. I thought myself in Elysium for half the first week; but the charm was soon broken, and I grew weary of turning night into day for no obvious reason, as all hours in the twenty-four were equally free from interruption, of listening to the *double entendres* of Mrs —— and Lady ——, and of playing commerce with a party of women impatient for the hour of eleven, which usually brought the men in a state very unfit for the conversation or even the presence of our sex.

"Under these impressions, I accompanied the same party to Lord ——'s, where I wrote a letter to Miss Chenevix, expressing my opinion of the society I was engaged in. This letter lay on the table while I retired to dress. —— —— and —— ——, who examined all my words and actions with the strictest scrutiny, each hinted a desire to know the contents. This inclination, in the more polished mind of the latter, would have died away, had it not been encouraged by the daring spirit of the former, who, collecting several of the female party, proposed, as an agreeable frolic, an action from which honour and principle alike recoil. The moment she obtained a half consent and a promise of secrecy, she heated her penknife and raised the seal. Pause a moment and consider the group. Agitated with a fear of discovery, conscious of being each in the power of the rest; *one*, mistress of the house, acting in direct violation of the laws of hospitality; *another*, condemned to read aloud the just censure of her own behaviour; a *third*, stung with resentment at a charge she could never refute without a confession of her own baseness; a *fourth*, in silent expectation of being held up to view in the light she deserved—all trembling with apprehension, ill-disguised under bitter smiles and affected indifference. As soon as they had finished reading, they resealed the letter, committed it to the post, vented their rage against its author, and reiterated promises of secrecy. These promises were kept like most others of the same nature. One of the ladies confessed all to her lover—that lover betrayed her to his friend—that friend imparted the secret to Mr St George, and he disclosed it to me. I felt no great resentment, particularly when I recollected that the fault was attended with its own punishment, even in the moment of commission: and I ever after behaved to the fair culprits with distant civility, though I never renewed with any one of them the slightest degree of intimacy. From the public they met with less indulgence. They were blamed, ridiculed, and even lampooned."

There is likewise a striking resemblance between the daily routine of Mrs St George's life and that of a fashionable beauty of to-day.

"As I rose late, I never found an hour in the day unoccupied, either by Mr St George's society, by dressing, visiting public places, consultations with the milliner, receiving company at home, or fulfilling my engagements abroad. Every study, every accomplishment was laid aside. I never opened a book except while my hair was dressing. I never touched a note, except when asked to play by St George. On domestic arrangements I never bestowed a thought: what was our income, and what our expense, I was equally ignorant. Scarcely could I find a moment to write to those I most loved. Both my temper and my taste would soon have been spoiled by this disposal of my time. Nothing is so quickly lost as the habit of occupation, which, till now, I had always in some degree maintained; now it was totally extinct. The injury my taste received from a recurrence of frivolous pursuits and the absence of reflection was still more evident; for I saw the Lakes of Killarney, about seven months after our marriage, with an indifference to its beauties I surely could not have experienced either before or since.

"Soon after, however, an event occurred which awakened all my dormant sensibilities, and conferred on me the purest happiness I had ever tasted. I had not long attained my nineteenth year when I became a mother. The delight of that moment would counterbalance the miseries of years. When I looked in my boy's face, when I heard him breathe, when I felt the pressure of his little fingers, I understood the full force of Voltaire's declaration:—

"'*Le chef-d'œuvre d'amour est le cœur d'une mère.*'

"My other affections appeared to require food, and, if not supported by adequate returns, I was sensible might expire; but this attachment seemed a part of my existence which could neither be increased nor diminished by any outward circumstances. My husband's delight in the birth of his son nearly equalled mine. My love for *him*, the father of my child, grew in strength, and I looked on myself as one of the happiest of women."

The decline of Mr St George's health soon put an end to this gay mode of life, and although "every day a new remedy was tried and a fresh physician called in," he gradually sank and died when they were at Lisbon, leaving Melesina a widow at twenty-two, with one child. That very same year she lost her grandfather, Archdeacon Gervaise, and was therefore quite alone in the world, so far as near relations were in question. She had, however, troops of friends. No woman ever had more, and of the right sort. She says, with wonderful simplicity, "that I often inspire affection is one of the chief blessings of my life." This faculty for making friends is very much marked in the pages of that portion of her journal which concerns her visit to Germany in 1799-1800, whither she went at the expiration of her first year of widowhood. It was a very independent undertaking for a woman of her age and appearance, belonging, moreover, as she did, to a generation which enforced the strictest observance of the laws by which women were hedged in. Yet Mrs St George, secure in her armour of innocence, and supported by the applause of her army of friends, bade defiance to the whispers of mock prudery, and took her fill of foreign travel unaccompanied by a chaperone. Everywhere she went she was received with open arms, having friends of her own or friends of friends at every legation. At Ham, near Hamburg, she was the guest of Baron de Breteuil; the whole family vied with one another in proofs of civility. And it was the same wherever she went; she was treated with the utmost kindness and respect. At Vienna she was the object of much attention, and after a week's residence had so many engagements that she was embarrassed in the choice of them. Her pleasantest recollections were of Lord Minto, the Hanoverian Minister, and Prince Schwartzenberg. At the house of the last named she heard Haydn's "Creation," which she thought the Germans applauded much above its merit. From Vienna she went to Baden, where she found it was the fashion for men and women of the best society to bathe together, "and," she adds naïvely, "they appear to enjoy the amusement very much. The gentlemen are in shirts and trousers; the ladies in their usual white morning dresses, and on their heads caps, handkerchiefs, laces and ribbons fancifully and becomingly disposed. It is the triumph of real beauty and freshness, as no rouge can be worn or paint of any kind. The bath opens a vast field for coquetry. A becoming dishabille, graceful attitudes, timidity, languor, and an affectionate confidence in your conductor, may here all be displayed to advantage. The lover leads his mistress, and has perhaps a secret satisfaction in finding himself with her in a new element: for Madame de Genlis observes, I think with truth, that to those who really love every new situation in company with the beloved has a certain charm. Many of those who have no lovers obtain, however, half a conductor, as every man who is not devoted generally gives each arm to a different lady. The old, the plain and the neglected sit round on benches, as it is dangerous for women to walk about in the bath without a guide. Spectators are admitted who view the scene from a little gallery. To them the heat and sulphureous smell is very unpleasant. The situation of this village is agreeable, among hills, which, though minute, are of a romantic character."

From Vienna Mrs St George made her way to Prague, and from there to Töplitz, where her intimate friend was the Princess Clary, to whom all Töplitz belonged. From Töplitz she returned to Dresden, where her friend Mr Elliot was the English Minister. During her stay here she came in for the visit paid by Lord Nelson, who was on his way to England accompanied by Sir William and Lady Hamilton. Mrs St George's account of these remarkable personages is an extraordinary narrative worth recording. It is written with the life-like fidelity which marks the well-kept diary, and photographs for the reader the scenes as they occurred.

It was when she was playing chess one evening with Mr Elliot that the news arrived of the arrival of the Nelson party, which included the three before named, and also Mrs Cadogan, Lady Hamilton's mother, and Miss Cornelia Knight, authoress of *Dinarbas*. The minute portrait of Lady Hamilton is not flattering, and hardly coincides with the lovely delineations with which we are familiar. "She is bold, forward, coarse, assuming and vain: her figure is colossal, but excepting her feet, which are hideous, well shaped; her bones are large, and she is exceedingly *embonpoint;* the shape of all her features is fine, even the form of her head, particularly the ears: her teeth are a little irregular but tolerably white; her eyes light blue, with a brown spot in one, which, though a defect, takes nothing away from her beauty or expression. Her eyebrows and hair are dark and her complexion coarse; her expression strongly marked, variable and interesting. Her movements in common life ungraceful; her voice loud yet not disagreeable. Lord Nelson," she tells us, "is a little man without any dignity, who, I suppose, must resemble what Suwarrow was in his youth, as he is like all the pictures I have seen of that general. Lady Hamilton takes possession of him, and he is a willing captive, the most submissive and devoted ever seen. Sir William is old, infirm, all admiration of his wife, and never spoke to-day but to applaud her. Miss Cornelia Knight seems the decided flatterer of the two, and never opens her mouth but to show forth their praises; and Mrs Cadogan, Lady Hamilton's mother, is—what one may expect. After dinner we had several songs in honour of Lord Nelson, written by Miss Knight and sung by Lady Hamilton. She puffs the incense full in his face, but he receives it with pleasure and snuffs it up very cordially."

In consequence of her friendship with the Elliots, Mrs St George saw a great deal of these strange visitors, and the more she saw the less she admired. She accompanied them to the opera, "where Lady Hamilton and Nelson were wrapped up in each other's conversation all the evening." There is a vivid account of Lord Nelson as he appeared, "*a perfect constellation of stars*, going to court." The Elector would not receive Lady Hamilton on account of her previous life, upon which Lord Nelson said to Mr Elliot, "Sir, if there is any difficulty of that sort, Lady Hamilton will knock the Elector down."

The night before she left Dresden, Lady Hamilton distinguished herself. It was after a morning performance; she had repeated her attitudes before a large company, none of whom remained to dinner except the Nelson party and Mrs St George. "Lady Hamilton, who declared she was passionately fond of champagne, took such a portion of it as astonished me. Lord Nelson, who was not behind-hand, called more vociferously than usual for songs in his own praise, and after many bumpers, proposed the Queen of Naples, adding, 'She is *my* queen; she is queen to the backbone.' Poor Mr Elliot, who was anxious the party should not expose themselves more than they had done already, and wished to get over the last day as well as he had done the rest, endeavoured to stop the effusion of champagne, and effected it with some difficulty, but not till the Lord and Lady, or, as he calls them, Antony and Moll Cleopatra, were pretty far gone. I was so tired I returned home soon after dinner, but not till Cleopatra had talked to me a great deal of her doubts whether the Queen would receive her, adding, 'I care little about it. I had much rather she would settle half

Sir William's pension on me.' After I went, Mr Elliot told me she acted 'Nina' intolerably ill and danced the Tarantella. During her acting Lord Nelson expressed his admiration by the Irish sound of astonished applause which no written character can imitate."[1]

The departure of the singular party took place the day following this exhibition, much to the satisfaction of their host, Mr Elliot, who was "very sensible of his deliverance." He would not allow his wife to speak above a whisper, and said now and then, "Now, don't let us laugh to-night, let us all speak in our turn and be *very*, very quiet."

Mrs St George returned to England in 1801, and on her way to her Irish home she made the acquaintance of Miss Anna Seward, to whom she was introduced by Lady Eleanor Butler, one of the ladies of Llangollen. Miss Seward's letter to Lady Eleanor gives a very flattering description of Mrs St George.

"Never was a first impression more lively; she absolutely dazzled me by the radiant expression of her eyes, while the graces of her address, the sweet and varied tones of her voice found immediate way to my affections. From circumstances I have not time to explain, I was *inextricably* obliged to pass Friday evening in a party less interesting than our *tête-à-tête* would have proved. Mrs St George was so good as to accompany me, and enchanted the private circle of quiet females with the constellation of her talents and graces. She danced, she sang, she conversed with fascinating grace."[2] Making due allowance for Miss Seward's sentimental rhapsodies, which carried her on to likening the object of her admiration to the Lesbian Maid and the first rose of Albion,

[1] Much offence was given by the frankness with which this amusing account is written, and a nephew of Lord Nelson took up the cudgels to defend his uncle's memory. In a pamphlet which is hardly worth the trouble of perusing, the dispute was accentuated by the introduction of a notice of Miss Cornelia Knight's autobiography which appeared in the *Quarterly Review*.

[2] Thirteen years later, Melesina, then Mrs Trench, writing to her son, Manners St George, alludes to this rhapsody of Anna Seward's. "Walter Scott, in reducing to six octavos the twelve folio volumes of Miss Seward's letters, has *cruelly* lopped her eloquent panegyric of your mother, who is dismissed with the laconic phrase of 'lovely and accomplished.' So there are no hopes of immortality from that quarter."

we may accept this highly-coloured portrait as essentially correct.

A calmer and more reliable authority, also of her own sex, describes Mrs St George at this period in equally flattering although more sober words. While visiting her property in Kildare, Mrs St George made the acquaintance of a Quaker lady residing at Ballitore. The impressions of Mrs Leadbeater are so well expressed, and give us such a perfect picture of Melesina, that although the extract is lengthy, I quote it in its entirety. These are Mrs Leadbeater's words—

"The inn on the high road from Dublin to Cork was completed, and was let to Thomas Glaizebrook. It attained a goodly reputation. One night, just as we were retiring to rest, a messenger came down from the landlord to say that a lady had arrived late, that the house was full to overflowing, and there was no room for her to take refreshment in, that she sat on the settle in the kitchen, reading, waiting until she could obtain an apartment; that she would be glad of the meanest bed in the house, being much fatigued; could we be so kind as to assist our tenant in this strait? My husband went up at once for her, and brought her down in a carriage here, when we found from her attendants that she was a person of much consequence. She retired to rest, after expressing grateful thanks, and we thought would pass away with the morrow. But not so. Her servants told us that she had an estate in the neighbourhood, that she had appointed her agent to meet her at Ballitore Inn, proposing to take her tenants from under the middleman to her own protection; and that she had been ten years the widow of a colonel, and had one son. I had seen but little of her the night before. When she entered my parlour the next day, I was greatly struck with her personal appearance. My heart entirely acquits me of being influenced by what I had heard of her rank and fortune. Far more prepossessing than these were the soft lustre of her beautiful black eyes, and the sweetness of her fascinating smile; her dress was simply elegant, and her fine, dark hair, dressed according to the present fashion, in rows of curls over one another in front, appeared to me to be as becoming as it was new. These particulars are not important except to myself; to me they are inexpressibly dear, because they retrace the first impressions made on me by this most charming woman, who afterwards gratified me by her friendship. Melesina St George, such was the name of the lovely stranger, spent two weeks in our house. She asked permission, in the most engaging manner, to remain here rather than return to the inn. Providence had been liberal in granting to her talents and dispositions calculated for the improvement and happiness of all around her, while her meekness and humility prevented the restraint of her superiority being felt, without taking from the dignity of her character. I was surprised and affected when I beheld her seated on one of the kitchen chairs in the scullery, for coolness, hearing a tribe of little children of her tenants *sing* out their lessons to her. I wished for her picture drawn in this situation, and for its companion I would choose Edmund Burke making pills for the poor. It was with difficulty I prevailed upon her to bring her little school into our parlour, because, as she said, she would not bring them into her own. Admiring her method of instructing, I told her she would make an excellent schoolmistress. She modestly replied, with her enchanting smile, not an *excellent* one, but she had no dislike to the employment, and had contemplated it, as a means of subsistence when the rebellion threatened to deprive her of her property. She came to Ballitore again and had apartments at the inn, where she entertained us with kind, polite attention, and amused her leisure with taking sketches of the views from thence with a pen and ink, not having her pencils with her, thus cheerfully entertaining herself with what was attainable."

The acquaintance thus begun, ripened into close friendship, a friendship which had a decided influence upon Mrs St George's after life, and has given to the present generation a correspondence between two interesting women which is full of interest. As before mentioned, Mrs Leadbeater came of a well known Quaker family, the Shackletons of Ballitore,

County Kildare. Mary Leadbeater was born in 1758, consequently was ten years older than Melesina. She was a singularly clever woman, well acquainted with the classics and general literature, and a writer of some repute. Her cottage dialogues, although now forgotten, enjoyed much popularity in the early part of this century, while her private journal, the "Annals of Ballitore," extending from 1766 to 1821, are most interesting from the variety of characters, incidents and anecdotes introduced, and the lively picture they present of her own time. So, too, with her correspondence, which is made doubly interesting by the contrast between the writers. This is no interchange of sentiment between two ladies moving in the same sphere of fashionable or even ordinary social life. The poles could not be more asunder than was the daily routine and social position of the two friends—the admired woman of the world, and the recluse of Ballitore. Herein lies the charm of these letters, which must be read in their entirety to be thoroughly enjoyed. Melesina tells her friend all she does in the gay world to which she belongs and in this Mary begins to take a certain interest, contributing in her turn that tone of patriarchal simplicity which in the early part of this century distinguished the Quakers, but has now quite disappeared with the coal-scuttle bonnet and the russet-brown frock.

This correspondence, which extends over a period of twenty-four years, never flags in interest. There was the all-absorbing topic of the people, whose ignorance and poverty Melesina made the most admirable efforts to ameliorate. That she succeeded was due in a great measure to the co-operation of Mary Leadbeater in every scheme suggested by her friend for the benefit of the poor.[1]

By a curious freak of fortune, however, for some years Mrs St George was unable to take any share personally in

[1] That Mrs Leadbeater contributed substantial aid as well as personal supervision, is clear from Mrs Trench's remarks when urging her friend to make money by her writings. "You see I am one of the slaves of Mammon; in truth, I think the mother of a lovely family, the wife of an enterprising, active husband, and the *benefactress* of the surrounding poor, ought to be reminded now and then of filling her pockets (if she condescends to wearing those Gothic appendages) as well as of extending her fame."

the good work. In the spring of 1802 the Peace of Amiens, which opened the Continent to English travellers, induced many to visit France. Mrs St George was one of the earliest visitors to Paris, where she was detained first by indisposition, and then by her marriage to Mr Richard Trench, son to Frederick Trench of Woodlawn, Galway.[1] The marriage took place at the French Embassy in 1803. They were on the point of returning to England when they were overtaken by the somewhat abrupt termination of the Peace of Amiens, and, by the orders of Napoleon, detained as hostages. They went, in the first instance, to Orleans. Here the newly-married couple had to remain for four years. There was, however, some relaxation made for Mrs Trench. While her husband was confined by his parole to Orleans and its immediate vicinity, she was allowed to visit different parts of the country, and, had she so wished, could at any moment have obtained a passport to England. She never made use of this liberty, but once every year went to Paris with always the same object, the release, if such were possible, of her husband. The letters she wrote when on these short visits are principally addressed to Mr Trench, and are full of little details calculated to amuse the *détenu*. The most interesting deals with her visit to Fontainebleau, whither she went to deliver a *placet*, or petition, to the Emperor for her husband's release.

"FONTAINEBLEAU,
"*Aug.* 1805.

"I arrived last night at eleven, much frightened (without reason) at passing the forest so late. To-day I went out before breakfast, not to lose any opportunity; waited from ten till three in the roads, courts and porter's lodge. Antoine, a millstone, a damper and an *épouvantail*, frightened at his

[1] The Trench family are another branch of the large tree of foreign refugees. Driven from their own country, they came to England in 1574, and in 1631 a grandson of the original emigrant passed over to Ireland, where he settled and prospered, branching out into the two noble families of Ashtown and Clancarty. The compiler of the Memorials of the late Archbishop of Dublin must, therefore, be in error when she states that Dr Trench was only Irish by the accident of being *born* in the country.

shadow, and equally endeavouring to frighten me. At three everyone said the Emperor would not go out to-day, and I found myself too weak to wait any longer, not having eaten a morsel. The Empress was walking in the garden and I went to her, requesting she would *appuyer* the *placet*, of which I gave her a copy. She received it graciously, and asked if I had presented the *placet* itself. Upon my saying not, she desired me to give it to her and *she would*. This I did, but consider it unlucky, as he is reputed to attend more to those immediately given to himself, than to those given in any indirect way. To-morrow I shall go again and try for an opportunity to tell the Emperor I am the person who presented a *placet* through the Empress to him. The Empress seems to me, as I at first thought her on my presentation, exceedingly attractive. The face was entirely covered by a fine lace veil and large rich bonnet; but her figure and *maintien* are highly graceful and beautiful. She recollected my having been presented to her three years ago. A poor woman gave her a petition on her knees immediately after: and her distress and anxiety to make the woman get up was very interesting. Everyone more than civil. I penetrated everywhere, in spite of the supposed difficulties."

To the Same.

"Fontainebleau,
"*Aug.* 1805.

"Yesterday I had the pleasure of giving you a second proof of affection, and whether it succeeds or not, nothing can deprive me of the satisfaction I receive from the act. *A travers* all the embarrassments and tumults of a *rétour de chasse*, guns firing, horses prancing, *la meute des chiens*, *piqueurs*, gamekeepers, guards; in short, a thousand objects, from each of which I should have fled on any other occasion. I delivered my *placet* to the Emperor, who received it willingly and graciously. He was just driving off in his *calèche*, after a successful hunt in the park of Fontainebleau. Now the little agitation and fretfulness of the business is over, I have leisure to look back and be surprised at the kindness and politeness with which I was treated, and the respect I uniformly received in circumstances the least likely to inspire it. With the smallest knowledge of the *local* customs or *entours*, I should not have suffered any fatigue or inconvenience: but being a total stranger, without one common acquaintance here, and Antoine a millstone, as I said yesterday, I had every disadvantage. It was not true, but a mistake, that I could not go into the court I mentioned yesterday. The Empress had ordered women should not remain there; but the wife of the *concierge* whose apartment was in it, offered me her *salon*, newspapers, etc., where I was quite retired, and much better lodged than travellers usually are anywhere. I never in the whole business met the slightest incivility, insinuation, freedom, or rebuff. I glided everywhere, whether others were refused or not, and I met with every mark of interest and *bienveillance*. By-the-bye, the *placet* itself was a most pitiful performance, ten degrees lower than my address, beginning '*Etrangère et seul*,' which had something like style and energy. It is singular, too, that one who was First Secretary, etc., *made* me, against my own opinion, make an official mistake in it—*Votre Majesté* and *Vous*, instead of *Elle*. How few people know their own *métier*."

The *placet* was not successful, and the poor *détenus* had to continue their constrained residence in France, which was made even more hateful by the death of their eldest and at this time only child, Frederick. Mrs Trench's grief and the impression left on her mind were deep and lasting. She would not believe La Bruyère's doctrine "*qu'on se console*," which, she says, "applies to every loss but that of a beloved child, who is not only the flower of one's present path, but the object of one's future hopes. Bruyère was not a mother. No *man*, no *father*, however affectionate, can conceive a mother's grief. This I always believed; now I am convinced of it." Very touching is her description of her first visit to the room where the boy died. "What a blank! What terrible silence! I went away. I came back. Again I went out. I tried to escape from my miserable self by wandering through the house; then I returned. Often in that room I turn involuntarily to the glass which reflected his last looks and expect to find some outline, some trace, some shade of him.

> 'He is gone, and my idolatrous fancy
> Must consecrate his relics.'

What relics? One poor, solitary lock of shining hair, the little simple clothes that he embellished: not a picture, not an image of that loveliness unparalleled."

The year after her affliction, the long-sought-for permission to return to England was obtained, and Mrs Trench found herself once more amongst her relatives and friends. From this time her life grew fuller: she paid several visits, generally alone, to London, and was much sought after in society. The record of her success is told to her husband with the utmost simplicity. She was a musician and sang delightfully. On one occasion she heard a lady seated behind her say, "She sang quite in the style of Braham." Very pleasant, too, is her account of a visit to an old friend (Mrs Morgan), who was a *little* more candid than was necessary. "Her lamentations over me at my having lost the prettiest and lightest figure she ever saw were really entertaining, adding, 'Ah, my dear!' (for she has some Irish phraseology) 'what a beautiful creature I remember you; and now even your face is grown fat and broad. Well, you will be always delightful to listen to.' I am very much obliged to her," adds Mrs Trench, "for remembering what she once thought me, but I had the weakness to feel a little involuntary melancholy."

During the years that followed her return from France, the friendship which Mrs Trench had always entertained for Mrs Leadbeater deepened into affection.[1] They met often, and in the correspondence before mentioned, some of Mrs Trench's most graphic touches are to be found. For the amusement of the recluse at Ballitore, she sketched humours

[1] Mrs Trench, whose passionate love of life and of the delights of friendship were equally strong, had that morbid shrinking from the advance of time which is often a noticeable feature in sensitive, highly-strung natures. Writing to Mrs Leadbeater, she says, "Oh, do not say you are growing *old*. I am not good enough to bear to hear my friends say that without great pain."

of the gay world. She gives her a lively account of a Mrs Williams, who put hundreds into King's pocket by dancing at his rooms. "I have not ventured to go since she has performed, for you cannot get a place near enough to see her without going at eight o'clock. She has taught her husband to dance; he is always her *vis-à-vis*, and he said to an old maid whom he heard abusing her for *exhibiting* as they call *everything they cannot do themselves*, 'Ma'am, if *you* had a husband that liked you should dance as well as I do that Mrs Williams should dance, I daresay you would do it too. She is my wife, and I hope she will dance as long as she is able.' The consternation of the old maid was great."

Another time she astonishes the quiet Quakeress with the doings of the fashionable world in which she moved; her anecdotes of the Prince Regent whom she disliked cordially are very piquant.

"The prince received the present of a snuff-box set with brilliants, on which were written, in a beautiful hand, three verses from the twenty-first chapter of the Book of Ezekiel. It was sent by the coach. She hears that his late illness followed an evening spent between a bottle of Noyeau and a bottle of alcohol. You know the Scripture, 'Woe to the land where the princes love strong drink.'"

It is not surprising that, hearing of all this wickedness, Mrs Leadbeater in her quiet retreat thinks the state of England "what *thou gavest me* a peep of," is indeed awful. She owns, however, she would like to know one thing—has the Duchess of York *one hundred and seventy dogs*? Her town friend writes back she is sorry she cannot answer this simple question, but rather imagines it to be an exaggeration.

"I remember hearing, ten years ago, Colonel——, a man nicely attentive to his own convenience, lament that eight or ten of them usurped every good place near the fire and made the drawing-room exceedingly offensive. She passes for being what is called a 'good sort of woman,' a person of whom nothing can be cited remarkable enough to merit praise or blame."

These bits of gossip are varied by household details put

very pleasantly. "I am in the fermentation of a domestic bustle with a true Irish contempt for lock and key;"—or very sharp criticisms on books, music and the stage. "Lady Wortley Montagu's letters are heartless, flippant, selfish and indelicate: Madame de Staël's *Germany* amusing to skim but not to read; Voltaire a voluminous but monotonous writer; Miss Edgeworth's diffuse and wire-drawn novel *Patronage*."

On the other hand, Mrs Leadbeater's *Cottage Dialogues* excite her warmest admiration, as, indeed, everything does which comes from that lady's pen.

"In whatever disposition of mind I may be when I receive your letters, their effect on me is the same—

> 'Round an holy calm diffusing,
> Love of peace and lonely musing.'

On another occasion she writes,—"The opening of your book on old age reminds me of an anecdote of the late Duke of Queensberry, old Q., which I have from an ear-witness. He was leaning over his balcony at his beautiful villa at Richmond, where there was every pleasure that wealth could purchase or luxury devise. He followed with his eyes the majestic Thames, winding through groves and buildings of varied loveliness, and exclaimed, 'Oh, that wearisome river, will it never cease running, running on? I am so tired of it!' To me," adds Mrs Trench, "this anecdote conveys a strong moral lesson connected with the well-known character of the speaker, a professed voluptuary, who passed his youth in the pursuit of selfish pleasures, and his age in vain attempts to elude the relentless grasp of *ennui*."

This constant variety of frivolity and seriousness, nursery anecdotes and philosophical disquisitions, great sweetness and matronly severity, joined to a decided turn for sharp, satirical observation makes the infinite charm of Mrs Trench's correspondence. Like all bright natures, however, she was ill-fitted to bear the rude blasts of misfortune. The trials which chequered her life were, moreover, those which, to one of her tender disposition (in which the heart played the leading part), became the hardest to endure. We have seen how deeply she grieved for the loss of her little Frederick in 1803, and now after ten years the wound was freshly opened by the death of "Bessy," her only daughter, at the engaging age of four. There is something especially pathetic in her brief notice of this sorrow in her Journal:—

"Friday, November 1st 1816. — My beloved child, my docile, gentle, joyous, affectionate Bessy, resumed by Heaven at seven o'clock this morning. . . ."

It is worthy of remark how the interval of years which came between the death of her two children seems to have strengthened and purified Mrs Trench's character, a result unfortunately not always found to accompany advancing age, which often rather intensifies than diminishes the impatience with which our faulty human nature looks upon any chastisement sent by Providence. The wild outbursts of despair and unreasoning complaint which marked Mrs Trench's first bereavement have no place in her later trial. Now the iron had entered into her very heart, and from this time it was filled with a deep and abiding sorrow. She wrote to an intimate friend (Hon. Emily Agar),—

"The lovely one is gone. I am more deeply wounded than religion permits. Pity and pray for me. My visit to you is not to be thought of. I would not sadden any society by my presence. My beautiful blossom, whose loveliness I had diminished in order to surprise you—foolish, wicked vanity—died as she had lived, loving everyone better than herself. A little before, she had asked her afflicted maid if *she* thought she would go to Heaven. Keep this note. I like to think she will not be forgotten."

To Mrs Leadbeater, the poor, stricken mother wrote as to one who could feel for her out of her own maternal heart.

"Bursleden Lodge, 1816.

"You are so kind to me, my dearest friend, that I should feel wanting in respect for friendship so tender if I suffered you to hear from common report that my lovely blossom is now in her little coffin. I have just kissed her beautiful marble brow, for she was beautiful, though I restrained myself from talking of her personal perfections. What is more important, she was heavenly-minded as far as four years and three months would admit. I am well in health, and I hope I am resigned, but you know how the loss of an only daughter who, to the weakness of mortal eyes, appeared faultless, and who had all the attractions which endear a child to strangers as well as friends. You know how it must darken the remaining years of a mother, past the age of hoping for any new blessings, but clinging too eagerly to those she already possessed. God bless you and preserve you from such affliction!"

Although Mrs Trench rallied from this, blow she never altogether recovered it. "I do not become less sensible of my loss, but I am more accustomed to it." Then she adds, translating from a German author:—

"I know I shall wear down this sorrow.
What sorrow does not man wear down? . . ."

More than a year after her little daughter's death, she wrote the following lines on returning from a dance,—

"I am not envious; yet the sudden glance
Of transport beaming from a mother's eye,
When light her daughter's airy footsteps fly,
Supremely graceful in the wavy dance,
Wakes with a start such thoughts as slept perchance,
Hushed to repose by the long lullaby
Of many a fond complaint and heartfelt sigh.
Again the host of keen regrets advance;
Again I paint what Bessy *might* have been,
Since what she *was* I never can pourtray;
So soft, so splendid shone my Fairy Queen,
A star that glittered o'er my closing day,
A light from heaven, whose pure, ethereal beam
Threw its long glories over life's dark stream.[1]

[1] Mrs Trench looked upon a daughter as a gift from God, a benignant star, a mother's companion in sorrow, her ministering angel in sickness. It is on her a mother relies to close her eyes, and to cherish that remembrance of her the scenes of busy life may soon efface from the breasts of others. This description would hardly apply to the present day when mothers have gone out of fashion!

In 1821 Mrs Trench lost her earliest friend, the Hon. Emily Agar, "the kind," "the generous," "the steady," "the wise," "the pleasant," "the pious," "the cheerful. . ." "Farewell, my Emily." She wrote some sympathetic verses to her memory, beginning,—

"I gaze upon thy vacant chair,
And almost see thine image there:
I view the slowly opening door,
And scarce believe that never more
Thy step of lightness there shall tend,
With cordial smile to greet thy friend,
My Emily.

. . . . . .

I saw thee in thy hour of prime,
I saw thee gently touched by time;
I saw thee as thy spirit fled,
I've seen thee since beside my bed.
A placid dream, pure, soft and fair,
A dream of love, a form of air,
My Emily."[1]

Another composition of hers, which has considerable merit, is the recasting of an old Irish legend which bears a family likeness to Childe Darien.

'Who will shoe my little foot? Who will glove my little hand?
All shivering and chill at your castle gate I stand.
The rain rains on my yellow locks, the dew has wet my skin;
My babe lies cold within my arms; Lord Gregory, let me in.

Oh, the night is far too murky, and the hour far too late,
To open for a stranger Lord Gregory's castle gate.

Oh, and don't you remember one night on yonder hill,
When we changed rings together, sore, sore against my will?
Mine was of pure gold, and yours was but of tin;
Mine was true to the heart, yours false and hollow within.
The rain rains on my yellow locks, the dew has wet my skin;
My babe lies cold within my arms; Lord Gregory, let me in.

Oh, the night is far too murky, and the hour is far too late,
To open for a stranger Lord Gregory's castle gate.

[1] The Hon. Emily Agar, daughter to Lord Clifden.

Oh, and don't you remember one night by yonder cross,
When we changed cloaks together, and still to my loss!
Yours was the woollen grey, and mine the scarlet fine,
Yours bore an iron clasp, and mine a silken twine.
The rain rains on my yellow locks, the dew has wet my skin;
My babe lies cold within my arms; Lord Gregory, let me in.

Oh, the night is far too murky, and the hour is far too late,
To open for a stranger Lord Gregory's castle gate.

Your castle gate is closed, but I behold your moat
And there your cruel eyes shall see my body float."

The specimens quoted show that Mrs Trench had a poetic mind. There are several fugitive pieces interspersed through her son's book which are so tastefully and tenderly written as to make one regret that her later poems have not been collected. The volume which has been put together only contains her earlier and decidedly inferior work. Her first poem, "Compaspe and Apelles," was published in 1805 with a modest preface in which she "talks of chords that should be struck by a more powerful hand than mine is." This self-depreciation is undoubtedly correct. Nothing can well be feebler than "Campaspe"; the author, however, disarms all criticism by her simple avowal "that she had chosen her subject badly," adding, "but I did not recognise this till the trifling attempt was finished." The "Assize Ball" which appears in the same volume was more successful. Mrs Trench, herself, preferred her prose to her rhymes, for the reason "that the want of precision, command of language and harmony, gained by a classical education and the study of the poetry of Greece and Rome, is more apparent in verse than in prose." There is undoubtedly a great charm in Mrs Trench's prose writings; her style is elegant, and she possesses the rare excellence of always choosing the correct word to express her meaning. Many of her letters, are equal in wit and power of observation to those of Lady Mary Wortley Montagu, while there is not one to shock or affront the most prudish reader. Her descriptions are life-like; and with one touch of the pen she gives a graphic portrait of an individual, or places a particular incident before your eyes. I make no apology for setting a few interesting extracts before my reader,—

"Why should a ready laugh, a general shake of the hand, and that difficulty of living alone or in a family circle, which makes all new-comers equally welcome, constitute a good-natured man? Good-nature is no great laugher. Nine laughs out of ten spring from a contemptuous feeling toward their object, or a triumphant consciousness of superiority. Good-nature is too affectionate to shake hands with every new-comer in the same cordial manner; and above all, good-nature can cheerfully pass her time alone: for her hours, always sweetened by the kindliness of her feelings, cannot be tinctured with *ennui*, while she can either serve or gratify another."

Here is another extract worth reading, "on meeting an old friend,"—

At last, after an interval of twenty-four years which succeeded a tolerably intimate acquaintance of seven weeks I saw Count Münster of Hanover again. We met like two ghosts that ought to have been laid long since. I witnessed the whole process of the difficulty of persuading him that I was I; and I thought him as much changed in his degree as he could have found me. When we conversed, all the persons we referred to were dead and gone; and our interview added another link in my mind to the chain of proofs that, after a *very, very* long interval, neither friends nor acquaintances ought to meet in this world."

## CONSOLATIONS IN LIFE.

"Among the many consolations, most of which fail to console, a few, I think, have been overlooked, which may, at least for a few moments, lighten the chain of years—that chain to which every revolution of the sun adds a new link—some painful and heavy, others brilliant and elastic. The treasures of recollection, that best cabinet of curiosities, better than diamonds or gems, or Alduses or Caxtons or visiting tickets, or even franks, all of which have been sought by indefatigable collectors—the treasures of recollection can only be obtained from the hand of time."

### ON HEALTH AND SICKNESS.

"An amendment in health disposes us to look on all around us with a favourable eye. I am not surprised that the gradual recovery of spirits, incident to humanity when it begins to 'wear down' a great sorrow, has sometimes induced men hastily to marry without much apparent temptation, when the affliction for a beloved wife was fading into calm regret. This action has been a theme for obloquy to all professors of sentiment, somewhat more than it deserves. It is rather a symptom of that easiness of being pleased which attends recovery of mind or body than one of fickleness."

### HER DESCRIPTION OF THE FASCINATION LONDON POSSESSESS.

"You, I am sure, wonder why I came to town, and why I stay there; but you must know London operates as a magnet when one is absent from it, and is full of the glue Madame de Sevigné speaks of as abounding in the society of *les devots du Faubourg*, I forget which, when one is in it. Be dissipated or domestic, sick or well, good or bad, wise or foolish, London once tasted will be required again and again.

"This is a mystery, and I leave it to wiser heads to explain. It is a good hint to country gentlemen not to be too anxious to give their wives a sip of this enchanted cup."

In 1821 Mrs Trench was in the city of her heart, and there witnessed the coronation of George the Fourth, of which she gives a graphic account.

"I opened my eyes on a hairdresser at a quarter before four, was *en route* in a white satin dress-gown and Court plume at five—at six was seated in the hall, after various difficulties, occasioned by the dulness of doorkeepers, and some danger from the circumstance of my being within a few yards of the gate at the very instant the Guards were called out to oppose the Queen. Tired to death at having been sent backwards and forwards by doorkeepers, I was at last near the right entrance, when I heard loud shouts, a few faint hisses and a cry of 'Close the doors.' The Guards are called out; the Battle-axes rushed in, and absolutely carried me in amongst them, and with wonderful alarm was the door closed against a woman—and a Queen.

"The show was all that Oriental pomp, feudal ceremonial and British wealth could unite. The processions in *The Curse of Kehama*[1] and in *Rimini*,[2] with the painting of *Belshazzar's Feast*, were continually recalled to my memory. The conflict of the *two lights*, from the blaze of artificial day mixing with a splendid sunshine, the position of the King's table, the pomp of the banquet, with its vessels of gold and silver, the richness of the dresses, and a thousand other particulars, rendered the resemblance so perfect, it seemed as if the feast had been in some degree copied from the picture. Thus does art seem to contain the germ of all that is developed in life.

"Our loyalty was noisy, and I think our roarings might have been dispensed with; for we roared not once, nor thrice, but at least a dozen times. We had great desire to roar for the horses also; but an energetic *hush* from those who conducted the ceremonial, silenced us with difficulty, as we attempted it repeatedly.

"The Archbishop of York, in his coronation sermon, assured us that, 'judging of the future by the past, we had reason to expect a reign of extraordinary virtue!' The Abbey, when looked down upon from one of the upper pews, appeared like a Turkey carpet continually changing its pattern."

Mrs Trench's health, which had for some time been a source of anxiety to her family, failed considerably from 1822, when she was attacked by a serious malady. From this time she seldom woke without what she calls her "penal visitation of headache," and spent a half-and-half life in the open air. She, however, kept up her ever-delightful correspondence with all its old spirit, carefully avoiding to give *bulletins* of herself. She also, when in London, occasionally went into society, as when, in 1826, she dined without fatigue

[1] *Southey's Poem.* [2] *Rimini*, by Leigh Hunt.

at the Bishop of Norwich's, where a ludicrous mistake occurred —best told in her own words.

"Going down to dinner with the prima donna, the Bishop said, 'Lord John Russell, take Mrs Trench.' I felt much pleasure at the thought of sitting by the historian, the political economist, the successful author, and prepared to treasure up his sayings and doings with that due degree of awe for his talents which is always a little unpleasant to me at first, though it soon subsided into a pleasant feeling of respect. Well, we sat down, and he talked of Harrow, and wished he had been at a private clergyman's, saying that he should have read more there and been much happier; that at Harrow he had been subdued, and that he always had wanted encouragement. 'How amiable!' thought I; 'how modest!' He went on to say, 'If I had been at a private clergyman's, I should have been quite a different person.' Still more modesty! 'How can a person who is so lauded,' thought I, 'have so moderate an opinion of himself?' Well, he drank his due proportion of wine with everybody, and watched their wants with a scrupulous attention. 'How very attentive to all the little forms of society,' thought I; 'this is so pleasing in an author of eminence.' In the evening he played cards, and I went into the music-room, and sang in quite another way from what I do when I am *afraid you* are *anxious* I should please. I came home and gave such an account of the author of *Memoirs of the Affairs of Europe from the Peace of Utrecht*, that all at home were dying to see him. 'Not that he said much to mark him out,' said I; 'but you could see the possession of talent under the veil of simple and quiet manners it pleased him to assume.'

"Well, the bishop had mistaken the *name* and I had been led down by one who passes for the greatest proser of his day, Lord John ——, and I had all my feelings of awe for nothing. So much for a *name*."

On her return from this, her last pleasure-trip, she heard of the unexpected death of Mrs Leadbeater. "June 26, 1826. —"Death was unexpected. I never thought of this word in connection with her, she was so serene, so happy, so active—

she never had mentioned her illness but so slightly. She had so many benevolent and literary plans, she was so loved and so sweetly loved again. Her instinctive fondness for me was a boon from Heaven, which I valued not half enough while I possessed it. How little gratitude did I show her for her unbounded kindness and partiality—not half so much as I felt! How many attentions to her were *to be* performed—how long they were deferred! how often wholly forgotten. Alas! I thought I should have her always—"

Mrs Trench survived her friend eleven months. She died at Malvern, May 1827, leaving a great blank in her circle of relations and friends. She had, in truth, a charming personality, uniting, in an uncommon degree, cleverness with amiability, worldly acumen with a generous acknowledgment of merit in others, strong family affections and domestic qualities with a love of society and social success.

MARGUERITE, COUNTESS OF BLESSINGTON.

[*After Sir Thomas Lawrence.*

# MARGUERITE POWER, COUNTESS OF BLESSINGTON

(*Born* 1790.—*Died* 1849.)

THE life of this woman, endowed as she was with natural gifts of singular excellence, and favoured in no ordinary degree by the good things of fortune, presents a curious example of that perversity with which some human beings (like the moth round the candle) rush upon their own destruction. According to the new theories, they are powerless to avert by any efforts of their own the downward tendencies which produce such fatal results. This unhealthy exculpation of all wrong-doing, by shifting the blame from the actual sinner to his progenitor, is not, borne out by fact. A more logical explanation is to be found in the want of early training and discipline, which lies at the root of many a wasted life. This want is to the individual what the lack of a rudder is to a boat—without it we are at the mercy of every wind and wave of capricious fortune. Marguerite Power was all through her chequered career to feel what it was to be tossed hither and thither without any definite guide but her own inclinations. She had no standard as to right or wrong, no settled belief, unless we can count as such a profound indifference to public opinion. Her impulses were all good, but her life was, if not an open scandal, an outrage upon the received laws of society. All this can easily be traced to the lax principles which prevailed in her father's house. Edmund Power of Knockbrit, in the County Tipperary, was a typical Irishman as existing a hundred years ago—hasty in temper, extravagant in habits, fond of play, horses, wine and revelry, inattentive to business, improvident in expenditure. He was a fine-looking man, of imposing appearance, demonstrative in the matter of frills and ruffles, much given to white ties and the wearing of leather breeches and top-boots. His sobriquets were—"Shiver the Frills," "Beau Power," and "Buck Power," the last being the distinguishing appellation of a man of fashion.

Mr Power had married the daughter of an unfortunate Mr Sheehy, who, for supposed complicity in rescuing some prisoners, had suffered the extreme penalty of the law.[1] Mrs Power seems to have been a gentle lady, who occupied herself principally in increasing her family. The Powers had numerous children and but small fortune. The times, moreover, were considerably out of joint, and it would have required a steadier head than Edmund Power possessed to steer clear of the rocks and quicksands which beset the path of an Irish gentleman. The Powers were a Catholic family, and, in consequence, Edmund Power was not on the roll of magistrates, no Papist being allowed to hold any office of trust.[2] Mr Power got rid of this disability by con-

[1] Edmund Sheehy, James Farrell and James Buxton were tried at the Kilkenny Assizes in April 1766, and true bills were found against them for the murder of John Bridge. They were executed a week after their sentence was passed. According to the barbarous custom of the time, their heads were to be severed from their bodies and spiked over the gaol. Mr Sheehy's relations tried to spare his widow this last trial, and were given a hint by the authorities that if, after the severance had been accomplished, any person was in readiness to bear it off, the soldiers would not be too zealous to prevent its removal. Accordingly, no sooner was Edmund Sheehy's head struck from his body than a rush was made by some one in the crowd, who seized the head and fled with it, the soldiers making a free passage. It was a woman servant who performed this act of devotion.

[2] It was not only the Catholics who were kept down by the dominant upper class, but the inferior clergy and smaller gentry of the Protestant religion were treated in a contemptuous, overbearing manner by those of higher rank. The case of Mr Higgins and the scene of bullying that went on at a Grand Jury dinner at Kilmainham is typical of the times.

Lord Santry gave the toast, "To the glorious memory of King William."

*Mr Rowley.*—And may he be hanged as high as Haman who refuses it.

*Lord Santry.*—No, that's too good for him. May he be starved to death.

*Rev. Mr Higgins.*—Pray, Mr Rowley, sir, let us have no cursing here; as much blessing as you choose.

*Mr Rowley.*—Sir, they can't be cursed too much who refuse, for it is to him we owe all our lives, liberties and property.

*Mr Higgins.*—Under God, Mr Rowley, under God.

*Mr Rowley.*—'Tis in God we move and live and have our being.

Then the glass came to Mr Higgins, who filled and gave the toast, "To all who loved King William when alive, and honour his memory now he is dead, and

forming to the established religion, whereupon he was appointed magistrate for two counties—Waterford and Tipperary. These appointments were purely honorary and extremely onerous—a magistrate in those troublous times having to turn out, in pursuit of rebels, at any hour of the day or night. The countryside was alive with Whiteboys, Steelboys, all manner of illegal associations, setting fire to houses, burning hayricks, maiming cattle. Mr Power devoted his time to upholding the law, very much to the detriment of his own affairs, which were utterly neglected.[1] He was led on by the *ignis fatuus* of the Irishmen of his time—a place under Government, which rested on the illusory promises of his noble patron, Lord Donoughmore. He could hardly have trusted to a more slippery protector. In lieu of a place, it was suggested to Mr Power that if he set up a newspaper he should have the monopoly of all Government proclamations. This advice, seeming to offer something tangible, was followed, and in an evil hour Mr Power removed his family to Clonmel, and started as editor of the *Clonmel Gazette*. He had at this time nine children, of whom four were girls, Marguerite being the second eldest, being born in 1790.

In her childhood she showed no signs of the beauty which was remarkable in the other children. She was pallid and weakly, and her delicacy, together with her extremely sensitive organisation and singular precocity of intellect, doomed

are truly thankful to God for the Revolution." This mightily pleased the company. Lord Santry next gave, "To all those honest gentlemen who make the law the rule of their obedience," to which Mr Higgins added, "And where they cannot obey will patiently suffer," which put my lord into a passion.

*Lord Santry.*—Sir, what do you mean by that?

*Mr Higgins.*—I mean, sir, that where we cannot obey and must not resist.

After some more observations from the clergyman, Lord Santry broke out again—"Do you come here, sir, to break the peace of the country, sir, and to bully the gentlemen of the country! You were once turned out of the community for breaking the peace of the county, sir, and we will have you turned out again, or I will not serve." And Mr Rowley and the others declared "it was intolerable a man should be here and huff the whole county," and Lord Santry wound up "that the Magistrates would go in a body and complain of the clergyman's conduct," adding "we will have you turned out again, sir."

[1] Mr Power's zeal in hunting Whiteboys sometimes carried him too far. On one occasion he shot a peasant at work in the fields under the idea he was a rebel. For this over-zeal he was tried on the charge of murder, but acquitted.

her, according to the superstitions of the country, to an early grave. The atmosphere in which the frail little creature grew up was most uncongenial to the development of her mind. Her father's temper was violent, and his outbursts shook the nerves of the sickly child. Her mother was incapable of discerning her finer qualities; and her brothers and sisters, strong in health, boisterous in spirits, were unfit companions for the little sufferer. She lived in a world of her own—a world of dreams and fancies, of perpetual speculation and restless inquiry, which never met an answer. At an early age her imagination began to work, and she would entertain the other children with the tales she invented. So remarkable was her talent in this way that her parents recognised and were proud of it, and would send for her to improvise for the amusement of friends and neighbours.

The change from Knockbrit to Clonmel, which was a source of delight to her brothers and sisters, was to Marguerite one of unmingled regret. She loved Knockbrit which was endeared to her by her passionate love of Nature, and always spoke of it with the greatest affection. In Clonmel troubles gathered thickly round her parents. The loss of two children impaired the health of her mother, while her father's temper grew so violent as to make him a terror to his family. The newspaper concern had been a complete failure. It was little read and entailed enormous expenses. Utterly unsuited as he was in every way to conduct such an undertaking, Mr Power's ruin was a foregone conclusion, while the frantic efforts he made to retrieve his position plunged him deeper and deeper. One of these efforts was a sudden rush into business as partner in the firm of Messrs Hunt & O'Brien, general merchants in Waterford. He expended large sums of money, procured by fresh mortgages on Knockbrit, for the purpose of building stores and warehouses. His incapacity for business was such that his partners, to save themselves from utter ruin, had to get rid of him. He had overdrawn the capital by several thousand pounds.

Meantime the usual course of extravagance was continued, with no attempt at economy. Mr Power kept a liberal table and entertained hospitably on the usual system of universal credit. In all this the children especially suffered from the deterioration of living in an atmosphere of debt and duns. Miserable shifts for keeping up appearances, and reckless dishonesty bore their fruit later, and in the wretched struggle and final break up of Gore House we have the reflex of Lady Blessington's early teaching. As a first evil result she had been taken from the boarding school where she and her sister Ellen had suffered keen humiliations from their father's irregularity in paying their pensions, and both girls were introduced into society at the ridiculous ages of fifteen and fourteen. Mr Power's embarrassment, which was only the normal condition of most Irish gentlemen of his time, did not interfere in the least with his social position. He and his family mixed in the best society of the adjoining counties, and here I have again to remind my readers that society in the last and beginning of this century was altogether on a different footing from what it is in our time—this social difference being altogether attributable to the increased facility of locomotion.

In 1804 it took two days and a night by canal and coach to travel from the south of Ireland to Dublin, and four days to reach London. Hence county families who were not overburdened with money were thrown upon themselves, and had to be content with what amusement could be got in their immediate neighbourhood. Large towns, like York and Bristol, Galway and Tipperary, had a season of their own. Tipperary, being larger and more important than Clonmel, was the chief gathering point for the adjoining counties of Waterford and Kilkenny.

Not many years ago there were many old people living who recalled the gaieties of winter seasons in the south, and the pleasant balls and parties given in the court-house. Here came all the best families living round about. The family coach was filled with fresh beauties, ready for fun and flirtation, while their elders carried themselves as befitted their position, and were ready to take offence at the slightest encroachment on their rights. The line of demarcation between the county and the townsfolk, which was drawn very rigorously in England, was strained to the utmost in the sister island. At the balls given at the Castle of Dublin by the Viceroy, there was an arrangement of cross benches upon which no one could sit but peeresses. The wives of solicitors were not admitted at the Viceroy's Court, and dancing was regulated with the strictest regard to social position. There was no relaxation of these rules in the counties. The upper ten kept together at the top of the room, danced with one another, and snubbed with courteous insolence the doctor's wife and the solicitor's daughters. The highest lady led the country dance, followed by the next in rank; and any infringement of the proper precedence of each one was jealously guarded and resented on the spot by the lady's partner, duels being often the consequence of such infringements. The family of Mr Power were received amongst the *élite;* the best people visited at their house, and the personal attractions of Ellen Power[1] made her the belle of every social gathering. Her beauty was of the statuesque order; her features Grecian in type; but she was somewhat cold in her manner, relying too much on her attractions. Her sister Marguerite, with far less beauty, had the art of captivating attention by her grace of manner, elegance in dress, and the gaiety and sprightliness of her conversation. She was also an excellent dancer. She had likewise the somewhat rare gift—which does not always attend beauty—of retaining her admirers.

A great feature of the county balls was the presence of the military, who were quartered in large detachments all through Ireland for the purpose of keeping down the rebellious spirit of the country. These Saxon warriors generally fell in love with the witchery of the Irish eyes, and were made captives in their turn. This history has been repeating itself since the days of Strongbow.

In 1804 the 47th Regiment was quartered in Tipperary, and the officers were made welcome to the society of the county. Two of these—Captain St Leger Farmer and Captain

[1] Miss Ellen Power married, in 1813, John Home Purves, Esq., son of Sir Alexander Purves of Purves Hall, Berwick. This gentleman dying in 1827, Mrs Purves remarried, in 1828, the Speaker of the House of Commons, the Right Hon. Manners Sutton, who, in 1838, was created Viscount Canterbury.

Murray—attached themselves to Marguerite, and in a short time both proposed for this child of fifteen. Marguerite preferred Captain Murray, but St Leger Farmer was the richer, and both her father and mother joined in forcing her to accept him, which she did, according to her own account, after terrible scenes, and with the utmost reluctance.

Her married life was miserable. It soon became plain to her that her husband was subject to fits of insanity, of which fact his relatives had acquainted her father, but this had been concealed from her. During the first three months of their marriage he treated her with personal violence. He used to strike her on the face, pinch her till her arms were black and blue, lock her up whenever he went abroad, and often leave her without food.

This is Lady Blessington's own account of her married life. Captain Farmer's brother, however, in a letter to the *Evening Packet* shortly after the publication of the above statement, contradicted it in every particular, denouncing it as a gross misrepresentation of facts. He writes: "So far as my brother and Captain Murray having both paid their addresses to the lady I believe to be true; but that she preferred my brother is an undoubted fact, inasmuch as it was in every sense a love match between them, no settlement being made or even promised by my brother or his family; for my father, having seven other sons, considered that in his purchase of all his steps he had received his share. . . ." He adds, "Having been my brother's school-fellow and constant companion, I can assert that as boy and man he never showed any signs of insanity."

There can be little doubt that the unhappiness of the Farmer marriage was due to the old story—faults upon both sides. Marguerite, a mere child in years, was destitute of experience, and possessed a love of admiration and a total want of good principles. Her conduct excited the jealousy of her husband, and drove him to frenzy. She escaped from his house several times, and ran home to her father's; but it was not until he went to India that a final separation was decided, and that Mrs Farmer returned to her family—she had then been married three years. The new arrangement did not bring her much comfort; her father was unkind; she was looked upon as an interloper, and as interfering with the prospects of her unmarried sisters. It was supposed that she had diverted the attentions of a certain Captain Jenkins, who, up to the appearance of the more fascinating Marguerite, had shown symptoms of matrimonial intentions in regard to Ellen. The same story repeated itself with Mr Stewart of Killymoon, who was in every way a desirable husband. Still, although Captain Farmer was constantly writing to urge Marguerite to join him in India, she persistently refused, and finally left her father's house: for the next nine or ten years she resided almost altogether in England. Different reasons have been assigned for Mrs Farmer separating herself from her family.[1] Scandal, which always hangs round a woman who lives apart from her husband, was soon busy with her good name, assigning to her different admirers—one of these was the Earl of Blessington.

This nobleman, whose career attracted more attention than it would have otherwise done, by reason of his marriage with Mrs Farmer, was a type of the reckless, extravagant Irishman of his generation. He was the son of Luke Gardiner, Viscount Gardiner, and the beautiful Elizabeth Montgomery, and when only six years old his father had him dressed up as a volunteer, and presented him to a concourse of people with a child's sword in his tiny hand. The pride his parents took in him, and the unlimited indulgence accorded to him spoiled a character which by nature had all the elements of refinement and benevolence, and the death of his father when the young heir was only ten years old, by leaving him practically his own master at so tender an age, completed the destruction of his best qualities. Before he was eighteen he had acquired a character for gallantry and extravagance. The first he established by eloping with Major Brown's wife, and the second by

[1] Mr Fitzgerald Molloy, in his recent life of Lady Blessington, states as a fact that she eloped with Captain Jenkins.

his emulating his contemporary, the equally extravagant Lord Barrymore, in his passion for theatricals and show of every description.[1] No expense was spared in the mounting of the pieces performed at his seat, Mountjoy Forest, in Tyrone. Here came on one occasion Mrs Farmer and her sister Ellen, then the wife of Captain Purves. The two ladies stayed at Rashe, a cottage on the Mountjoy estate, which was fitted up with the most lavish extravagance. This was hardly a step to silence the tongues of the scandal-mongers, Lord Blessington being at this time a married man although his wife was too delicate to be of the party. The intimacy was continued after Mrs Farmer went to reside in London, where she had a house in the now unfashionable quarter, Manchester Street, her brother Michael living with her as a sort of chaperon. Intercourse with the world had improved Marguerite's natural gifts, and had likewise developed her beauty. She was a fascinating and lovely woman. Lord Blessington evidently thought so; his continued presence in her drawing-room and assiduous attentions giving rise to much comment, especially as, now that he was a widower, his attentions would have been gladly received in many distinguished quarters. The irony of fate, however, made him the lover of one who could derive nothing but an unpleasant notoriety from his devotion. So long as her husband was alive, Marguerite's position was doubtful. In 1817 an end came to all the gossip and the scandal; Captain Farmer terminated his unfortunate existence by falling from a window after a hard night's drinking, and his wife was free to accept the high position offered her by Lord Blessington. They were married at the church of Bryanston Square as soon as decency permitted, the witnesses being her

[1] Major and Mrs Brown being both of the Catholic faith, no divorce could be obtained; after the death of her husband, however, Lord Blessington, to his credit, married Mrs Brown, to whom he was sincerely attached. She died at St Germains in 1814. Lord Blessington, whose delight in all shows extended to funerals, brought over to Dublin the remains of his wife; they lay in state at his mansion in Henrietta Street, under a magnificent pall of black velvet embroidered in gold (this pall had done duty previously at the funeral of Marshal Duroc, so it may only have been hired). On each side of the coffin were seated six female mourners or mutes who had accompanied the corpse from London. The total expense of this display amounted to £2500.

brother, Robert Power, her brother-in-law, Captain Purves, Sir William Campbell and T. G. Pole. And now began a halcyon time for Marguerite. An adored wife, with an assured position and unlimited command of a large income, she must have sometimes felt as if in a dream, and have dreaded to awake and find herself back again in the frets and worries of her earlier life. At the time of his marriage her husband had a rent-roll of twenty-two thousand a year, a fine estate in Tyrone, a rare old mansion in Henrietta Street, Dublin,[1] and a splendid town residence in St James's Square, which he had recently furnished for the reception of his bride with the most reckless extravagance.

Her private apartments were hung with Genoa velvet curtains, trimmed with gold bullion fringe; the furniture—sofas, chairs, tables—was of silver. Lady Blessington, in one of her later works, speaks of her husband's love of splendour being not conformable with good taste. She might have used a stronger expression in speaking of his wanton, mad extravagance. At this very time, when he was having his bride's sitting-room hung with bullion fringe, he was steeped in debt, and years were to elapse before the unfortunate purveyors of the silver furniture received their money. Like many another who has passed from the tight curb of poverty to the ease of affluence, the newly-made Countess, in a few years, out-Heroded her lord in the magnificence of her ideas. She became so fastidious in her tastes that it was almost impossible to please her. She did not, however, lose the kindness of heart which had always distinguished her. Previous to her marriage, great changes had taken place in the family circle she had left at Clonmel. Her mother was dead, her father had married again without improving his circumstances, her younger sister had grown up, as also two of her small brothers. From these, and others of more distant kin, there were constant applications for assistance, and to all the most generous aid was given from

[1] Blessington House, in Henrietta Street—a fine stone mansion, the windows and doors adorned with fluted columns, the ceilings, panels, and architraves after the manner introduced by Adam. The house has now been modernised and utilised for chambers belonging to the gentlemen of the law, its title being Queen's Inns. In 1894 all the Mountjoy property round Dublin was sold for £120,000 to the Honourable Charles Spencer Cowper.—Abridged from the *Irish Builder*.

Marguerite's purse. She was happy herself, and wished to include those she loved in her newly-found happiness. So far as her social life was concerned, Lady Blessington showed an extraordinary facility in accommodating herself to the duties of her new position. As Lord Blessington's wife, she found herself called upon to preside over a brilliant circle, including some of the most eminent men and women of the day, distinguished alike for rank, talent, beauty and fashion, and belonging to every shade of politics and every class of society. It was a difficult task for one unaccustomed to the shoals and quicksands which beset the path of an untrained navigator in such deep waters, yet she managed to steer clear of anything approaching to shipwreck. Her beauty exercised a potent spell. So, too, her grace of manner, which at this period of her life, before she grew literary, was singularly frank and unaffected. The instant a thought crossed her mind it seemed transmitted by some electrical agency to her face; the girlish joyousness of her laugh—*éclats* of Jordan-like mirth, *petits rires folâtres* adding to her fascination; her voice, too, that greatest charm in woman, won her many admirers. "With all her beauty," said one who knew her well, "and all her talent, the witchery of her voice to me was her most exquisite attraction."

For three years Lady Blessington held her court in St James's Square—years of great excitement and continuous gaiety, but nevertheless tinged with some mortifying recollections. The society that gathered round the brilliant hostess in the palatial mansion was lacking in one element, and that one especially dear to Lady Blessington's heart. It is true that in later years she was to feel what it was to be ostracised by her own sex; this was not the case at the time alluded to—ladies of rank and estimation came to St James's Square, but not in profusion; they were scattered like hidden gems in a heap of sawdust. Still she had some female support; there was not that terrible array of black coats, and nothing but black coats, which was the distinguishing feature of the assemblies at Gore House. Another annoyance to Lady Blessington was the coldness evinced towards her by

Lord Blessington's sisters—one of these, wife to the Bishop of Ossory, refusing even to see her. These crumples in the rose leaves of her life made Lady Blessington fall in with a sudden whim, which seized upon her husband in 1820, that they should shut up the London house and go to Paris to get ready for a lengthened tour through France and Italy. The preparations for this expedition were on a scale of magnificence ill suited to the already straitened income of Lord Blessington, but with him extravagance had now amounted almost to a mania. Nothing stood in the way of gratifying the whim of the moment, and, according to him, it was the business of his solicitors to supply the money, and of his creditors to wait until he chose to pay them. His travelling retinue befitted a great English prince rather than an impoverished Irish nobleman. He took with him a French cook and *batterie de cuisine*, together with lady's-maids, footmen, house steward, courier and valet. The French stood open-eyed at this wonderful *cortége* and the amount of luggage that was necessary for such a party, including the appendages, without which the now luxurious Countess never travelled. To make the royal progress complete, and to prevent the *ennui* which might arise from too much of their own company, the Blessingtons invited three young people to be of the party—her ladyship's youngest sister, Mary Anne Power, a pretty, sprightly girl: Count Alfred D'Orsay, and Charles Mathews,[1] son to the elder Mathews. Count D'Orsay, who played later on such a prominent part in the life of Lady Blessington, had been known to Lord Blessington from his childhood, his father, General D'Orsay, being one of his oldest friends.[2] Neither was he to Lady Blessington a new acquaintance. In the first year of her marriage he had come to London with his brother-in-law, the Comte de Guiche,[3] who

[1] Young Mathews, afterwards the celebrated actor, was at this time destined for the very different profession of an architect. He did not join the travelling party till they had reached Naples, when he returned with Lord Blessington, who had gone to visit his Irish estates for a few weeks, and invited the son of his old friend, Charles Mathews, on a visit, ostensibly to study painting, in reality that his comic talents might dispel the *ennui* which even the brightness of foreign life could not dissipate.

[2] General D'Orsay was one of the handsomest men of his day. When serving in the *Vieille Garde*, he had the soubriquet of "*le Beau D'Orsay.*"

[3] Afterwards Duc de Grammont.

had brought him to St James's Square. Being then little more than a boy, his fascinations did not make so much impression as they did later. On one occasion he was invited to dine at Holland House, where he was seated next to Lady Holland, who supposed the handsome stranger to be a shy boy who was awe-struck by her majestic self. Owing to the considerable development of her person, her ladyship was continually letting her dinner-napkin slip from her lap to the floor, and, as often as she did so, she smiled blandly but authoritatively on the French count, and asked him to pick it up, which he did politely several times. At last, however, tired of the exercise, he said, to her great surprise, "*Ne ferai-je pas mieux, madame, de m'asseoir sous la table afin de pouvoir vous passer la serviette plus rapidement.*"

Since those days D'Orsay had developed into a youthful Apollo. "*Cupidon déchaîné,*" Byron called him later on. His powers of fascination equalled, if they did not surpass, his personal charm, and the union of the two made the irresistible D'Orsay. It was a singular infatuation that induced a man of the world like Lord Blessington to commit the folly of domesticating this handsome guest, and placing him in familiar contact with a woman of Marguerite's peculiar temperament, prone as she was to admiring all that was beautiful and noble. It is said that those the gods wish to destroy they blind, and considering Lord Blessington had experienced in his own person the consequences of such an intimacy, his blindness was, to say the least, extraordinary. During the period that the Blessingtons remained abroad—which covered the space of seven years—Count D'Orsay continued their guest. During this time, the other members of the party went their different ways. Mary Anne Power married the aged Count de Marsault; Charles Mathews grew tired of being the comic man, ever ready to invent jokes to amuse his hosts, and returned to make his name on the stage. Alfred, however, held his ground; it was in truth too good a berth to be easily relinquished by a man of the Count's luxurious habits. With each year the friendship of his hostess, and the infatuation of his host increased, until at last Lord Blessington put the seal to his previous folly by conceiving the project of making D'Orsay the husband of his daughter and heiress, Lady Harriet Gardiner. The first inception of this monstrous scheme (it may have been suggested by the Count himself), took form in 1823, when his lordship lost his only son and heir, Viscount Mountjoy, a boy of ten years old, who hitherto had always lived with Lord Blessington's grandmother, Lady Mountjoy. At this time Lady Harriet was only eleven years old, and resided with her aunt, Miss Gardiner, in Ireland. There was therefore an interval of years to elapse before the project could be accomplished. The time was spent in wandering about Italy. At Genoa the party met Lord Byron, who at first was reluctant to be drawn into any intimacy, but he could not long resist the spell which Marguerite could weave round the hardest heart, and soon he was on terms of close intimacy with the household. talking sentiment with her ladyship and calling D'Orsay *cher* Alfred. Lady Blessington was in a state of wild enthusiasm for this king of lions—she rhapsodises by the yard concerning his perfections, sneering occasionally at his weaknesses. She gives a very life-like portrait of his personal appearance, his finely-chiselled lips, grey eyes, one visibly larger than the other; his handsome nose and fine teeth. "I have never *seen finer*," she says, "nor a smoother or fairer skin." His figure was so thin as to be quite boyish, and his lameness was little perceptible had attention not been called to it by his own visible consciousness of the infirmity, a consciousness that gave a *gaucherie* to his movements.[1] Lady Blessington grows very hysterical as she gushes over her "hero," who, on his part, was affected unto tears at parting with friends he had only known a few days. The farewell was of the tenderest and saddest; presents were

[1] In connection with this consciousness of his infirmity, the writer remembers hearing an anecdote related by Count Zorzi, who, as a child, often saw Byron, who was *un habitué* of his mother's drawing-room. The boy, who for his years was a close observer, noticed how Byron would glide from one seat to another, until he made his way to the chimney-piece; here he would fall into an attitude, his elbow on the mantelpiece, his locks of hair thrown back, his offending foot well out of sight. Not till this carefully-prepared attitude had been arranged did he take any active part in the general conversation.

interchanged. Lady Blessington presented him with a ring of considerable value, and he in return gave her a pin with a small cameo of Napoleon, which he told her had been his constant companion for years. He wrote, however, from Genoa to ask it back on the plea that he was superstitious, and had recollected that memorials with a point are unlucky. He requested her acceptance of a little chain of Venetian manufacture, the only peculiarity of which was that it could only be obtained in Venice. It has often been said that very few even of our best friends speak of as they do to you. Writing to Moore, Lord Byron says, "Your other allies I have found very agreeable personages—Milor Blessington and *épouse* travelling with a very handsome companion in the shape of a French count, who, to use Farquhar's expression, in the 'Beaux Stratagem,' has all the air of a *cupidon déchainé*. Miladi seems highly literary, to which, and your honour's acquaintance with the family, I attribute the pleasure of having seen them. She is also very pretty—even in a morning—a species of beauty upon which the sun of Italy does not shine so frequently as the chandelier! Mountjoy seems very good-natured, but is much tamed since I recollect him in all the glory of gems and snuff-boxes and uniforms and theatricals and speeches in our House (I mean of Peers), and sitting to Strohling, the painter, to be depicted as one of 'the heroes of Agincourt with the long sword, bridle, saddle-whack, fal de la.'

There is a latent sneer running through all this that does not quite correspond with the tears at parting, and in another letter his lordship was kind enough to describe D'Orsay as one who seemed to have *all* the qualities requisite to have figured in his brother-in-law's ancestors' memoirs, by which he meant the memoirs of the Count de Grammont perpetrated in the days of Charles II. by Antoine Hamilton. On the other hand, no one ever has given the least idea of the real Byron—how he looked and talked so well as did the Count. Amongst his other talents he possessed the art of peppering and caricaturing his friends. He wrote a journal which he showed to Byron, who declared it to be the most extraordinary production, giving as it did a "most melancholy but accurate description of all that regards high life in England." At this time D'Orsay had not much knowledge of English society, except what he had seen during his three years' residence under Lord Blessington's roof. During this period the travellers had visited all the principal towns in Italy, the Blessingtons keeping up a sort of princely establishment. At Rome they had a palazzo at £100 a month, and gathered round them a brilliant society. The Italians are not, except in some exclusive circles, too particular, and the oddly-constituted party did not excite more surprise than the equally curious trio who later visited Italy, Sir William and Lady Hamilton, and Nelson. While they were at the Palazzo Nigroni, an addition was made to the family circle by the arrival of Lady Harriet Gardiner. Her father (who had never relinquished his favourite scheme of marrying his unfortunate daughter to Alfred D'Orsay) had arranged that the wedding should take place as soon as she was of marriageable age. She was barely sixteen when she was taken from the care of her aunt and brought to Rome and presented to her future husband. The marriage, however, did not take place in Rome, owing to difficulties made by the English Ambassador. The whole party therefore moved on to Naples, where the wedding took place at the English Embassy. The real story of this miserable drama has, I fancy, never been told. One can hardly believe that Lord Blessington's obstinacy could have led him to wantonly sacrifice his child's happiness unless some other influence was at work. Speculation, however, is at fault, and nothing can be said with either profit or advantage on the subject, except that Count D'Orsay, apparently for the sake of her fortune, consented to contract a marriage with a girl for whom he did not entertain even a feeling of kindness. Mr Patmore's excuse for him places the Count in a worse light, as is often the case with friendly endeavours to wash a blackamoor white. He says, "D'Orsay when a mere boy made the fatal mistake of marrying one beautiful woman, while he was, without daring to confess it even to himself, madly in love with a still more beautiful woman whom he could not marry. Discovering his fatal error when too late, he separated from his wife almost at the church door." But how about living under the same roof with "the still more beautiful woman," and outraging his wife's feelings by his open neglect of her while eating her father's bread.[1]

The intimate friend and biographer of Lady Blessington, who has exercised a most judicious reserve as to this subject, admits that he was most painfully impressed by the position that Lady Harriet D'Orsay held in her father's house. "She was exceedingly girlish-looking; rather inanimate, silent and reserved. She seldom spoke, was little noticed, and was treated in every way as a mere schoolgirl. I think her feelings were driven inwards by a sense of slight and indifference, and by the strangeness and coldness of everything around her." He goes on to charge her father with all the blame of this unfortunate incident. "It was his act that had led to these misconstructions, misconceptions, animosities, aversions and estrangements." This may be, but one cannot but think that there were two other actors in this domestic drama who were quite as much, if not more, culpable than the half-crazy Earl. The curtain, however, was soon to come down. A year after the ill-starred marriage, the Blessingtons, accompanied by the Count and his young wife, left Italy for Paris, with the intention of making a long sojourn. The magnificent hotel belonging to Marshal Ney was engaged at a high rent, and soon Lord Blessington was busy at his usual work of spending money. He seems on this occasion to have exceeded his usual extravagance. Lady Blessington, writing to friends in England, dilates with evident pleasure upon what she playfully calls "our new toy," and describes how her husband surprised her by the decorations and fitting-up of her apartments, which were kept secret until quite finished, when the doors were thrown open and the splendours revealed. "The whole," she says, "is in exquisite taste, chastely beautiful; a queen could desire nothing better."

Not many weeks after this was written, an end came to

[1] By the marriage settlement, £2100 a-year was settled *absolutely* upon Count D'Orsay. This annuity was at the time of the enforced sale of Lord Blessington's property consolidated into a lump sum of £80,000, which was paid over to his creditors.

all the sin and the folly. Riding in the Champs Elysées, Lord Blessington was seized with a fit and brought home unconscious. He died in a few hours. His affairs were in terrible confusion. The journeys, purchases, retinue of servants, arranging surprises for his wife—all this mad extravagance was now to bear its fruit. His schedule of debts, with its overpowering crop of mortgages, is in its way a curiosity. To Lady Blessington, however, a settlement of two thousand a year was secured. He likewise left her different legacies of jewels, furniture and carriages, as also his house in St James's Square, the sale of which, it was calculated, would add five hundred a-year to her income. This hope proved fallacious. The property was so inextricably involved in litigation that Lady Blessington ultimately relinquished all claim to it into the hands of the executors.

At the time of her widowhood, 1828, Lady Blessington was in the zenith of her beauty. That very year Lawrence's portrait of her was exhibited at the Academy, and Mr Coventry Patmore describes seeing the original standing before her own presentment.

"Then I saw," says Mr Patmore, "how impossible it is for an artist to flatter a beautiful woman, and that in attempting to do so he is certain, however skilful, to fall into the error of blending incompatible expressions in the same face—as on this occasion the original stood before the picture she fairly killed the copy. There is about the latter a consciousness, a pretension, a leaning forward and a looking forth as if to claim or covet notice and admiration, of which there was no touch in the former. At this time she was about twenty-six. Unlike all other beautiful faces I have ever seen, hers was at this time neither a history nor a prophecy."

Such gifts of beauty, and more than beauty — fascination — which are thus set forth by Mr Patmore, and which are endorsed by many other contemporary writers, naturally drew upon the beautiful and well-endowed Countess an amount of attention which, had she been wise in her generation, should have warned her that it would be well for her to step carefully over the snares and pitfalls that lay in her way. She might have known, for she had suffered before, that success is oftentimes more dangerous than failure, insomuch as it is sure to excite envy, and there is no guarding against the tongue of the envious. Unfortunately Marguerite's prudence was her least possession. She had hardly established herself in her house in London when she made her first mistake. Prompted by generosity, who shall say? She offered a home in her house in Seamore Place to Count D'Orsay and his young wife. This, to say the least, was ill-advised, and the false step which inaugurated Lady Blessington's return to London life struck the key-note of her future position. It may be that, as Mr Fitzgerald Molloy, her latest biographer, avers, there was nothing in the relations between the Count and his step-mother-in-law that could afford ground for cavil. Putting grave accusations altogether aside, there still remains the question of the happiness of the girl wife, and that this was materially affected by the humiliating part she was made to play as a cypher where she should have been mistress, nobody can reasonably deny. Neither can we blame her for at last asserting herself by insisting upon a total separation from a husband who was openly neglectful of her. In 1831 Lady Harriet D'Orsay left her step-mother's house, and there is no reason to suppose that they ever met again. Count D'Orsay remained in London, having apartments of his own near Seamore Place. His constant presence, however, at Lady Blessington's, where he acted as master of the house, coupled with their appearing always together in public, showed an imprudent disregard for public opinion and, on Marguerite's side, a total lack of delicacy, especially after the intimacy had been publicly censured by the scurrilous press of the day. We are told by Mr Molloy that she suffered keenly from the attacks made upon her character in the *Age* and the *Satirist*. If this were so, the remedy lay in her own hands. She could have checked, if she had so wished, the tide of scandal that now flowed against her. Her name was in everyone's mouth, and the great ladies who had visited her ceased altogether to do so. The supposed partner of her indiscretions was, however, visited with no such severe ostracisms. To him the doors of the most fashionable and correct houses remained open; his popularity as a leader of fashion was at this moment at its zenith.[1]

D'Orsay was now in the prime of his beauty. Looking at his portraits, one fails to catch where lay the charm which gave him the reputation he possessed in his own day, and which has handed down his name to us as a celebrity whose memory will live when those who did more valuable work are forgotten. We must, however, remember the conditions of the time in which he lived. Society was differently constituted from what it is nowadays. The area was far smaller, entrance to this charmed circle being impossible except for those entitled by birth. The competition, therefore, was restricted, and whereas it would be now impossible for any man of fashion to dominate as did D'Orsay in his day, the task was then comparatively easy. For the rest, nature had given him as many good gifts as to the Admirable Crichton. He was a good swordsman, a fine horseman, a fair shot, an accomplished artist, a clever sculptor, and his literary capabilities, had he cultivated them, would have placed him in the front rank of writers. Such manly tastes obliterated the touch of effeminacy associated with his dandyism,[2] and made him equally popular with men as with women. Gronow describes him driving his tilbury in the Park,—"He was like some gorgeous dragon-fly skimming through the air, and although all was dazzling and showy, yet there was a kind of harmony which precluded any idea or accusation of

[1] To be D'Orsay's tailor was more profitable than to be His Majesty's, and Stulz, who had the honour of making the well-fitting coats worn by the Count, owed his rise to the extensive orders he received from D'Orsay's admirers. "On one occasion a *nouveau riche*, wishing to give himself a fashionable air, applied to Stulz to dress him in as close an imitation of the Count as was possible. He tried on the coat and considered himself anxiously in the looking-glass. His uneasiness at not looking one bit like the aristocratic object of his admiration became every moment more pronounced. 'Mr Stulz, how is this? The coat has not the same air as the one worn by Count D'Orsay.' Mr Stulz shrugged his shoulders. 'Well, sir,' he said, 'you see nature must do something.'"

[2] Another contemporary describes him as taking the most extraordinary care of his beauty. His bath was perfumed, and he used an enormous dressing-case, which it took two men to carry. This case accompanied him on all excursions.

bad taste. All his imitators fell between the Scylla and Charybdis of tigerism and charlatanism, but he escaped these quicksands." A writer of the day gives us a very life-like sketch of the Count's personal appearance,—"He was rather above six feet in height, and in his youth might have have served as a model for a statuary. His neck long, his shoulders broad, waist narrow, and, although he was somewhat under-limbed, nothing could surpass the beauty of his feet and ankles. His dark chestnut hair hung naturally in long, waving curls, his forehead was high and wide, his features regular, his eyes large and of a hazel colour. He had full lips and very white teeth, a little apart, which sometimes gave to his generally amiable face a rather cruel, sneering expression, such as one sees in the heads of the old Roman emperors."

It was while living at Seamore Place that Lady Blessington entered upon her literary career. So early as 1822 she had published a small volume of sketches, which had the success due to its author being an admired beauty.

Despite a certain facility which she possessed, in common with many other women, for scribbling, it was a mistake (one of the many she made) for Lady Blessington to take up the *rôle* of a fashionable novelist. For a woman who spent her life as she did in society (where she was the stimulus of much mental activity), it was morally impossible to make any literary effort worthy of the name.

The writer who holds even the public of his own time, to say nothing of future generations, is not made out of the smart man or the fashionable woman. In the deteriorating process of amusing themselves or the world around them, they fritter away any good gifts they may have; and the best result they can hope to attain is a mere ephemeral success.

It is no reproach to Lady Blessington to say, that hardly anyone of the present day has ever read, or perhaps heard of, *The Two Friends, or, The Victims of Society*, which was one of her best attempts. Sir Walter Besant calls this "a horrid book," and doubtless, according to the standard of to-day, this judgment is correct. It is undoubtedly a poor excuse for Lady Blessington's feeble twaddle, to say that she was not worse than the average writer of her time who delighted our grandmothers. Lord Normanby was a fashionable author in 1830, and who could now read *Contrasts?* So too with Mrs Gore's tedious novels, full of aristocratic ladies speaking slip-slop French. I doubt if anyone could get through *The Wild Irish Girl* without an enormous amount of skipping. Miss Edgeworth's fashionable tales are somewhat prosy, and yet these works excited a furore on their first appearance.

For many years Lady Blessington continued to fill the shelves of the circulating library. She wrote *The Confessions of an Elderly Lady*, *The Sorrows of a Governess*, and *The Memoirs of a Femme de Chambre*, besides *Grace Cassidy*, *Lionel Deerhurst*, *Country Quarters*, *The Repealers*, etc. Most of these portrayed the follies and vices of people in high life, the characters being supposed to be portraits of persons well-known in society. This gave them a peculiar zest, especially as what was called a key was handed about privately. This would seem to have been hardly necessary, as the disguised names were singularly transparent. Take, for instance, Lord Rey for Earl Grey, Lady Yesterfield—Lady Chesterfield, Lady Lacre—Lady Dacre.

Her ladyship likewise contributed largely to the flood of Keepsakes and other Annuals which flooded the market, and took the place that society papers and periodicals now fill. Being, however, costly, they could be only purchased by the upper ten. They were of all sizes—Friendship's offering was small; the Keepsakes larger, and *Finden's Tableaux* and other Annuals full size. The illustrations were by the best artists. Chalon's especially are worthy of notice. One of these publications, *The Belle of the Season*, with several beautiful illustrations, bound in red silk, and letterpress by Lady Blessington, lies before me now. It is the story of a young girl, written in exceedingly sloppy verse. But then, it was the hand of a countess which wrote the lines—and so a guinea was cheerfully paid to read such twaddle as,—

"Your daughter's charming, on my word,
While you—I vow I heard Lord Lyster,
Say—you looked like her elder *sister*.
My son has just come from the East,
But has not suffered in the least.

Well, Lady Mary's quite a belle
And dressed, I must say, à merveille.
Any attachment? *entre nous!*
Too young—ha, ha! that's so like you.
*Au revoir chère amie.* Adieu."

This feeble production had, nevertheless, an extraordinary success, for the reason that under her usual thin disguises Lady Blessington introduced the Marchionesses of Conyngham and Anglesea, Lady Charlemont, Mrs Norton, the Duke of Leinster, Sir Robert Peel and Mr Sheil.

We have Jerdan's[1] authority for stating that her literary work brought her in at one time from two to three thousand a-year. This amount was, he adds, due more to her title than to her merit as an authoress, which, viewed critically, cannot be considered as even near the first rank. He and Greville both credit her well-arranged parties as being the great factor in her literary success. Having her publisher now and then, says Jerdan, to meet folks of a style unusual to him, had something to do with the acceptance of her novels. Greville, who is always "nasty," lays bare "the springs and the machinery which sustain her artificial character as an authoress—first and foremost, her magnificent house, her luxurious dinners—acting, he seems to insinuate, on the weak minds of Messrs Colburn and Longman." If this somewhat exaggerated statement is true, one can but applaud Lady Blessington for laying out hospitality to such good account. Three thousand a-year is great interest for a few dinners!

There is no doubt that Lady Blessington had recourse to her pen to keep up such an establishment as Gore House, Kensington Gore, whither she had removed in 1836. Gore House had already a literary record, having belonged to

[1] Jerdan was a man of exceptional power. He was the editor of the *Literary Gazette*, in which he wielded a critical flail of unexampled severity. He was said to have been the lover of the unfortunate L. E. L.

Wilberforce. It was a delightful mansion, with the additional charm of an old-fashioned, walled-in garden, with terraces and mulberry trees. Here Lady Blessington was joined by her two nieces, Marguerite and Ellen Power, the daughters of her brother Michael. Count D'Orsay had his own studio and apartments as in Seamore Place close at hand.

Lady Blessington's name is more intimately associated with Gore House than with any of her previous residences. Here she and Count D'Orsay realised a long-cherished wish of collecting round them a circle of the most brilliant, artistic and literary men in London. Of this circle Lady Blessington was undoubtedly the centre—like Madame de Staël, she had the art of conversation, and, like Madame de Swetchine, the tact to make others feel that they were contributing their best gifts to the entertainment. "She was unsurpassed," says Mr Molloy, "in eliciting from even the most modest tyro whatever there was within his shell of reserve that could add to the general enjoyment."

Greville bears testimony to the splendour of the house, the excellence of the dinners, and the frankness and cordiality with which Count D'Orsay did the honours; he adds, however, that the society "is not so agreeable as, from its composition, it ought to be. There is a constant coming and going, eating and drinking, with a corresponding amount of noise, *but little or no conversation*, discussion or interchange of ideas and opinions, ensuring a perennial flow of conversation." This want, according to Greville, was, "that the woman herself who must give the tone to her own society is *vulgar*, ignorant and commonplace. Nothing can be more dull and unattractive than her conversation, which is never enriched by a particle of knowledge, or enlivened by a ray of genius or imagination."

Greville's editor, Mr Reeve, makes an effort to soften this sweeping judgment by suggesting that Mr Greville probably mistook Lady Blessington's Irish cordiality for vulgarity. He likewise gives his own impression of her insuperable tact and skill in drawing out the best qualities of her visitors.

N. P. Willis, the American author of *Pencillings by the Way*, gives us a far pleasanter account of an evening at Lady Blessington's. He describes Lytton Bulwer, whose *Pelham* had just made a sensation, coming in at midnight, and rushing up to Lady Blessington, with the heartiness of a boy out of school. "I liked his manner extremely, and he was welcomed as the best fellow in the world. There was a German prince, with a star on his breast, Tom Moore, Horace Smith and others. Lady Blessington was the only lady present. She looked on the sunny side of thirty (she was close on forty). She wore blue satin, cut low, and folded across her bosom, showing her exquisite shoulders, while her hair was dressed close to her head, parted simply on her forehead, with a rich *ferronnière* of turquoise. Her features are regular, and her mouth, the most expressive of them, has a ripe fulness and freedom of play peculiar to the Irish physiognomy and expressive of the most unsuspicious good humour. Add to this a voice merry and sad by turns, but always musical, and manners of the most unpretending elegance, and you have the prominent traits of one of the most lovely and fascinating women I have ever seen."

He goes on to say that it would be impossible to convey an idea of the evanescent spirit of a conversation of wits. It was carried on into the small hours, Horace Smith getting on his crutches some time after three in the morning.

Another writer described her "seated in her arm-chair talking in her soft Irish voice, with her sweet Irish laugh rippling like a little brook. Her conversation was not very witty nor exceedingly wise, but it was in good tone and taste, mingled with humour, which escaped everything vulgar or bordering on it."

Dr Parr was another of her admirers. He talks of her luxurious laugh, quite ineffable; that her eyes were meteors, not stars, however bright.

This was the woman as the world saw her in society, or in the Park driving in her green chariot, gracefully built and lightly hung, the panels gorgeously emblazoned with arms and supporters. The horses were a pair of superb bay chestnuts. The coachman was in velvet breeches, fine, full-bottomed, well powdered wig, his burly legs in silk stockings; two footmen standing behind of equal height and equal calves. It was a sight to look at, and to watch the raising of the hats, and the clustering of men round her ladyship and her pretty nieces. But never a woman! either abroad or at home. Some there were who came in the morning hours on business of their own—to get help with editors, for subscriptions and so forth—but even those who were under obligations for her ever-generous assistance would not risk putting in an appearance at the evening gathering, as this might possibly militate against being invited elsewhere.

We know how Johnson held forth to his circle of listeners at Streatham, how Horace Walpole fluttered about Mrs Vesey's, picking up the best crumbs of conversation, to retail them in his admirable letters, but would it be worth while nowadays to have a note-book as Boswell had. There are no crumbs to pick up. Fifty years ago we should have had our aprons full. There was a keen encounter of wits at Holland House and Gore House.[1] There were smaller gatherings at Lady Charleville's in Cavendish Square, at Lady Cork's in Burlington Street, and breakfasts at Roger's, where the wit was of the best.

There was this difference between Holland House and Gore House, that everyone *wanted* to go to the first, and everyone *went* to the last. As to the popularity of the rival hostesses, the balance of opinion favoured Lady Blessington. She had much of the *esprit* of Lady Mary Wortley Montague, and a great deal of the *finesse* of those ladies of the great world so vividly pourtrayed by Horace Walpole. No doubt, the Bohemian element which pervaded her *salon* lent to it a certain charm. The coldness with which Lady Blessington was regarded by ladies, "the whispers and the open talk," says Sir Walter Besant, "did not make the house less delightful, but they placed it 'outside' society."

[1] A good authority, writing on this subject, says:—"One was not unfrequently reminded by the wit combats at Gore House of the days of the Chevalier de Grammont, when the whole band of wits—Dorset, Sedley, Etherege—diverted the *beau monde* with their sallies, repartees, quaint observations and sharply-pointed epigrams brought to bear on striking peculiarities of well-known persons of quality within the category of *précieuses ridicules*."

Amongst the shifting crowd of visitors at Gore House we find all shades of politics, every sort and condition of professional man—literary, artistic, lawyer and physician, scribblers, journalists, draughtsman and dramatist. Here came Lords Normanby, Carlisle and Strangford, the D'Israelis, father and son, Landseer, Theodore Hook, Tom Moore, Macready, Charles Dickens, John Forster, Walter Savage Landor, Samuel Rogers, and Prince Louis Napoleon. The list would fill a book. Both Lady Blessington and Count D'Orsay had undertaken as a sort of mission the duty of bringing together all who were rivals in the same pursuits, and for this purpose they laboured assiduously, it may be with too much effort. Their aim was somewhat akin to that pernicious system pursued by Mrs Leo Hunter—every lion, native or foreign, being eagerly sought out and brought to roar at Gore House. Lively spirits and the amusement of the moment were cultivated more than at Holland House, where the wits had it all their own way. The handsome, irresistible D'Orsay, with his good humour and liveliness, kept the ball rolling. It has been conceded on all sides that D'Orsay's wit and powers of facetiousness were unrivalled. He abounded in humour. and excelled in repartee. His air of aristocratic nonchalance lent piquancy to the grave irony of his remarks. He was also an adept in the art of quizzing those who offered themselves to ridicule through some trick of voice or peculiarity of any kind: his singular composure of mien and manner gave a zest to these performances, which were for the rest highly to the taste of Lady Blessington, who enjoyed, as only an Irish nature can, banter and quizzing. The holding up to ridicule the peculiarities of an invited guest, is a decided outrage on good taste and feeling, and cannot be excused by any amount of fun to be got out of the situation or by any elegances of "mien and manner," which, in fact, rather increase the offence. Take, for instance, the making a butt of Count Julien le Jeune, which was a stock piece at Gore House. It may have been amusing—we are told it afforded infinite merriment — but such a scene could hardly bear much repetition. This gentleman (an intimate friend of the host and hostess) had figured in the French Revolution, and for political reasons was exiled from his own country. It seems to us somewhat of a poor joke that this old man should be invited night after night to recite for the company the story of his political afflictions, which he had embodied in a poem of considerable length. This he would do with all the diffident airs of a young lady dying to sing and protesting she cannot. At last persuaded, he would place himself at a table with wax lights, pull the roll of paper from his pocket, and begin his recital of his "*Chagrins Politiques*" in a lugubrious voice, like Mdlle. Duchesne's *pleurs dans la voix*. The *salon* would be crowded with distinguished guests; on the left hand of the poet was Lady Blessington, in her well-known arm-chair, looking most intently, and with apparent solicitude, full in the face of the dolorous reciter. On the other side of Monsieur Julien, somewhat in front, sat Count D'Orsay, with a handkerchief occasionally lifted to his eyes, and ever and anon an exclamation of pain was uttered by him at the recital of some particular *Chagrin*. At the very instant when the accents of the reciter were becoming most lugubrious and ludicrous, and the difficulty of refraining from laughter was at its height, D'Orsay was heard to whisper as he leaned his head over the back of the nearest chair, "*Pleurez donc!*"

Doctor Quin, a well-known figure of the day, added his quota to the general effect. Whenever D'Orsay seized upon some particular passage, and exclaimed, "*Ah, que c'est beau*," then Quin's "*Magnifique, superbe, vraiment beau*," would be heard in solemn accents, and a call for that moving passage over again preferred and complied with. At the conclusion of *les Chagrins* Julien's eyes would be bathed in tears, and in this melting mood was he conducted by Count D'Orsay to the *fauteuil* of Lady Blessington, and there received compliments and consolations.

Custom had probably hardened Lady Blessington to ostracism by her own sex, but no use could accustom her to the ever-increasing necessity for work if she was to keep up the extravagant household, the green chariot and the expensive society. She got, says her biographer, no sleep at night, knowing that there was nothing to meet the large expenses going on but her two thousand a-year which was a drop in the big ocean of extravagance. To add to her troubles, her literary success, to which she looked as a means of rescue, was beginning to wane. It had been mainly due to adventitious circumstances, her name being so much in people's mouths, her friendship with editors, and many causes. An enigma, Greville calls it in his biting cynicism, but nevertheless acknowledges that hundreds were paid for her books; that they were translated into French and German and made popular in the States. All this was now to cease. The public had suddenly tired, and publishers were beginning to fight shy of her ladyship's three-volume dulness. The poor lady could not read aright the reluctance shown by Colburn and Longman to continue the supply, and kept on pestering them with manuscripts which cost her many a sleepless night when the lights were out and the guests departed to their downy pillows.

To add to her difficulties, she had in an evil hour allowed herself to be drawn into accepting the post of editor or editress of Heath's *Book of Beauty*, one of the many annuals then in fashion, "trashy things for which all the beauty, taste and talent of London were laid under contribution, and by means of notoriety, puffing and stuffing, and untiring industry, and practising on the vanity of some and the good-nature of others the end is advanced." The rage for these books was, however, at one time equal to any run of the present day. The public could not get enough of them until the demand created a glut, and then came the inevitable decline which was probably due to the appearance of the periodicals. Heath's *Book of Beauty*, which was a really charming production, lasted until 1846. The portraits of the fashionable beauties were illustrated in a manner we could not now have at any price. There were contributions from some good writers, poetry, stories, imaginary conversations. There was plenty of material, printed on lovely satin paper and bound elegantly in silk, either blue or brown. I have some volumes of these books before me now, one for 1837, another for 1843, etc. The first is the best, but it is wonderful to note the contrast in the appearance and dress of the women to those of the present day. How sweet and feminine they were, with their pretty, gentle faces and soft curls. Their dress, too, so modest and airy with the clouds of tulle and lace. It was not wonderful that they made conquests so easily. There were no complaints *then* that men wouldn't marry, they were only too eager to secure these sweet creatures. If, however, the portraits are most of them charming, so much praise cannot be given to the letterpress. The amount of silliness and vapid nonsense written in prose and verse in these elegant annuals is appalling. Nor is this astonishing—fifty-three contributions had to be supplied! As may be imagined, they could not all be good. In the early volumes there are some fugitive pieces by Barry Cornwall, Moore, Dr Beattie, stories by Lytton Bulwer, and other excellent writers; but even these seem to feel half ashamed of the company they are in. While Lady Blessington occupied the editor's chair, she made unceasing applications to every literary man, woman and child of her acquaintance to furnish copy for the *Book of Beauty*. Every new acquaintance was put under requisition, the principal quality necessary being not the merit of the writers but the quality of their station. In the volume for 1843 seventeen titled authors and authoresses contributed their noble names. Amongst them we find two marquises and a marchioness. Who would grudge a guinea a year to have such a galaxy? When any of her recruits failed, Lady Blessington fell back upon her nieces, Marguerite and Ellen Power,[1] who were always ready to turn off at a moment's notice any amount of "lines" on Lady Mary's angelic features or the Honourable Jane's transcendant loveliness; while for stories she could rely on her own facile pen. An end, however, came to these vapid productions; even the aristocratic authors grew stale. The public would have no more of the

[1] Ellen Power married Mr Henderson. Marguerite died unmarried. In the volume of letters published after his death, Charles Dickens pays a high tribute to the sweet disposition and generous character of Marguerite, whose early death pained him much.

Imaginary Conversations or of Mrs S. C. Hall's Irish donkey boys, and the whole thing collapsed. Heath died insolvent, heavily in debt to Lady Blessington. So far as she was in question it was all round a failure, involving her in great pecuniary loss and all manner of annoyance, quarrels with publishers, jealousy of rival authors and authoresses, enormous correspondence, and much ill will. Her life in fact was rendered miserable.

Another means of adding to her income had now to be found, and for the moment this was supplied by the proprietors of the *Daily News*, a paper just started (1846), under excellent management—Charles Dickens as editor, John Forster in the literary department, while Lady Blessington was entrusted with the doings of fashionable society. For this she asked £800 per year, which was thought too much, and she was offered and accepted £260 for six months. Dickens threw up the editorship, to which Forster succeeded. His straightforward character was adverse to jobbing of any kind, even when it was to help a friend. And although it pained him sorely, he cancelled the engagement with Lady Blessington at the end of the six months. All this time Count D'Orsay had been pursuing his course of fashionable frivolity: his coats were the admiration of the dandies; his horses were as well groomed, his tilbury as well appointed as if no duns were daily clamouring for payment at the doors of Gore House. In 1841 his liabilities had reached the enormous sum of £107,000, of which about £80,000 was secured on the Blessington estate. The utmost patience had been shown towards him by Stulz, to whom he owed a fabulous sum, as also to Hoby, whose fame in a certain pattern of boot he had made. It was this last, however, who had the ingratitude to arrest his benefactor as he was walking in a pair of the identical Bluchers. Having done this much, Hoby relented, and allowed his debtor to remain at large on the condition of giving up certain securities. After this warning as to the perfidy of those he had benefited by his custom, the Count considered it would be wiser to remain in the safe seclusion of Gore

House, whither he removed from his apartments. The doors were kept safely locked except on Sundays, and the Count took his daily exercise in the garden, until that day came round, when he once more appeared in the Park, in all the elegance of a perfect and unpaid-for costume. Some ill-natured person had, however, the malice to hint that time was beginning to tell upon the handsome Adonis. He was reminded in *Fraser's Magazine* "that a dozen years or more had passed since Byron had called him a *cupidon déchainé*, and that he was nearer to that bourne whence no traveller returns, by what Tacitus would call *ingens spatium humanae vitae*."

> "Believe me, dear Count, that twelve years do not pass,
> And leave not some signs as they go:
> They may fly with the wings of the hawk—but, alas!
> They are marked by the feet of the crow."

One good result was attained by the Count's imprisonment. For the first time in his life this incarnation of selfishness realised that he must put his shoulder to the wheel if he wanted to regain the dear delights of the outer world. Unfortunately he found, as many others have done, that while he was sipping the flowers of pleasure, his chance of the tangible goods of life had escaped him. He was too old for diplomacy: too fine a gentleman for a statesman's secretary—even a consulship was refused. Failing these genteel employments, our Count turned his attention to modelling and painting, and in the last he made his mark. In a short time he executed one hundred and fifty portraits of his friends and celebrities, including some of undoubted merit. One of the best was of the Duke of Wellington.

It was too late, however, for even this source of income to be of any real use in stemming the crash which was close at hand. Troubles came faster and thicker on the doomed household. In 1848 the terrible Irish famine put the crowning touch to Lady Blessington's ruin. Since 1847 she had earned nothing by her pen; the doors had to be locked against her creditors as well as the Count's, and she too only went abroad on a Sunday. In the spring of 1849 a sheriff's officer succeeded in making good his entrance, and put in an execution at the suit of Howell & James for a comparatively small sum. This was, however, only the beginning. Creditors flocked in on all sides, bills were overdue at the bank and bonds were out in all directions. Count D'Orsay fled precipitately, leaving Lady Blessington to bear the brunt of the storm. A few hurried arrangements were made. The sacrifice of Gore House and its contents was insisted upon, and as soon as this was agreed to Lady Blessington and her nieces took farewell of all their former greatness. A few faithful friends, the true-hearted John Forster amongst the number, came at night-time to say farewell, and to help, as far as in their power, the needs of these forlorn ladies, who were only allowed to take a few necessary articles of clothing with them on their journey. What a contrast to Lady Blessington's luxurious progresses of former days. Their destination was Paris, where they joined the Count, who had taken rooms. Soon the papers announced the sale of the costly effects. "Magnificent furniture, rare porcelain, marble, bronzes, jewellery, services of rich-chased silver and silver-gilt plate, superbly-fitted dressing-case, collection of ancient and modern pictures,[1] fine engravings, extensive library of upwards of 5000 volumes and other useful effects, the property of the Right Hon. the Countess of Blessington, retiring to the Continent." The auction, which took place May 10th, 1849, was an event in the world of fashion. The rooms were crowded. The arm-chair in which the hostess used to sit was occupied by some Jew broker, "busily engaged in examining a marble hand extended on a book," the fingers of which were modelled from a cast of those of the now absent mistress.[2] Everywhere were to be seen the friends who had been *habitués* of the house and enjoyed its profuse hospitality.

[1] Lady Blessington's portrait by Lawrence (as here shewn) was sold to Lord Hertford for £336. It had originally cost £80. Lord Blessington's portrait brought £68.

[2] Mr Madden, who was present at the auction, comments on the want of feeling shown. "People poked the furniture, pulled about the objects of art and some made jokes on the scene."

Lady Blessington's French man servant wrote to her that the only person who seemed to be at all affected was Mr Thackeray—"*il avait les larmes dans les yeux.*" This indifference on the part of the former guests was after all but natural, such friendships being mere social contracts of mutual entertainment which cease with the circumstances which call them into existence; nor can promiscuous hospitality, such as prevailed at Gore House, ever expect more than a passing recognition. Each invited guest feels the feast has been made not for him but for everyone, and treats his host accordingly. Both Lady Blessington and Count D'Orsay knew their world thoroughly, and expected but little from it. In her *Night Thoughts* there occurs these passages, "When the sun shines on you, you see your friends. It requires *sunshine* to be seen by them to advantage—while it lasts we are visible to them, when it is gone and our horizon is overcast, they are invisible to us." Again, "Friends are the thermometers by which we may judge the temperature of our fortunes." If Lady Blessington had ever doubted the truth of this fact, she experienced full confirmation of its accuracy from the hand of Louis Napoleon, who in his days of adversity had received the most extensive hospitality and assistance from both the Count and herself. His return was now a lukewarm reception and an invitation to dinner. In spite of this douche from the President, as he then was, Lady Blessington's mercurial spirits revived in "frivolous Paris." This was in a measure due to the good result the auction had on her affairs—the sum of eleven thousand pounds net being realised, while her whole liability was fifteen. There was a hope that, given some prudence and the re-establishment of rents in Ireland, her embarrassment might only be temporary. With revived spirits she took an apartment in the Rue du Cirque, Champs Elysées, into which she intended to remove, accompanied by her nieces and the Count, when, without much preparation, she was summoned to another life. The sudden seizure resembled, curiously, that of Lord Blessington some twenty years previous. She had returned from dining with the Duc and Duchesse de Guiche,[1] and went to rest without complaining; early next morning she was seized with spasms of the heart, and died in a few hours. It does not appear that, beyond much hysterical demonstration, D'Orsay was affected. His vapourings over his loss are somewhat disgusting. She was to me a mother, he would say—perhaps he meant mother-in-law, but his wife had long since made ties of another sort for herself, so efforts in that direction would have been more than useless. He lingered on in Paris, trying vainly to induce Louis Napoleon to give him an appointment of some sort, but in vain. After a little he was overtaken by a malady which precluded all hope of recovery. The loss of his limbs must have been a sad trial to this weak, frivolous being; but in his time of need women who had filled up his hours of ease ministered to his wants. He was tenderly nursed by the Duchesse de Grammont (his sister) and by Marguerite Power, who devoted herself to his service. Thackeray saw the Count before this illness seized upon him and has left a lively sketch of the "*cupidon dechainé*" in his apartment, which served for *atelier* and sleeping-room.

"I went to see poor D'Orsay yesterday. He has got an *atelier* not far from his sister's house, and he has filled it with pictures, looking-glasses, trophies, and a thousand gimcracks. His bed is in the corner, surmounted by a medallion of Lady Blessington, a view of her tomb, the star and sword of the Emperor Napoleon, and a crucifix. He sleeps as a child, and looks with a happy admiration at the most awful pictures hung up of his own painting, and at his statues and busts, in which he possibly has some assistance. He has done one of Lamartine, who has composed a copy of verses to his own bust, of which he says that the passer-by regarding it—(it is to be on his own tomb)—will ask, Who is that? Is he a statesman? Is he a warrior? Is he a prophet? Is he a priest? Is he a tribune of the people? Is he an Adonis? Meaning that he is every one of these things. And these mad verses written by a madman, D'Orsay says, are the finest verses that ever were written in the world. Marguerite

[1] Nephew to Count D'Orsay.

has translated them in the finest translation ever made, and the bust is the grandest that ever *wasn't* made by an amateur. Are we mad too, I wonder?"

Lady Blessington was buried temporarily in the vaults of the Madelaine, but later removed to the churchyard of Chambourcey, St Germain en Laye. Here she reposes. In the mausoleum upon which Count D'Orsay devoted so much of his time for more than two years, there is a spacious chamber containing two sarcophagi, for D'Orsay lies there also.

The portraits of Lady Blessington were legion—almost every painter of note in her time wished to "limn" her lovely face and form. Lawrence, whose presentment is here reproduced, gives us a charming representation; Chalon's is full of grace, and Borall's portrait, as Francesca, was lovely as either. Besides these there are endless sketches and miniatures; Maclise's spirited drawing in the Fraserian Gallery must not be forgotten.

SYDNEY OWENSON (LADY MORGAN).

*(From a Miniature by Behnes in the possession of her niece Mrs Geale.)*

## SYDNEY OWENSON, LADY MORGAN

(Born 1774 - died 1859.)

AND

## OLIVIA OWENSON, LADY CLARKE

(Born 1779 - died 1859.)

THE name of Sydney Owenson, Lady Morgan, is to the reading public, familiar as a household word. The story of her life has been told many a time in endless variety, in large and small volumes, long and short articles. It would seem there was no need for repeating so well-worn a theme, which, through so much handling, must have acquired somewhat of a chestnutty flavour. Such an atmosphere of romance, however, surrounds the story of both Sydney and her more beautiful sister, Olivia, there is such a dramatic ring in many of the incidents, that like a rich mine it may be dug over and over again without exhausting the supply of rich matter. The literary side of Sydney's life presents great attractions for those who are interested in studying the changes which have taken place, during the last half century, in the literature of the day.

The childhood of Sydney resembled, in some points, that of Marguerite Power. Like her, debts and difficulties surrounded the cradle of the future authoress. Her father, Robert Owenson, the gentleman player, as he was called (whose own story has a tinge of romance), had adopted the stage as a profession, with a fair share of possible success. He was a handsome man, with extraordinary versatility, and was drawn to the stage by an irresistible impulse, which led him to give up the tangible advantages afforded by his wealthy patron, Mr Blake. Like all young actors, his goal was London, where his kinsman, O'Grady, introduced him to Garrick, who, however, did not engage him. He excelled in Irish parts, such as *Major O'Flaherty* in "The West Indian," and the Irish always quoted him as their best actor. His popularity was unbounded.

"Visions of old Owenson," says one who knew him well, "why float ye before our eyes? Years have passed, a long segment of human life has gone since last we saw you, but your goodly figure rises in white-headed, red-nosed beauty before our mental optics, fresh as a daisy in spring; still ring in our ears the glorious choruses of your songs—amatory, convivial, political, jocular and uproarious—in all the dialects of Ireland, from the antique Milesian down to the disguised English of Connaught. Various and miscellaneous were your stores." One of his most popular songs ran:—

"I lave my pate to Darby Tate,
My face to the O'Gradys;
And I lave my legs to Daniel Beggs,
To flaunt among the ladies.
So Modereen a-roo, a-roo, a-roo—
Modereen a-roo—a-roo, afandy."

Fortune smiled fitfully upon the young actor, who was eager to mount the ladder of fame. In an evil hour he allowed himself to undertake the management of a music-hall, or place of entertainment, in Dublin, and with the usual result—debts, difficulties, followed by lawsuits, which dissipated any profits, soon plunged him into a hopeless struggle, which lasted many years, crushing the very life of the poor, quiet Mrs Owenson[1] who had run away from her Shropshire home with the handsome young actor. We first make the acquaintance of the two little girls in the rambling, old-fashioned house in Dublin where poor Mrs Owenson spent her sad days. The whole scene is so instinct with life as to be almost a living picture. "My sister and myself," writes Lady Morgan, "were one day playing in the court in front

[1] She was Jane Mill of the family of the Mills of Hawkesley.

of our dreary house when a noddy[1] drove up to the gate and a parson stepped out, carrying a green bag under one arm, and a huge book and a little portmanteau in the other. We ran on before him as he advanced, and the noddy man ran after him, holding out an English sixpence between his thumb and finger, and crying, 'Is it wid a tester you put me off? And I come from Stoneybatter wid ye . . . and that is worth the hould *thirteen*[2] any day in the year, and you a parson, reverend sor.' 'I'll give you no more,' said the reverend sor, while *we* paused with our hands behind our backs and our eyes raised to the parson. 'Then I'll have ye before the court of conscience,' was the reply, when his reverence, accidentally crushing the bag under his arm, a sound was emitted from a pair of bagpipes. Fearing the pipes were injured, he drew them from the bag, and played a few notes of Moloney's jig, which struck the man and the children as magic music. 'Will ye give us a little more af ye plaze?' His reverence complied. The children danced, the noddy man fell in, the servants rushed out and began to dance too. When the music stopped the ecstatic charioteer held out the sixpence, saying, 'Plaze, your reverence, take it; by the piper that played before Moses, I could not touch a farthin'. Sure I would drive ye back to Stoneybatter for nothin' at all save a tune on your beautiful pipes.'"

Says Thackeray, "Is not this like a bit of Sterne?"

The poor Shropshire lady found the struggle too hard for her quiet nature, and while her husband was fighting against the buffets of evil fortune, she slowly faded out of life, her one sorrow the leaving of her two friendless little girls. She could not have had much confidence in an erratic genius like Owenson fulfilling the difficult position of guardian to a child such as Sydney had already shown herself, but at first he did the best thing in placing both children at an excellent school kept by a French Huguenot lady, Madame Terson, at Clontarf,

[1] Noddy was the vehicle used in Dublin. It was in shape something like a phaeton, having a flap in front. There was a stand of noddys in College Green, round King William's statue.

[2] The English shilling was *thirteen pence*.

near Dublin. Unfortunately, after a few years, this lady dying, they were removed to another, and finally taken home. Troubles were coming fast and thick upon the poor gentleman player. He had been driven from Fishamble Street by Daly, the rival manager, and had engaged in a disastrous speculation at Kilkenny, with the result that he had, in the phrase then common, to go into "hiding," leaving his two daughters and their maid, the faithful Molly, who had been their nurse, to bear the brunt of angry creditors, and the humiliation of being refused re-admittance to Mrs Anderson's school. This condition of affairs, which would have crushed most girls of her age, seems to have roused all the energy latent in Sydney's character, and brought out all that was best in her nature. Her letters to her father, encouraging and consoling him, her tender, motherly care for her young sister who is to be shielded from all "rough work," her humorous sketches of Molly—all this fills the reader with admiration for this young creature, barely sixteen, who sets herself up as the saviour of the family. *Aide toi le ciel t'aidera* is an old motto which perhaps Sydney Owenson had written in her copybook at Madame Terson's, and now was to prove. An old friend of the family, an excellent clergyman, was touched by the generous spirit of the girl. He exerted himself in her behalf, and procured her a situation as governess in the family of Mrs Featherstonehaugh,[1] of Bracklin Castle, in the County Westmeath. In a letter to her father she describes her first introduction to the family. It is a delightful picture, graphically touched off. A farewell dance was given by her French dancing-master, Monsieur Fontaine, in her honour, at which she danced until the horn of the coach which was to convey her to Westmeath was heard sounding at the top of the street; then all was hurry and confusion. She had no time to change her short white muslin skirt, nor her white shoes with sandals. A cloak was thrown over her finery, a bonnet was crushed upon her head, and she and her bundle were handed in charge to the guard. Her appearance must

[1] The name can be spelt either Featherstone or Featherstonehaugh.—Lady Morgan's *Memoirs*.

certainly have startled Mrs Featherstonehaugh, but it seems to have made no impression unfavourable to the new arrival: she was received most kindly, and from that time treated quite as one of the family.

The Featherstonehaughs always moved to Dublin for the winter season. They had a handsome house in Dominic Street, and saw much society, both fashionable and literary. The friends Sydney made under their roof were excellent rungs in the ladder she was beginning already to ascend. She was not of a nature that would be content with taking a back seat, and her powers of fascination soon were recognised. Few governesses, indeed, are endowed with her social talents, and it is possible that, in a steady-going English family, they would not have been allowed scope for so much display. Her experiences are in curious contrast with those of Charlotte Brontë. Sydney, however, had the rare gift of knowing how to accept kindness and to be grateful for good intentions. In living with others, especially in a more or less dependent situation, this is a grand secret for happiness.

Mr Owenson, who had a great deal of Irish pride in his nature, was hurt at seeing his child in what he considered an inferior position. He obtained her a post more worthy of her talents, as companion and reader to the Dowager Lady Moira. Sydney, however, would not accept the post. She was attached to her pupils, a favourite with everyone, and perfectly happy. Moreover, she had already entered upon her real vocation. Fired by reading an account of Miss Burney's clandestine publication of *Evelina*, Sydney resolved to emulate so excellent an example. The result, in the first instance, was somewhat disappointing. Her first novel, *St Clair*,[1] did not, like *Evelina*, take the world by storm; but then we must remember she had not a father to secretly pull the wires. All things taken into consideration, it was surprising how, with no one to help her, Sydney succeeded in finding a publisher willing to undertake the risk. It is true she derived no advantage beyond a few copies. Still she had made the first step, and, as she was a quick writer, she followed it up

[1] St Clair was published in 1803.

by a second venture, which was more successful. *The Novice of St Dominic*, which was published by subscription, was brought out by Sir Richard Philips, of St Paul's Churchyard, a well-known bibliopole. It made a certain mark, was well received, and when he was dying, Pitt had it read to him three times over. It would not repay perusal now.

Miss Owenson having finally determined to adopt literature as her profession, and finding that leisure to carry out her intention was absolutely necessary, she, with much sorrow on both sides, took leave of her kind friend, Mrs Featherstonehaugh, and the pupils, to whom she had never been a governess in the true sense of the word. She returned to her father's house, and occupied herself diligently with the production of the book with which her name is principally associated—*The Wild Irish Girl.*

Sydney Owenson, at this period of her life, before the world and flattery had spoiled her, seems to have been a very attractive girl. Thackeray, with a gallantry rather unusual in his utterances towards the nation, declares that it is easy for an Irishwoman to be charming; he adds, "and this young Irishwoman was good-looking, quick, impulsive, not without a streak of genius, desirous of pleasing and of being pleased, singing Irish songs, playing the Irish harp, telling droll stories, amusing society by her vivacity and harmless vanity, and *overshadowing* no one by any eminent superiority." "We cannot but admire," adds Thackeray, and praise from his sharp pen is worth having, "the prudence and energy with which this mere girl first goes out as a governess, then resolves to imitate Miss Burney to relieve her improvident father; how she does not allow the flattery of social and literary success to enervate her and cause her to relapse into idleness, because she has the facile luxury of great houses open to her."

Thackeray, who seems to have studied Sydney's character closely, admits that she *flirted freely*, but kept out of scrapes. Her prudent conduct in this regard he ascribes altogether to her having an *English mother.* Wherever the prudence came from, the flirting was of Irish growth. Except the Spanish, no women flirt so prettily as do Irishwomen. "They begin," says an English writer, "in their cradles; it comes, in fact, as second nature, and forms part of the desire to be all things to all men which predominates in the Celtic nature." Sydney had been coquetting all her life. She was a mere school-girl when Dermody, the crazy, handsome, rhyming *protégé* of her father, fell madly in love with her. It is said she returned his affection, but that his wild, fantastic notions as to the marriage tie, or rather no tie, presented an insuperable obstacle, and in the end drove the poet to the solace of the native beverage. Sydney, if she were in love with him, soon recovered. She flirted with everyone—from the Viceroy to the crossing-sweeper. Even over the dry, English publisher, Sir Richard Philips, she at once threw her lasso, and drew him into her net. Their correspondence is all veiled flirting; her letters full of brightness and coquetry, his somewhat antiquated. He addresses her, in a tone of high-flown gallantry, as "*a dear, bewitching, deluding syren.*"

Sydney, however, was not to be caught by sweet words. She had a very keen eye to her own interest, and when Sir Richard hesitated as to accepting *The Wild Irish Girl* on the score of its decidedly advanced national tendency (Lady Morgan was all her life a staunch patriot), the plucky authoress lost no time in applying to Johnson (Miss Edgeworth's publisher), who offered three hundred pounds for the book. When Sir Richard heard this his hesitation vanished. He put forward his prior claim, and secured the right of publishing, but he had to advance his terms, or his bewitching syren would have deserted him. The book caused a *furore*. It went to seven editions, was translated into French, and praised to excess. "Books," says Miss Julia Kavanagh, "have their youth like women and men—a youth which is always enchanting." *The Wild Irish Girl* possessed this charm. It was full of faults, yet its romantic interest, its improbabilities and its enthusiasm gained it a popularity far better written books could not command.

Its phenomenal success was due more to the fact that the Irish question was one of supreme interest than to its own intrinsic merits. It has not borne the test of time, and it is almost impossible now to read it without weariness.

*The Wild Irish Girl*, however, quite satisfied the generation for which it was written, and placed its writer at once in the coveted position of a fashionable novelist. When she went to London, which she did at the instance of her publisher, she was made the lion of the moment, and was invited here, there and everywhere by persons of rank and fashion.

At that time there was flourishing in society a certain animated little old lady, who gave Sunday parties in Burlington Street, who was a link between the eighteenth and nineteenth centuries. Lady Cork, as Miss Monckton, had been one of Mrs Montagu's Blue-stocking Club, had known Mrs Delany and Fanny Burney, Oliver Goldsmith and the Homecks, been called a pretty little dunce by Dr Johnson, and had been painted by Sir Joshua in a pastoral attitude, seated in a garden, a dog at her feet. This remarkable old lady had retained her ardour for company and the enjoyments of life, and her zest for society was as keen as when, sixty years previous, she had gone to a fancy ball as an Indian Sultana, attended by four blacks.[1] Mr Luttrell, the wit, likened her to a shuttlecock, "all cork and feathers," while others speculated in an unfeeling fashion upon her great age.[2] This

[1] At Mrs Cornely's masquerade, February 26th. 1770, Miss Monckton, Lord Galway's daughter, appeared in the character of an Indian Sultana, in a robe of cloth of gold, and a rich veil. The seams of her habit were embroidered with precious stones, and she had a magnificent cluster of diamonds on her head. The jewels she wore were valued at £30,000.

[2] John Wilson Croker, who had an ill-natured fancy for convicting women of suppressing or falsifying their ages (in them not an unpardonable failing), gave himself endless trouble to investigate the actual truth as to Lady Cork's age. In 1835 he discovers that in *Lodge's Peerage** the date has been mis-stated, and in 1836, when she wrote him a most charming little note inviting him to dinner on her ninetieth birthday, this captious critic's only idea was to convict her idea. "I found," he says, "by the register of St James's Parish, that she had understated her age by one year." Lady Morgan is likewise accused by Cyrus Redding of concealing her age, as if that were a heinous offence. "I never could get at it," he says, and then he describes how he fished to elicit some clue. One day, when visiting Lady Morgan, she told him the Countess of Morley had just left. "I wish I had seen her," remarked Redding. "I knew her when she was Lady Boringdon. She must be about your age." "I don't know her age." "Older than you?" "I don't know." "The time I speak of was between 1811 and 1814." "I don't know her age." So he adds, "I could make nothing by the motion." And why should he?

* Lodge gives the date of her birth 1747 !

lady invited to her house all sorts and conditions of men and women, no matter what was their creed, party or calling. Provided they could contribute in any way to the general amusement, they were free of her hospitality, and most diverting stories ran round society as to her pursuit of lions, and her methods of making them perform.[1] Her gatherings were somewhat of an *olla podrida*, as it was well known she would have invited a half-naked savage to her parties if by so doing she could make people talk. For the rest, she was a most interesting personality, having such a distinct connection with the past century. She had often been to the Court of Marie Antoinette, and had never forgotten what the old Princesse de Joinville had told her, that *la propreté* was the beauty of old age. She therefore always dressed in white, wearing a white crape cottage bonnet and a white satin shawl, trimmed with the finest point lace. She was never seen with a cap, and although so old, her complexion, which was *really* white and pink, not put on but her own, was most beautiful.

The first time that Sydney presented herself at Lady Cork's assembly, she was so overcome with nervousness as to be hardly able to ascend the marble staircase with its gilt balustrades. She felt, she said, like Maurice Quill at the battle of Vittoria, who wished some of his greatest enemies were kicking him down Dame Street. The kind reception of her hostess soon dispelled this feeling, and made her quite at home. She was presented to one great personage after another with a flourish which savoured somewhat of the show-woman exhibiting a dancing dog or monkey. "*Allons, mademoiselle, parlez donc. Vous allez voir, mesdames, comme elle parle.* Now, my dear, fancy you are at home, and take off the Irish brogue for us. She does it inimitably. Ah, where is Sheridan? Let someone go and find Sheridan. That's Monk Lewis over there. You

[1] A very amusing story is that of Lady Cork hearing, on the morning of one of her assemblies, that Sir Anthony Carlisle, the fashionable surgeon of the day, had just dissected and preserved the female dwarf, Coechenie. The news suggested to her ladyship that this might afford amusement for her guests of a totally novel description. She posted off to Sir Andrew, who was out. Lady Cork then asked the servant for the little child. "There's no child here, ma'am." "But I mean the child in the bottle." "Oh, this is not the place where we bottle the children, ma'am; that's in the master's workshop."

have heard of him, but you mustn't read his books. They are exceedingly naughty." After this Sydney's Irish harp was brought in, and she was asked to exhibit. Her nervousness had, however, returned. The large pier glasses which lined the walls of the room reflected her solitary little figure surrounded by a gaping crowd of strangers, all waiting for her Irish howl.[1] She was on the brink of tears, and the howl was a failure. At supper, however, she revived. Mr Kemble, who came late, addressed her (drawing at the same time a copy of *The Wild Irish Girl* from his pocket),—

"Little girl, why did you write such nonsense, and where did you get those d——d hard words?" This extraordinary rudeness roused the Celtic nature, and with a flash of her blue eyes, Sydney answered,—

"Sir, I wrote as well as I could, and I got the hard words out of Johnson's dictionary." Sydney, who by the way was not a little girl but a fully-fledged young lady, scored by this quickness of *repartee*, and the story was repeated at all the clubs, adding greatly to her prestige. She had more invitations than she could accept; Lady Charleville, the Marchioness of Abercorn, and her first patroness, Lady Cork, made much of her, and their example was followed by the lion hunters of the day, who vied with each other in paying her every attention, so that it would have required a head of marble to keep cool upon her young shoulders. Nevertheless, we find her letters to home most natural in her enjoyment of these honours—and who would not have enjoyed such distinctions as compliments from royalty itself?—and at the same time there is the same warm interest in every household detail, the same loving care of sister Livy, and respectful attentions to her father, which proves her heart was untouched by her rise in the world. One of the most charming features in Sydney Owenson's character was her intense affection for her sister Livy, untinged as it was by one spark of jealousy of

[1] Lady Cork's drawing-room was charmingly arranged; it was literally filled with flowers and large looking-glasses, which reached from the top of the room to the bottom. At the base was a brass railing, within which were flowers, which, reflected in the glass, had a very pretty effect.

Recollections of LADY CLEMENTINA DACRES.

her very superior attractions. The younger Miss Owenson was both beautiful and highly gifted. Her delicate health, sensitive nature and remarkable beauty unfitted her for making the same struggle for success as did Sydney, who was eminently suited for the more rough-and-ready work of life. It was, therefore, fortunate that the more retiring younger sister, early in her career, secured the affections of an excellent man with ample means to give her every comfort, and what to her affectionate nature was especially welcome—a home for her father. As the wife of Sir Arthur Clarke, there was no more harassing cares for "Livy's future," and a great anxiety was shifted off Sydney's shoulders. She had, however, trials on her own account. Mention has already been made of the flirting propensities which amused without touching the heart of the volatile authoress. In the words of the old ballad, "All men were to her like shadows"; the sufferings of her victims troubled her in no wise. Her day, however, came at last. There is no doubt that her affections were given to Sir Charles Ormsby, a man of position fortune and family, and that a marriage with him would have gratified her ambition and satisfied her heart. That she fully expected an offer from her lover is evident; that he did not make it is inexplicable, as there is strong evidence that he was deeply attached to her.

Seeing that Sir Charles, after going to the extreme verge of flirtation either would not, or could not, cross the brink, she most wisely determined to break off all intimacy with a man who possessed so faint a spirit; but this effort cost her much, and left traces through her life. It was when smarting under this disappointment that a proposal of a very different character was made to her, and that she listened to it for a moment was no doubt due to the wish she had to escape from the scene of her mortification. Lady Abercorn, one of her newly-made friends, was fascinated by the brightness and cleverness of the Irish authoress. She and Lord Abercorn thought it would be delightful to have her as a perpetual visitor. Their children were all married, and this young lady would help them to get through their lonely hours. They were very great people, and very kind people, and the offer was no doubt a good one; but Sydney, after some reflection, did not fall in with the proposal; the idea of being an appendage to a great man's household did not suit her. She was making an independent income, and liked her liberty better than hanging on to a noble patron; but in the end her scruples were overcome. The Abercorns altered their proposal to one less irksome. She was asked to spend a portion of each year either at Baronscourt or Stanmore Priory. Her friends persuaded her to accept this; her father especially urged her to do so. He belonged to the time when patrons were necessary stepping-stones to fortune, and he was more of a snob than his clever, plucky daughter. He wished with all his heart to see his child in such a fine position, and his wish was gratified. Still, to say the truth, it was a mistake, this taking up of a gilded servitude, and Sydney soon tired of it. The position was accompanied by a thousand vexatious circumstances. The noble pair bickered constantly, and Miss Owenson was expected to sit in the cross fire of their humours, and to find good spirits and sprightly conversation when they were dull. There were, of course, compensations. She had the advantage of the very best society, not alone courtly, but literary, and it was under Lady Abercorn's auspices, and very much through her gentle ministrations, that Sydney at last landed in the safe harbour of matrimony. That she was a consummate flirt her best friend cannot deny. The taste had grown since her disappointment, and she felt a pleasure in making the race suffer for the fault of one man. Sir Charles Morgan, however, was too much in earnest to allow this game to be played with him. "I cannot let you make a shuttlecock of my heart for your amusement," he says in one of his letters, and this earnestness prevailed much with the coquette. But it would have gone hard with him had he not been helped by such an able ally. Reading between the lines of the biography, one can see that from the first Lady Abercorn had set her heart on the marriage of her two *protégés*. At first Sydney took the matter much as a joke, and although she accepted the doctor she led him such a tantalising dance that he probably would have broken away altogether only for her ladyship, who took the affair into her hands and settled it in a very summary manner. One January morning the young lady was sitting in her room at Baronscourt, when to her entered Lady Abercorn, and told her "to come upstairs and be married, for there must be no more trifling, my dear Glorvina. . . ." And so Glorvina was led away to her patroness's dressing-room, where everything was prettily arranged for the ceremony—parson surpliced, bridegroom waiting, no possible chance of escape; and in this wise was the Irish girl caught and caged.[1]

Once married, the flighty little authoress made an excellent wife. and in all essential points the pair were admirably suited to one another. Sir Charles was sensible, clever and quiet; his solid qualities were of infinite use in tempering her too redundant vivacity, which he kept in check. He advised her in all points, and occasionally overawed her. Her attachment to him was decidedly strong and sincere, and they were a pleasant, hospitable, happy couple, eminently social especially after they cut the Gordian knot which bound them to their distinguished patrons, and set up house for themselves in Dublin, having a small house in Kildare Street, which soon became known as a centre where society gathered. At that time there was a touch of foreign life in the little Irish capital, and a pleasant interchange of fun and frivolity, as when Lady Morgan, wishing to give an evening party, threw up the windows of her drawing-room and invited her friends as they passed to join the revel. We hear of her at the Viceregal gaieties, where she scorned to appear in the necessary uniform of train and feathers, "preferring to glide about with her luxuriant hair bound by a solid gold fillet, her face all animation, and with a witty word for everyone." She was exceedingly vain of her toilet, being addicted to very *prononcé* colours, bright blue satins, and much adornment of lace. Neither did she disdain to abandon the pen for the needle, and generally made her own dresses. As may be imagined, she soon

[1] The wedding ring was too large, and before the evening the bride had lost it. It was never found. Sydney would not hear of Sir Charles replacing it, by what she maintained would be a sham wedding ring.

became a well-known character in Dublin, and always received an enthusiastic cheer when she appeared in the dress-circle at the theatre. Thackeray has immortalised her in his "with Lady Morgan drinking tea," and Moore has chronicled different pleasant dinners with Curran, Shiel, Edward Moore and the Clarkes. Lady Clarke was the chief attraction of the Kildare Street gatherings. The prettiness of the girl had developed into the beauty of the woman, to which she added conversational powers so superior to those of her novel-writing sister, that one cannot help suspecting that the work which went in the name of one was a joint production. A visitor to Dublin a few years later gives the following amusing account of the Morgan household:—"A number of pleasant people used to assemble of an evening in what has been called 'Lady Morgan's snug little nutshell in Kildare Street.' When I first made the acquaintance of the lady of the house she was in the height of her popularity. I found her occupied in preparing for the Press her novel of *The O'Briens and the O'Flahertys.* In this work, as she told me, I am made to figure as a certain Count—a great traveller—who made a trip to Jerusalem for the sole object of eating artichokes in their native country."

The same writer[1] goes on to say:—

"I once joined a group at a masquerade in which both sisters figured. Lady Morgan was a Marquise of the Court of Louis XV., a character which, from habit of her interlarding her conversation with French epithets, became quite natural to her. Lady Clarke enacted the part of an Irish lady of the last century on whom the Pope had bestowed the title of Countess of the Holy Empire. She wore a high-crowned hat, and that description of riding-habit called a 'Joseph.' It was of a bright snuff colour, and had metal buttons as large as crown pieces down the front. I personated a Macaroni of the same period, fresh from Italy; but I did not do justice to my part, from the desire I had to catch some of the pleasantries which the Irish countess was dealing out to all around.

[1] Recollections of the Earl of Albemarle.

OLIVIA OWENSON (LADY CLARKE).

[*From the Original Miniature by Behnes in the possession of Mrs Geale.*

"Lady Clarke used to sing some charming Irish songs. They were for the most part squibs on the Dublin society of the day. I find, from inquiries I have made, that not a copy of any of them is to be found. A verse of one of them, giving a sketch of the Irish metropolis of my day, runs somewhat thus:—

'We're swarming alive,
Like bees in a hive,
With talent and janious, and beautiful ladies.
We've a Duke in Kildare,
And a Donnybrook Fair,
And if that wouldn't plaze yez, why nothing would plaze yez.
We've poets in plenty,
But not one in twenty
Will stay in Ould Ireland to keep her from sinking;
They say they can't live,
Where there's nothing to give.
Och! what business have poets with ating and dhrinking.'

"The authoress of *The Wild Irish Girl*, justly proud of her gifted sister Olivia, was in the habit of addressing every new-comer with, 'I must make you acquainted with my Livy.' She once used this form of words to a gentleman who had just been worsted in a fierce encounter of wits with the lady in question. 'Yes, ma'am,' was the reply, 'I happen to know your Livy, and I would to heaven your Livy was Tacitus.'"

Sir John Malcolm says that without having the pretensions of her better-known sister, she was far more witty, and quite as agreeable. "I was never so entertained," he writes, "as by this little, shy-looking woman playing and singing her own funny songs. One, a parody of Miss Stephens' "Home, Sweet Home," was made by Lady Clarke on *Home*, the celebrated pastry-cook of Dublin, *his name* naturally lending itself to the parody,—

'No one makes pastry—makes pastry like Home.

"She sang it," Sir John Malcolm declares, "delightfully, and was especially happy in the last verse.

'All *the sweets* of this world are centred in *Home*.'

"She has a thousand others of the same kind; in one she most funnily describes her clever sister:—

> 'She is, though I say it, an elegant artist,
> A Radical . . . and a great Buonapartist.'"

In a notice in the *Athenæum*, mention is also made of Lady Clarke entertaining the company with snatches of old Irish songs, and reminiscences of the "Beggar's Opera." She had a fund of good spirits, and much dramatic talent. As her daughters grew up, she cultivated their musical gifts, and originated a series of clever performances by marionettes or puppets, who performed operettas sung by the Misses Clarke. These were highly popular, the Viceroy and his staff always attending. Lady Clarke occasionally wrote the prologue for 'The Royal Operatic Marionette Theatre,' and excelled in this class of versification, which owes much to the *àpropos* of the illusions which are not so well understood by another generation. She had undoubtedly a talent of this sort. When the British Association visited Dublin in 1838, a most elaborate account of what was, in fact, a most brilliant gathering of savants appeared in the pages of the *Athenæum*, which also chronicled the wise speeches of Drs Lardner and Coulter, Sir John Franklin and Professor Agassiz from Neufchatel.

It seemed, however, there was another side to all this philosophy, and that the learned doctors were not insensible to the charms of the Irish ladies. Their surreptitious flirtations were very humorously described in a short poem called "Fun and Philosophy," which appeared in the *Athenæum* when all was over. It was from the pen of Lady Clarke, and gives the "popular view" of the intellectual gathering:—

> Heigh for Ould Ireland! Oh, would you require a land,
> Where men by nature are all quite the thing,
> Where pure his peroration has taught the whole nation
> To fight, love and reason, talk politics, sing?
> 'Tis Pat's mathematical, chemical, tactical,
> Knowing and practical, fanciful, gay.
> Fun and philosophy, supping and sophistry,
> There's nothing in life that is out of his way

He makes light of optics, and sees through dioptrics,
He's a dab at projectiles,—ne'er misses his man;
He's complete in attraction, and quick at reaction
By the doctrine of chances he squares every plan.
In hydraulics so frisky, the whole Bay of Biscay,
But if it flowed with whisky, he'd stow it away.
    Fun and philosophy, supping and sophistry,
    There's nothing in life that is out of his way.

To him cross over, savant and philosopher,
Thinking, God help them! to bother us all;
But they'll find that for knowledge, *'tis at our own college*
Themselves must inquire for—*beds*, dinners or ball.[1]
There are lectures to tire, and good lodgings to hire,
To all who require and have money to pay;
    While fun and philosophy, supping and sophistry,
    *Ladies* and lecturing fill up the day.

Here's our *déjeûner;* put down your shilling, pray,
See all the curious bastes after their feed.[2]
Lovely lips, Moore has said, must evermore be fed,
So this is but suiting the word to the deed;
Perhaps you'll be thinking that eating and drinking,
Where wisdom sits blinking is rather too gay.
    But fun and philosophy, supping and sophistry,
    Are all very sensible things in their way.

So at the Rotundo, we all sorts of fun do,
Hard hearts and pig-iron we melt in one flame.
For if love blows the bellows, our tough college fellows
Will thaw into rapture at each lovely dame.
There, too, *sans* apology, tea tarts, tautology,
Are given with zoology to grave and gay.
    Thus fun and philosophy, supping and sophistry,
    Send all to England home, happy and gay.

From the time of her marriage, Lady Morgan's literary career assumed a different aspect. Her union with a man of the undoubted ability of Sir Charles, who was a writer of much refinement and elegance, had a distinct influence as regarded

[1] A notice to this effect was posted on the walls of the college.

[2] The breakfast was given in Glasnevin Gardens to more than 1400 persons. An essay was read by Professor Agassiz. The ladies were not admitted until after the philosophers (*i.e.*, the bastes) had been fed.

the improvement of her somewhat slip-shod style.[1] From the time of her marriage her position as an authoress grew more assured. It was Sir Charles's office to act as his erratic little wife's amanuensis, correcting her wanderings into divers tenses and other feminine aberrations, while, at the same time, he took care not to interfere with the fidelity of her pictures of existing life, or to curb the vivacity of her fancy. *O'Donnell*, which she published in 1814, two years after her marriage, shows evidence of this careful pruning. It lacks, however, much of the charm that distinguished *The Wild Irish Girl*. The authoress, in her preface, says it deals with the flat realities of life. The hero is, nevertheless, genuinely romantic. Sir Walter Scott, in his diary, mentions having "amused myself very pleasantly reading Lady Morgan's novel, *O'Donnell*, which has some striking and beautiful passages, and in its comic parts is rich and cultivated; there is, however," he adds, "a want of story always fatal to a book on the first reading, and it is well if it has a second chance, poor novel."[2]

*O'Donnell* was published by the new fashionable publisher, Henry Colburn, who had inaugurated an entirely new system of publishing. In the year 1814 the publishing business was in the hands of Murray, Longman and Colburn, who later on was joined by Richard Bentley. Murray's position was unchallenged; as "the Prince of Bibliopoles" he drew round him talent of no ordinary kind, and deserved the confidence of the public. Colburn, on the other hand, was a new man. He was said to be of a mean, pettifogging spirit, a

[1] Sir Charles contributed to the *Athenæum* as well as to the *Examiner*, and gave to both papers "a considerable amount of backbone," as Mr Grote was wont to say. "After his marriage, Sir Charles gave up almost altogether medical practice, and devoted himself exclusively to political and literary pursuits. The *Monthly Magazine* contains some of his pleasantest contributions, and up to the week of his death he wrote in a celebrated literary review. On the coming in of the Whigs, he was made one of the Commissioners of Irish Fisheries, and his reports were remarkable for their cleverness. He was also the author of two valuable works, which have undergone translation in French and Italian—*The Philosophy of Life*, and *The Philosophy of Morals*. To Lady Morgan's books of travel in France and Italy he contributed the chapters on Law, Medical Science and Statistics, and the last joint-publication of the devoted couple was *The Book without a Name*. Sir Charles was very accomplished—a writer of much ability, an honest politician, an amiable and enlightened man. He was never at a loss for a witty or wise passage from Rabelais or Bayle."—From the *Examiner*.

[2] This remark of Sir Walter Scott's was repeated by a young lady to Lady Morgan. She answered good-humouredly, "Yes! I have not much invention."

dealer in petty arts and small stratagems which ensured success where no intrinsic merit existed. The arts he resorted to were then considered unworthy, because they were unknown. He may be said to have invented the art of influencing the public by the means of extensive puffing and advertisements. Advertise, advertise was his motto, and, judged by the standard of to-day, an excellent method. It did not however, find favour with the uncompromising critics of Colburn's time.

In an article in *Fraser's Magazine*, entitled, "The Art of Puffing," Mr Henry Colburn and the small fry of authors composing the Tag-rag and Bobtail Club, headed by Thomas Campbell, the bard of hope, are very roughly handled. "Literary puffers and trumpeting booksellers should form themselves into a special guild and choose Henry Colburn for their head, for it is he who has not only invented, but brought the present art and mystery of puff manufacture to its existing condition and consistence. Does he not keep clerks and writers, whose exclusive employment is, as he says, 'Solely to look after the papers and the advertisements;' and does not the little man boast of being able to stuff his inconceivable trash down the reluctant maws of the public? . . . This achievement is of easy execution for the manly shoulders of Henry Colburn. *He* is proprietor of the *Court Journal*, the *New Monthly Magazine*, the *Naval and Military*. He has a share in the *Literary Gazette*, and every newspaper opens its columns for the puffs of this *clean-handed* gentleman, save only the *Times* and the *Morning Herald*. '*Mister* Henry Colburn,' however, continues to put money into his pockets (and very fast he keeps it there), and Mr Richard Bentley means to do so likewise, reasoning, as he does, that there are more fools than wise people in the world, and that, if even half his trash were to be sent to the candle and snuff shops, the other half would find a sufficiently ample market, for the odds are in favour of the gullibleness of fools. The secret of success, therefore, is involved in the right use of one grand cabalistic word—Puff. Ay, Puff! Puff! Puff!"

Another writer is even fiercer in his attack upon the successful publishers.

"Have ye ever perused one of the compositions of Messrs Bentley and Colburn, known, ye gods, men and booksellers, by the name of 'puffs,' in which the 'denounced,' or the 'disowned,' or the 'd——d,' or any other of the admirable productions of that class and order are depicted as works of superhuman genius—talent more than mortal energy can devise. Price, one pound, one shilling. *N.B.*—None are genuine unless they have the mark of Colburn & Bentley on the title-page. And being enticed in the simplicity of your heart by these flattering pictures, you are handed, for your sovereign and its silvery attendant, the volumes, with the certain fate of discovering that the book so beplastered is stupid beyond belief, ignorant and abominable, and with affectation not to be endured."

"Here are three examples out of a hundred puffs which Messrs Colburn and Bentley have manufactured for the purpose of carrying off their editions of this egregious stuff."

The *Morning Chronicle* leads the way:—

"The new fashionable poem, Mr Bulwer's 'Siamese Twins,' has become the most popular phrensy since the publication of 'Don Juan.' The first edition is, we understand, already exhausted. We have not heard whether any alterations are to be made in the second, or whether that singular passage describing the introduction of *the twins* at Almack's by Lady Jersey's ticket is retained."

The article goes on to describe the manufacture of the fashionable novel then in vogue, with its elaborate system of *Keys*[1] to the real names of the titled personages who

[1] In the recollections of Cyrus Redding a curious story is told of the use made by Colburn of *the Key system*:—"'Authors and publishers,' says the writer, 'were in those days much more *a unity* than they are now.' Calling one day upon Colburn, who published Disraeli's first book, *Vivian Grey*, he said to me,—'I have a capital book out, *Vivian Grey*. The authorship is a great secret—a man of high fashion—very high—keeps the first society. I can assure you it is a most piquant and spirited work, quite sparkling.' Colburn always regarded, in publishing, the fashionable taste, no matter how absurd, for the fashionable was a buying taste, and no Lintot looks farther. I remarked that the characters were not drawn from life, for I had already run my eyes over the work. 'Two or three characters might,' I said, 'be from the life, but they were exaggerated, or almost wholly imaginary.' This Colburn did not like, but remarked that

figure as *dramatis personæ*, an invention, this, of "the two princes paramount of puffers and quacks, Messrs Colburn and Bentley."

All this vituperation boded well for the commercial success of Colburn. For years he commanded an extensive share of public favour, and published the works of the best writers. He did not care what price he gave, provided he could keep certain authors like Lytton Bulwer and Harrison Ainsworth to himself, and prevent other publishers getting hold of them. He gave Lady Morgan £600 for *O'Donnell* and double that sum for *Florence M'Carthy*. The first named was attacked fiercely in the *Quarterly Review*, the writer being supposed to be John Wilson Croker, a countryman of Lady Morgan's. Later on it was well known to be the work of the venomous Gifford.[1] The extraordinary license allowed to reviewers at

people of fashion might read, and would understand them for realities. Three or four days after this, walking down Oxford Street, I saw one of Colburn's establishment coming out of Marsh's, in Oxford Street. It was here that Mr Disraeli published incog. a periodical paper called the *Star Chamber*, in the columns of which the author had extolled his own book. The messenger had a number of pamphlets under his arm 'What have you there?' The pamphlets were in yellow covers, about twenty pages of matter. The word 'key' was signified by a wood-cut of a key, and below the cut were the words 'to *Vivian Grey*—being a complete exposition of the royal, noble and fashionable characters who figure in this most extraordinary work.' There was a second wood-cut of a curtain, partly drawn aside, displaying in the perspective a drawing-room filled with company attitudinising. 'Oh,' said I, 'why did not Mr Colburn publish this as well as the book itself?' 'That would not answer," was the reply. I did not on the instant remember that Marsh was the publisher of Mr Disraeli's *Star Chamber*. I took away one of the pamphlets, and found it filled with extracts from *Vivian Grey*, and remarks, some of feigned censure, to give critical verisimilitude, others were puffs of the work, highly laudatory. At the end of the key there was a clue to living personages, whose names were affixed to the real and imaginary characters in the work, all extracted from Mr Disraeli's *Star Chamber*, which affected great mystery as to the authorship, the aim of which was obvious. 'We know,' so it ran, 'who the author of *Vivian Grey* really is.' Then in the before-mentioned paper followed the names of living characters. Mr Foaming Fudge, Mr B——m; Lord Alhambra, Lord P——; Colonel Dalmington, Colonel L——n. All this was intermingled with a little critical censure here and there, and above all surpassing wonderment at the noise the extraordinary work was making in the world. "Such were some of the artifices made use of to get the book into notoriety, and they were successful."

[1] Hazlitt, who suffered terribly from Gifford's attacks, wrote in scathing terms of his enemy:—"There cannot be a greater nuisance than a dull, envious, pragmatical, low-bred man who is placed, as *you* are, in the situation of editor to such a work as the *Quarterly Review*. He exults over unsuccessful authors, he hates successful ones; he is angry at the faults of a work, more angry at its excellence." Here is a sample of how the unfortunate writers were treated:—"In these days of cant and humbug, of fraud, folly and foppery, of idle words, vast pretensions of vain and blatent hollowness, of Robert Montgomeryism, Lytton Bulwerism, Colburn and Bentleyism; in these days when Thomas Campbell passes

the beginning of this century, and the paramount importance accorded to their opinions, is a marked feature in the history of literature. That such turgid, unsparing criticism was not without good effect upon the writers of the day is incontrovertible; nevertheless, its influence for good was seriously impaired by the offensive character of many of these reviews —the personal animosity which it thinly veiled, and the decided political bias which was the ruling motive of many a virulent attack. In the attacks made on Lady Morgan during her literary career, this party bias has to be taken into account. She was a staunch, uncompromising patriot; an advocate for emancipation, civil and religious.

And although, strangely enough, these well-known principles did not interfere with her friendship with the most aristocratic of the upper ten, it drew down upon her the wrath of the Tory party, who were the principal upholders of the Conservative *Quarterly* and *Fraser's Magazine*. From these papers Lady Morgan got no quarter. The intrepid lady faced her adversaries boldly.

A few years later, in the May number of *Fraser's Magazine* for 1833, she made a spirited remonstrance to Mr Fraser on his omission of her name in the essay on female character:—

"Oh, fie, Mr Fraser! 'tis shameful, 'tis scandalous, shocking and spiteful,
To think, in your Essay on Females, that else had been perfect delightful!
You have falsified all your pretensions to gallantry, grace and gentility,
Or the chivalrous spirit that honours every gem of true female nobility;
You have forfeited credit and character, fitting a popular organ,
By omitting the name of matchless *moi-même*, Ladi Morgan.
Only think what a wrong to the fair sex, who hail *me* their pride and
their glory;
Only think what a loss to mankind! but this comes of your being
*a Tory*,

for a Greek scholar, Thomas Babington Macaulay for an enemy to quacks, and James Mackintosh for an historian, modesty is unlooked for, and so novel, that an approach should be hailed with joy." S. C. Hall draws down the flail upon his unfortunate person by announcing that the first sheet of the *Amulet* (one of the many periodicals) was reserved "for my friend Mr Bulwer," afterwards Sir Edward Lytton Bulwer. "Hear ye this, readers of annuals and poetical books, and let the words sink deeply into your ears. *Bulwer*, ay, Bulwer *ipsissimus*, postpones *his* aid until next year. He must have the *first* sheet, forsooth," etc.

For you know that the Duke, Peel and Eldon, and others on whom you're dependency,
All declare "they have no chance of power while my lady maintains the ascendency."
And so I shrewdly suspect my Lord Roden or Sir Richard Vyvyan
Have prevailed on you, Mr Fraser, to bury my name *in oblivion*."

But if Lady Morgan could put such a good face upon her annoyance, Sir Charles was by no means so plucky. In 1830 we find him writing to Cyrus Redding of the false, calumnious and diabolical attack upon Lady M—— in the *Times*. "What is he to do? Is it wise or prudent to answer, or to let it alone—four columns in the *Times!* At such a moment could it have been purchased, and if so, by whom?"

*Ida of Athens* followed *O'Donnell*. It was severely handled in the *Quarterly*.

*Ida* was succeeded by *France*, which appeared in 1817, and met with great success, but again the *Quarterly* flew at her throat, treating the work with a severity quite unjustifiable, and which would not be tolerated nowadays. This persecution of a woman roused great indignation. Lady Morgan's suspicions fell upon Croker. Mr Peel, afterwards Sir Robert, who then held office in Dublin, writes to Croker, "Lady Morgan vows vengeance against you as the supposed author of the article in the *Quarterly*. You are to be *The hero* of some novel of which she is about to be delivered. One of her warm friends has been trying to extract *from me* whether you were the author of this obnoxious article or not, but I disclaimed all knowledge, and only did not deny that it was to be attributed to you because I thought you would be very indifferent to Lady Morgan's hostility. I was excessively amused by hearing that the female circle of Dublin generally attribute the article to Vesey (Fitzgerald)."

From a subsequent letter it is pretty evident that a great portion of these "obnoxious reviews" were written by Gifford. Lady Morgan, however, having no suspicion of this, fulfilled her threat in regard to holding up her supposed enemy,

Croker, to the derision of the world. Her portrait of him as Crawley in *Florence M'Carthy* was at once recognised, and his tough withers were wrung with mortification.

The amount of literature turned out in the little house in Kildare Street was truly surprising, and supports the idea, suggested by a recent writer, that Lady Clarke, who had a charming facility with her pen, sometimes assisted in the process of manufacture.

*France*[1] was successful, running into several editions in spite of the hostile attitude assumed by the press, which had, to use a vulgar expression, "rounded on" Lady Morgan. An amusingly-written, but unkind and satirical review, appeared in *Fraser's Magazine*, in which great capital is made of her ladyship's innocent vanity. The tone may be gathered from the following, which is a fair sample of the personal nature of reviews in those days :—

"This late book is decidedly your (Lady Morgan's) best, because it may be in some sort considered the mirror of your iconic nature. We have clearly before us the charming arts by which you bewitched Lafayette the General and Careene the cook, Rothschild the banker and Beranger the *chansonnier*, David the sculptor and Celliers the executioner, the romanticist with the open shirt collar, and the classicist with no collar." All through her literary career Lady Morgan seems to have been exposed to the most insulting, coarse, ungentlemanlike attacks. Her age, her personal appearance, her dress, her domestic affairs were commented upon in a manner which fortunately is absent from the criticism of to-day. It was cruelly unjust and yet not inexplicable! Lady Morgan had an aggressive character, which showed itself in her writings. She was fearless; she braved sarcasm and slander, and kept good her stand against her enemies; she was not to be put down. At one time she had the *Quarterly*, the *Times*, the *Age* and *Fraser's* all assailing her, but she was equal for them all. When a

[1] *France* appeared in 1817. It excited considerable interest abroad. Lebrun translated it. The Baron F. P. C. Dupin, addressed a letter to Lady Morgan. "*La France telle qu'elle est, et non la France de Lady Morgan*" was the title of another pamphlet; also, *Observations sur l'ouvrage intitulé la France, par Lady Morgan, par Defauconpret.*

writer called Morgan Rattler attacked her *France* with some severity, she replied in rhyme :—

"But oh, Mr Fraser, that you should with dire dereliction of duty,
Betray such a want of good taste and of homage to talent and beauty.
Though the *Quarterly* showed me no quarter, and you and your friend
Morgan Rattler
Set me down as a *tiresome* twaddler, a *pert, pretty, pragmatical* prattler."

*Italy* succeeded *France*. Colburn gave the Morgans two thousand for it, and in addition presented Lady Morgan with a parure of amethysts, so charmed was he with *Florence M'Carthy*, the proofs of which he was reading. On their way to Italy, Sir Charles and his clever wife remained some time in Paris, from which place she wrote the following characteristic letter to Lady Clarke, which puts the real woman before us with her innocent vanity and warm heart for those at home :—

"*Tuesday, Paris*, 29, 1818.

"MY DEAR LOVE,—I give you one word more. No letter yet arrived from you—'*tis two months to-morrow since you wrote*. The public news is at a stand. The old ministers cannot go out because no *one* will take their place; even *Cuvier* the naturalist, whom the French call '*plat et suple*,' has refused being Minister of *the Interiur*. The King *cries* all day long. The other day he had *de Cage and Richelieu*, the two rival ministers with him, but could not get them to pull together. He said at parting with them, '*Mon chere de Cage, je vous aime, Mon. le Duc je vous estime*.' 'The Duchess of Devonshire comes to me to-morrow night, and some Russian Princess, whose name I can neither pronounce nor spell, but sounds like *Kourikan*. We dine on Tuesday next at Mr Lattin's. Mrs Solly (Morgan's sister) has got a magnificent hotel, and means to dash *not* a little. She is mighty kind, good-natured and pretty. We dined with them on Sunday last. They have 2 cooks, French and English. Morgy has one of *his bad colds*, and I am grown thin again for want *of sleep*. I cannot discover the cause, but my rest has quite abandoned me. I am beginning to think 'tis the strong coffee. The weather is *intensely cold*, but clear and bright. The poverty of the lower classes excessive, and all commerce at a stop for the present. Not the slightest commotion is, however, expected, and all safe and secure for the present!!! I had a sort of little triumph at the *Athénée* the other night when I went to hear *Constant's Oration* on Sir S. Romilly. I came in late, every place was occupied. The Princess *Jablanowska*, who sat in the front, s^d pretty *loud* who I was. Everyone got up; a clearance was made in a moment; everyone offered me their seat, and a chair was at last placed for me near the *Princess*, who enjoyed all this amazingly, and could talk of nothing else all night, for she took us home with her, and we remained with her till midnight. Once more, god bless you all. Morgan says a word from Clarke on the state of *medical* affairs—and bit of Irish *politics*—he has effected a great cure here of a *bilious woman* who *was in extremity*. What *coloured* eyes and hair has the young Dandy?

"Love to the Macarthies. Does the puppet show go on?"

*Italy*[1] roused a storm of indignation; its authoress had not been very measured in her language, and she had somewhat injudiciously attacked old institutions and ceremonials dear to the heart of the nation. Francis Joseph, Emperor of Austria, would not allow Lady Morgan to set foot within his dominions, and from the Vatican the book was strongly censured.[2] This attitude on the part of the Catholic Church can cause no surprise. It is, however, curious that the work was attacked with equal warmth by the English Protestant Press. This continued persecution at length roused Lady Morgan's anger, and the letter she addressed to the "Reviewers of *Italy*," much too long to insert here, is a most spirited remonstrance. It is amusing to find her Irish ladyship attributing the attacks of the reviewers to the wire-pulling of the Government—the Irishman's panacea for all grievances. "The Government," she says,

[1] *Italy*, 1824. Translated into Italian and German "*una risposta a Lady Morgan nella sua opera L'Italia. . . . Facchini*; also *Le Morganiche lettere scritte à Miladi Morgan*, 1824.

[2] Lady Morgan was fond of alluding in grandiloquent terms to this prescription, calling herself "the proscribed of Emperors and the excommunicated of Popes."

"gave the word to all subaltern scribes to tear down and attack whatever I should print, and the public must allow that the rag-a-muffins of the '*ancient pistol,*' who, like Sir John Falstaff, had misused the Kinge's Press, have done their spiriting faithfully if not gently. They have attacked me in every point where the woman was most susceptible, the author most sensitive—my profession and private character, my person, principles, friends, kindred; even my dress. They have done everything to injure me save *praise me*, and, after all,—

> "*It is their slaver kills—not their bite.*"[1]

Nothing daunted by the bites she received, and secure in the favour of the public Lady Morgan next took a flight into the regions of Art. Her *Life of Salvator Rosa* was a new departure into a subject of which one of her editors considered she had no real knowledge, but he adds, "This ignorance is shared by many of her sex, who publish catalogues with remarks that only the ignorant would accept." *Salvator Rosa* was preceded by *The O'Briens and the O'Flahertys*, one of her best novels, and in 1829 *The Book of the Boudoir* appeared.[2]

In addition to these larger undertakings, both she and Sir Charles contributed constantly to the *New Monthly Magazine*, writing all sorts and kinds of articles, from the political to the frivolous.

A change was, however, at hand, and as great

[1] Byron was much struck by the injustice with which Lady Morgan was treated by the *Quarterly*. Writing in 1818 to Murray, he says:—"What cruel work you make with Lady Morgan. You should remember that she is a woman, though, to be sure, they are now and then very provoking; still, as authoresses they can do no great harm, and I *think* it is a pity so much good invective should have been laid out upon her."

[2] *The Book of the Boudoir* was savagely attacked in *Blackwood's Magazine*, but the sale was not in the least injured by this fact. Colburn, who was highly gratified by the success of *The O'Briens and O'Flahertys*, was all anxiety to secure another work from Lady Morgan's pen to succeed the successful novel—strike while the iron is hot being his plan. With this intention he called on her, just as she was leaving London—the carriage was at the door and all packed. Suddenly the publisher caught sight of an untidy, dirty-looking parcel of writing that the servant was thrusting into the pocket of the chariot. "What is that?" cried the excited bibliopole, and, snatching it out of its concealment, carried it off with him. It was *The Book of the Boudoir*.

thunder-storms follow upon protracted atmospheric disturbance, so a final rupture in domestic or friendly relations is invariably preceded by a series of minor grumblings. A coolness had for some time been in the air between the Morgans and Colburn. The lady was unreasonable, so said the publisher — the publisher was grasping, said the lady. This carping and grumbling came to a decided quarrel as to Lady Morgan's second volume of *France*, a work in which her peculiar genius had the fairest play and development. There had been no understanding with Colburn about it, but he considered, so he afterwards said, "that Lady Morgan was bound to him in literary matrimony," and, like the usual husband, acted towards her with cool security. "Having written to him more than once, without receiving any reply, Lady Morgan transferred her MS. to Saunders and Otley, who gladly accepted it, and then the storm broke. Colburn (whose value for a writer always rose when he was about to lose him) was frantic, and vowed if she did not immediately break off with Otley, and return to him, she would suffer both in her pecuniary interest and her literary fame." Lady Morgan snapped her fingers at these threats, but her indifference changed to anger and annoyance, when Colburn had placards printed with this mortifying heading,—

"LADY MORGAN" *at half-price.*

The announcement ran, "In consequence of the great losses sustained in publishing her works, which had never sold, the publisher was obliged to dispose of the residue of the stock at a great reduction."

Saunders and Otley at once took alarm, and asked to be released from their bargain, and the whole matter came into Court, when Mr Colburn admitted he had been so enraged at losing Lady Morgan's work that he had tried to damage her literary reputation and the sale of the book, and offered every apology, as well as retracting what he had said.

*France* was followed by the publication of *Dramatic Scenes*, Saunders and Otley again being the publishers. *Sketches or Dramatic Scenes* consists of three drawing-room plays, *Manor Sackville, The Easter Recess*, and *Temper*. Although readable they have no particular merit.[1] This was her second attempt at the drama. A play of hers was produced at the Theatre Royal, Dublin, the year before she was married. Her gifts, however, did not lie in this direction, and neither the more ambitious attempt nor the last venture made any mark. The *Dramatic Scenes* are, in fact, somewhat vulgar, and did not escape without some severe handling.

What seems, however, to have affected Lady Morgan infinitely more than any adverse criticism, was the spiteful remarks which appeared in a book written by a petty German prince, who gave to the world his impressions of his tour through Europe. Why she should have attached so much importance to the ill-natured remarks of a vain, disappointed man like Prince Puckler Muskau, is hard to understand. His business seems to have been to rake up any piece of scandal regarding every person or family with whom he came in contact. He had a bad word for even those who were kindest to him, and a good word for very few. The praise or blame of such a man was of small importance. The consciousness, however, that there were such worthless specimens of human nature, such evidences of ingratitude, put Lady Morgan out of temper. She writes to Mr Redding :—"The last instance of the return of evil for good is the book of Prince Puckler Muskau. This person was recommended to my attention by a lady of high consideration in London. My house here is open to all strangers and foreigners of respectability. It is the only house that is so in Dublin, and never has any one benefited more largely by my humble hospitalities than did this German Prince. You have, by this time, read the return he has made me in every page. He begins by accusing me of frivolity and falsehood, and yet, at the very time he details all these follies, it appears, on

[1] In dramatic scenes she introduces Sir Arthur and Lady Clarke, Sir Charles and herself playing a game of cards known as "forty-five."

his own showing he was daily partaking of Sir Charles's and my hospitalities and attentions." Then she returns to her usual suspicion that her enemy Colburn was jobbing something in all this.[1]

Lady Morgan might have consoled herself with the reflection that she did not get off worse than many others who had shown the ungrateful Count hospitality. If he described her as a little frivolous woman, neither pretty nor ugly, he used far coarser language in regard to the fashionable London ladies, and had he ever ventured to show his face there again he would have received a good horse-whipping.

Amongst the few people he spared, Lady Clarke and her daughters can be named. "They sing and act delightfully; the mother, with her talent for the drama, cutting out and contriving admirable dresses out of heterogeneous material." The daughters, he writes, have an inexhaustible fund of grace and vivacity extremely un-English—eminently Irish. When he took them to an equestrian[2] performance at a circus, their *naïf* delight was charming; "the youngest never turned her eyes from the most terrific feat, she trembled all over with anxiety and eagerness, and kept her hands clenched the whole time."[3]

[1] It appears to have been a rooted idea in the minds of both Sir Charles and Lady Morgan that Colburn was their deadly and secret enemy, ever working in the dark to upset them. Spiteful he may have been, but he was totally innocent of any dark plot in regard to the severe articles in the *Times*, which were altogether due to the personal dislike of the editor, Mr Barnes.

[2] Olivia afterwards married Mr Savage, the popular author of *The Falcon Family*. Olivia and José Clarke were called by Lord Carlisle Lady Morgan's harmonious nieces. The latter, Mrs Geale, had a voice of singular beauty, with a tenor register. She sang Moore's Melodies as they are not sung nowadays, having received instruction from the poet himself. Her singing will always be remembered, by those who had the pleasure of hearing it, with delight. She was also an accomplished artist. Her marriage with Mr Geale was thoroughly romantic—the young people having only Love *pour tout potage*. Lord Carlisle, however, who was, when Lord Morpeth, an admirer of the fair Josephine, came to the rescue and smoothed the path of the lovers. Mr Geale's sisters, by right, should have a place in the beauties of the nineteenth century. They were a singularly handsome group, and are mentioned in Fisher Murray's novel, *The Viceroy*, as the belles of Dublin. During Lord Anglesea's Viceroyalty, Lady Somerville later made the conquest of Lord Fortescue, the Lord-Lieutenant, in 1841. Mrs Williams was equally handsome, and in *her* daughters the heredity of beauty has been carried on—Lady Charles Wellesley, Dowager Lady Gresley and Mrs Farmer of Nonsuch having all received a share of the divine gift.

[3] Prince Puckler Muskau and his book are long since forgotten. He lives, however, in *Pickwick*, where he figures as Count Smorltork, at Mrs Leo Hunter's party, gathering materials for his great work on England.

Prince Puckler Muskau's praises of her nieces did not, however, mollify Lady Morgan, who considered his mention of the young ladies an "atrocious breach of the delicacy appertaining to private life." That we would not think so now is only another proof of "*autre temps autre mœurs.*"

In 1830 there was a general turn-out (a literary strike, it might be called) of the staff of the *New Monthly*, who shortly after started a magazine called the *Metropolitan*, which lasted a few years, and then took its place in the limbo of forgotten periodicals. Sir Charles and Lady Morgan contributed constantly to the *Metropolitan*. Both husband and wife were exceedingly industrious, and no greater proof can be given of Lady Morgan's popularity with the public than the constant appearance of her name in all contemporary literature of the period. Quantity, however, is not quality, and that there was a falling off in the latter goes without saying; still, most authors prefer to have their name kept before the public. For this reason we must suppose Lady Morgan was flattered at being bracketed with Miss Letitia Landon for the second number of the "Lays of the Twaddle School" (not a complimentary title), a sort of lyric lilt instituted by Fraser to give vitality to his magazine. The lilt between the two ladies consists in each singing her own praises in verse. As "The Lays" are quite forgotten, it may amuse our readers if we reproduce the one in question here.

## LAYS OF THE TWADDLE SCHOOL.

### No. II.

*L. E. L.* Memento . . . servare mentem . . .
Ab insolenti temperatam
Lætitia . . . HORACE, Ode iii., lib. ii.

*Lady Morgan.* Alle fonte tornava
Trovò Morgana ch'intorno alla soglia
Faceva imballo e ballando cantava
Piu leggier non si volge, al vento foglia
Di ciò chi quella donne si voltava.
BOIARDO, "Orlando Inamorato."

*L. E. L.* Who can sound the Sapphic shell
Like the Lesbian L. E. L.?

*Lady Morgan.* Saucy sparrow—cease such jargon,
Sappho's self is Lady Morgan.

*L. E. L.* Suckled by the Muses—well,
As Anne de Vignes, so was L. E. L.

*Lady Morgan.* Suckled! Born, too, in the bargain
Of the *Nine*—was Lady Morgan.

*L. E. L.* Far from Brompton to Bow Bell
Swells the fame of L. E. L.

*Lady Morgan.* Fame, from Stamboul to Stillorgan,
Blows the trump of Lady Morgan.

*L. E. L.* Nature did herself excel,
In the gifted L. E. L.

*Lady Morgan.* Fatal as the glance of Gorgon,
Is the eye of Lady Morgan.

*L. E. L.* Genius has no parallel
For the soul of L. E. L.

*Lady Morgan.* Genius!—All, says Doctor Corgan,
Centred shines in Lady Morgan.

*L. E. L.* Della Crusca's glories fell
At the feet of L. E. L.

*Lady Morgan.* Aphra Behn and Moore are o'er gone,
By the lyre of Lady Morgan.

*L. E. L.* Golden violets![1] Who can smell
Their bright hues but L. E. L.?

*Lady Morgan.* Liberty's impassioned organ,
Is the pen of Lady Morgan.

*L. E. L.* Jerdan says, "If *they'd* but sell,
"Sure specs were works by L. E. L."

*Lady Morgan.* At half price were all my store gone,
None would lose by Lady Morgan.

[1] The title of one of L. E. L.'s books.

*L. E. L.* Glory's most impulsive spell,
Is the song of L. E. L.

*Lady Morgan.* Lafayette had ne'er to war gone,
But for note from Lady Morgan.

*L. E. L.* Churchyard Cupids chime their knell
To the strains of L. E. L.

*Lady Morgan.* Lovers from La Trappe to Lurgan,
Lisp the lays of Lady Morgan.

*L. E. L.* Swan-like, dying damoiselle,
Sings a dirge from L. E. L.

*Lady Morgan.* A very Cook made Calembourgs on
All-inspiring Lady Morgan.

*L. E. L.* Regent Street and proud Pall Mall
Venerate young L. E. L.

*Lady Morgan.* France—adored as Demogorgon,
In "*my France*" is Lady Morgan.

*L. E. L.* Florence! My Castalian cell,
Halcyon home of L. E. L.

*Lady Morgan.* O'er "*Italy*" like shooting star gone,
Flares the fame of Lady Morgan.

*L. E. L.* Morgante mio! sylphid spell,
Morgan links with L. E. L.

*Lady Morgan.* Patronised as poets par'gon
Is L. E. L. by Lady Morgan.

*Both.* From British bardesses now bear the belle,
Learned Lady Morgan, love-lorn L. E. L.

To this doggerel is appended a note by Lady Morgan :—

"DEAR MR EDITOR,—I entreat that this elegant elesion may be elementarily exemplified by the exemplary editor.—His obedient servant, LADY MORGAN."

There is a good deal of fun and hard hitting in the above, although the allusions are not always clear to us of this generation. That the lays were not appreciated by the readers of Fraser is evident by the cessation of the issue after a few numbers.

In 1837 the Morgans resolved to leave Dublin, and make their home in the great centre of civilisation—London. It is not difficult to understand why they came to this determination. Dublin was growing more and more provincial. Sir Charles had never liked it, and only remained in deference to the wishes of his wife, who clung to her sister and nieces. Time, however, had brought changes in the domestic circle. Her favourite niece, Sidney, had married the Rev. Mr Lawrence, and was settled in Norfolk. Sir Charles had lost both the appointments he held in the Irish Fisheries, and Lord Melbourne had promised Lady Morgan a pension of three hundred a-year. She now gave her consent to the wish of her husband, and the migration took place, not without a wrench at parting, from the cherished circle in Great George's Street. The elasticity of her Irish nature soon asserted itself, and we find her writing to Lady Clarke:—"I am just returned from looking at a charming *maisonette* in William Street; no houses opposite, and all looks rude and wild—a thing that would be a field (if it could) and a low wall round it; but then there is to be a pretty square by-and-by." It is funny reading this when we think of the busy thoroughfare at Albert Gate and the fine square hard by. The *maisonette* was soon to be the rendezvous of all the best literary and artistic society in London: everyone crowded to Lady Morgan's "at homes," where the music was of the best, and everyone worth knowing was sure to turn in. The hostess had the rare art of making even the most insignificant guest really at home, so that everyone came away pleased.

For six years Lady Morgan led a thorough society life, which was quite to her taste. Her letters and diaries are full of the celebrities she met, and the compliments she received. Now, it is Mrs Edward Lytton Bulwer, handsome, insolent and unamiable; Disraeli, an egregious coxcomb; the Duchess of St Albans (Miss Mellon), coarse, full-blown, receiving morning visitors in white silk; or she sends a copy of verses from Horace Smith, turned out in his regular jingle-jangle style:—

"O dear Lady Morgan, this pain in the organ
Of sound, that the doctors call Larynx,
Is a terrible baulk to my walk and my talk,
While my pen its extremity ne'er inks.

All this I don't mind, but one pang lurks behind,
Nay, it sticks in my gizzard and kidney,
Though I know it's not *sage*, I'm transported with rage,
'Cause I can't be transported to *Sydney*.

When my daughters come back, from your dwelling, alack!
What lots of *facetiæ* they can tell us,
While I, within clutch of a feast I can't touch,
Am condemned to the tortures of Tantalus.

When last you came here you had illness severe,
*Now I* must call in the physician,
We would meet, but the more we're despised (What a bore!)
The greater our indisposition.

O Morgan's fate, do not bother my pate,
With these Fata Morgana probations.
If ye can't make me well, rob Sir Charles of his spell,
And his spouse of her rare fascinations."

Her social success did not interfere with Lady Morgan's literary occupations. She continued to write with her usual facility, Sir Charles exercising his discretionary powers of pruning the redundancies and softening down the extravagances. *The History of Pimlico, The Book Without a Name, Woman and Her Master*, all belong to this period. *The Book Without a Name* being a collection of articles, the joint composition of husband and wife, which had appeared from time to time in different periodicals. It is very amusing reading, and contains "The Macaw of a Lady of Quality dictated by himself," which is the story of a young officer, the Honourable George Fitzforward, to whom the bird belonged. It shows a thorough knowledge of the world of fashion. It was a mark of *bon ton* to be able to say in a note of invitation, "We shall be few and good; you will meet Macaw Fitzforward and Donna Popinjay." "If you have not seen 'The Donna' and heard George Fitzforward tell an Irish story, you have heard nothing." Not the least amusing part of the story lay in Lady Cork's imagining it was a *bona-fide* bird. She had heard Moore and Lytton Bulwer speaking of Lady Morgan's "Macaw." What could it be? She had never seen it. She wrote at once to Lady Morgan to send the bird to her house, "like a good soul"—she will make much of it. She was equally pleased when she found out the truth, and talked of nothing else for a month. This was all very pleasant, and the Macaw is undoubtedly very amusing, although now quite forgotten.[1]

Lady Cork was very fond of birds. On one occasion she invited all the clever birds of her acquaintance to a party, in order that she might judge which of all the parrots and parroquets was the cleverest. The fortunate bird was to carry off a little gold collarette with a medal attached. Lord Conyngham sent a wonderful bird, who talked beautifully; but Lady Clementina Davies, who tells the story, says her parrot was still more remarkable, for it possessed the admirable talent, not only of talking, but of talking sense.

History repeats itself, and not long since a story went the round of the society papers dealing with the partiality Her Majesty the Queen entertains for parrots and parroquets. Desiring to obtain one who could talk *sensibly*, like Lady Clementina's, Her Majesty desired a bird-fancier to bring a certain number of parrots for inspection, and the one who should say the most sensible impromptu observation would be the one selected. The birds arrived well covered up. The coverings being removed in the presence of the Queen, one grey parrot, wise in his generation, made the sapient remark, "*My eye! what a lot of parrots!*" Needless to say, he was at once selected.

Crabb Robinson, who met Lady Morgan in the height of her popularity, was not favourably impressed by her con-

[1] The Macaw was Lady Cork's own bird. Lady Morgan introduced herself as Lady Titmouse; the conversations are amusing, but it is a little drawn out.

versation. She was good-natured and lively, he says, but seemed too conscious of her own importance and superiority. She offended him by her remarks upon German philosophers like Kant.

"But does your ladyship know anything about them?" he asked rudely. It was in this way she always provoked rude attacks by a sort of unconscious assertion of manner.

Time, however, that ruthless invader of all human happiness, was lying in wait with its wallet full of sudden changes. The usual inevitable death-roll set in; one by one the gems in the once bright circle of dear ones, relatives and friends, began to drop away. Her charming niece, Olivia Savage, was the first, in 1843, and soon after, Sir Charles was carried off unexpectedly by an attack of his heart. The entry in her diary is affecting in its true ring of sorrow and loneliness.

"Oh, my husband. . . . I cannot endure this; I was quite unprepared for this. So ends my life. . . . The winter fire kindles for me alone . . . the chair, the lamp, the books, the paper-cutter—all these are here this November. Gloomy wretched November! how I used to long for social, home-girt November. Now I spend it wandering through this deserted house." And again she says later, "Time, applied to grief, is a worldly commonplace. Time has its influence over visible grief; it softens sighs and dries tears, but *le fond* remains the same. Time gives you back the exercise of your faculties and your habits, but the loss of that which was part of yourself remains for ever."

In the following year she lost her dearest and faithful friend, her adviser, consoler and *confidante*—her always beloved and cherished sister. . . . No wonder she said, "The meaning of life was to her gone." Nothing could console her, although, with a characteristic touch, she writes, "that all old friends and new *acquaintances* have been to my door to offer sympathy, but I am beyond the reach of solace. . . ." Still, in time she revived. We all do. Our poor human nature craves for brightness and so the veil lifts as time and sunshine creep in once more. It is never the same, however, and it is more to banish the memory of what we have lost than for actual enjoyment that the old and the stricken seek the temporary oblivion that society offers; but, at the best, old age is nothing but an ever-recurring obituary. 'Friend after friend departs," until, like Moore's solitary guest, we find ourselves in the banqueting-room with the lights extinguished, the garlands faded, and no one left but our sad and desolate self. . . ."[1]

One is almost glad to find Lady Morgan, in 1856, engaged with all her old spirit in a controversy with Cardinal Wiseman as to the authenticity of St Peter's chair, which her ladyship had, in her usual haphazard fashion, pronounced to be a spurious manufacture, the *basso relievo* representing, she said, the Feast of Mahomet. The Cardinal, who took twenty years to compose the pamphlet he issued in 1855, sarcastically remarks that Lady Morgan, being a writer of romances, had the right, so long as she exercised *that* character, to *invent* amusing tales to gratify her readers, and then proceeds to demolish her shallow hypothesis gathered from her friend Dénan. Although, no doubt, the Cardinal was in his right, yet one cannot help sympathising with the weaker vessel, when in her reply she reminds her adversary of her strong advocacy of the Catholic claim to freedom. "My romances were not written merely to amuse the reader. They were written *for* and *in* the great cause of *Catholic Emancipation*—the theme and inspiration of my early authorship, and the conviction of my after life." It must be owned that here she had the Cardinal on the hip. The controversy as to St Peter's chair attracted a good deal of attention. A writer of the day remarks that Hogarth has

[1] "The Dublin papers mention the death of Lady Clarke, wife of Sir Arthur Clarke, M.D., and only sister of Lady Morgan, an amiable and accomplished woman, entitled to a remembrance. In the *Athenæum* there is a notice of her as a contributor of light, cheerful verse (see her 'Fun and Philosophy'), and as the writer of a comedy, 'The Irishwoman,' which had considerable success on its appearance in Dublin some twenty or five-and-twenty years ago. The comedy we have forgotten, but Lady Clarke herself ever passed with us as a worthy representative of 'the Irishwoman.' No person was better fitted by nature to grace and adorn society—light-hearted, brilliant, full to overflowing with animal spirits, she was more to be welcomed there. Yet the wife and the mother was content to shine in a narrower sphere—to do the drudging duties of life, and to gladden with her good spirits her own family and fireside. In a sentence, she was a high-principled and true-hearted woman."—From the *Athenæum*, September, 1845.

painted the battle of the pictures; Parney chronicled *la guerre des dieux*; the witty Dean of St Patrick's added a bright leaf to his chaplet of immortelles by his battle of the books; it was reserved for Lady Morgan to strike a blow in the battle of the chairs.

It might well be termed her last blow, although, like Napoleon's Old Guard, she rallied after each misfortune, and tried to fill up the constantly-recurring gaps in her regiment of friends by new recruits. It was weary work, and it was easy to see her heart was no longer in the world and its ways. Social questions, however, interested her keenly, from a statue erected to commemorate Moore's memory to the opening of Albert Gate. Her last work was the "*Odd volume*" produced in 1859. In January of that year she wrote to her old friend, Mr Redding, to thank him for a friendly notice of the book :—

"*January* 16*th*, 1859,
"WILLIAM STREET, ALBERT GATE.

"DEAR MR REDDING,—I feel most grateful for the manner in which you have mentioned my blessed husband, and the justice you have done to his merits. For myself, I am overwhelmed by your partial and friendly notice. I must tell you at this moment I am very unwell and confined to my room by a severe cold, but in the hopes that I may be better on Monday next, the 18th. If you are inclined to come and pay me a visit at two o'clock, and take some soup and a cutlet with me at that hour, I should be most happy to see you.—Yours always most truly, SYDNEY MORGAN."

Mr Redding found her on that Monday painfully changed. She was exceedingly weak in body, and her recollections appeared defective. Amongst other things, she told him she had made up her difference with her old publisher, Colburn, who had been to visit her.[1] In March of that year, however, she had so far rallied from her weakness as to be able to give

[1] "Lady Morgan made an extraordinary statement in regard to Mr Colburn, who, she said, after the reconciliation, called one evening to ask her to sign a paper giving some young publisher the right to produce her *Life of Salvator Rosa*. It happened that on this particular evening she had a musical party, and in her

her usual commemoration of St Patrick's Day (for she was an Irishwoman who never shirked her nationality). A week later her last illness set in, and on April 16th, 1859, ended fatally. Her death made a gap in social and literary circles. Her house had long been the resort of all best known in society—her own powers of conversation being to the last the magnet that drew round her others brilliant and clever as herself. The sarcastic severity of tongue, which had made her formidable to friends and foes in early life, softened with years. She used to say it was only the young who were pitiless in their judgments, and when she heard anyone repeating bitter things she would say, "*Ah, ma chère, ne vous chargez pas de haines.*" Perhaps there is no record of a woman achieving such a sudden and brilliant success as did Sydney Owenson, and this and the enormous amount of flattery she received must be taken into account in judging her harmless vanity, which for the rest had the merit of being perfectly frank—it never touched the heart which to the last beat warmly for her friends.

Lady Morgan's portraits represent her as a handsome woman—that by Lawrence is most captivating. It is hard to reconcile this with the statements of those who knew her in the flesh, and who assert the contrary. One is forced to the supposition that the painters flattered her with the brush, as did her other admirers with the tongue. On the other hand, there is a consensus of opinion amongst contemporary writers that Lady Clarke was a most lovely woman. Her miniature from which the present engraving is taken is from the original miniature by Belmes, which has been kindly lent by her daughter, Mrs Edward Geale, as likewise the miniature of Lady Morgan, which is very characteristic. Sir Charles Dilke has some charming miniatures of both Lady Morgan and Lady Clarke; and in the National Portrait Gallery, Dublin, there is the original picture by Berthen. The sketch by Maclise in

hurry signed the document without looking at its provisions. Later, she found that she had assigned not *one* but all her copyrights, and, only that Mr Colburn died shortly after, she would have been engaged in a Chancery suit to recover her rights."—*From Yesterday and To-day*, by Cyrus Redding, Vol. II.

the Fraserian Gallery is admirable; it is accompanied by lines written by Dr Maginn :—

"And dear Lady Morgan, look how she comes,
With her pulses all beating for freedom like drums,
So Irish, *so modest*, so mixtish, so wild,
So committing herself, as she talks like a child,
So trim, yet so easy, *petite* yet big-hearted,
That truth and she, try all she can, won't be parted.

# CAROLINE ELIZABETH SHERIDAN, MRS NORTON

AFTERWARDS

# LADY STIRLING-MAXWELL OF KEIR

(*Born* 1808—*Died* 1877)

THE transmission of talent is not always the rule—at least it is supposed to skip a generation before reappearing. In the Sheridan family it was handed down from one generation to another. There was Thomas the first, the smoking, drinking, jolly clergyman, who lived at Quilcapgh, and was such a joker that he lost his living for a jest. He was the friend of Dean Swift, who gave the literary bias, according to Mary, the cook maid, to the family—

"And Saunders, me man, says you are always jesting and mocking,
Mary, said he one day as I was mending my master's stocking;
My master is so fond of that minister that keeps the school,
I thought my master a wise man but that man makes him a fool."

The clergyman had a son, Tom Sheridan, whose passion for the stage led him in an evil hour to be lessee of the theatre in Smock Alley, and round whom all the misfortunes which could fall upon a luckless manager fell. His troubles brought him one piece of good fortune—a charming wife in Frances Chamberlaine, daughter to Dr Oliver Chamberlaine. This young lady, having a pretty talent for writing, espoused the luckless manager's cause, which he, finding out, in duty

HON. CAROLINE NORTON.

[*After Sir Edwin Landseer.*

bound, married his anonymous defender. The story is a pretty one, as told at full length in the Sheridan annals. For Frances Chamberlaine I own to having a strong partiality. Had she been a trifle better looking, her story would have been written in these pages, albeit there is nothing in her life of stirring interest. She was a clever woman and a good woman. What would you have more? She shared all the troubles of her erratic husband, and loved him faithfully to the end, helping him with the productions of her very versatile pen. Her novel *Sidney Bidulph* had a great success in its day and her comedy, "The Discovery," a long run. She died, poor lady! in France just when brighter days were dawning.

Her son—Richard Brinsley, the delightful, fascinating Brinsley, round whose name lingers the romantic halo associated with the ever-charming Miss Linley — was a typical Irishman, so far as we know him. He made the great mistake of being a chartered buffoon. A joker can never be taken seriously. His son, Tom Sheridan—poor Tom as he is often called—never wrote nor acted; neither was he a brilliant talker nor a professed joker, yet he was a very pleasant fellow, and everyone liked if they did not love him. His own father once said he would rather be remembered as the parent of Tom than the writer of the "School for Scandal."

Tom Sheridan, poor fellow! died at Madeira and left a wife and six children. His wife, who was of a good family (Callander) had a turn for writing, and composed a novel called *Carwell*, which dealt with some particular form of disease, and was the parent, so to speak, of the novel with a purpose. Mrs Sheridan's reputation was, however, more that of a woman of the world than a novelist. She was still in the prime of her beauty when she introduced her lovely daughters, and the group recalled to the mind of the artistic Fanny Kemble a full blown-rose and rosebuds all growing on the same stem. The loveliness of these women was set off by a singular charm of manner, much vivacity, wit and fascination, joined, especially in Lady Dufferin's case, with wonderful sweetness and humility. She seemed quite unconscious of her own charm in comparison to the superior attractions of her sisters. "Georgy" (the Duchess of Somerset) "is the beauty, she would say, and Carry" (Mrs Norton) "is the wit, and I ought to be the good one, but I am not." It was true that Lady Dufferin's beauty was of a different type from that of her sisters', but they were alike in their tall, stately figures. Lady Dufferin, the eldest, had a really divine figure, the very perfection of grace and symmetry; her head was beautifully set upon her shoulders, and although her features may have been less regular, her expression was angelic. She had also the charm of a sweet voice, sang delightfully, and composed some charming airs.

The Duchess of Somerset had deep blue or violet eyes, black hair, black eyebrows, perfect features and a complexion of lilies and roses. Those who knew them in life are all of the same opinion, that although speaking critically not so handsome as either of her sisters, Mrs Norton in a room produced a more striking impression by the force of the poetical genius with which she was gifted. In her childhood, Caroline had given so little promise of beauty that her mother, "who had a right to be exacting on such a point, almost despaired." As she grew up, however, she blossomed into a stately style of loveliness, "grandly classical," her rather large and heavy features recalling the grandest Grecian and Italian models, to the latter of which her rich colouring and blue-black braids of hairs gave her an additional resemblance. Gibson the sculptor always said he had seen many handsome women in his time, but none so lovely as Caroline Norton, and Shelley corroborated this testimony—"I never met a woman so perfectly charming with so variable but always beautiful expression." She was a brunette with dark burning eyes like her grandfather, Tom Sheridan, to which she could impart at will the softest, most bewitching, seductive expression. Her voice was exquisitely tender, a most excellent thing in woman, and when she spoke, every expression—grave, gay, ironical, melancholy, sportive, proud, indignant—fleeted across her fine face. Of whatever company she was a member, she was the principal feature, all gathering round her.[1] She was not a musician as the word is now understood. She possessed, however, the art of charming her audience by the manner in which she spoke her words in a deep contralto voice, accompanying herself with a few desultory chords on the piano; and this, combined with the beauty of her face, was sufficient to bring everyone crowding round the piano.

As may be imagined, the house at Storey's Gate, which Mrs Tom Sheridan had taken, was crowded by all the fashionable men of the day, who clustered like flies round the young beauties. D'Israeli records in his diary meeting them at a reunion at the Lytton Bulwers', and going with them to a fancy ball at Hanover Square Rooms—the two elder sisters appearing as Greek slaves. Years after, when old and in retirement, the image of these beautiful women would rise before the weary politician, and he would speak of his early days of intimacy with them. Lady Dufferin was his great admiration, more beautiful even than her beautiful sisters—"Dreams," he would say, as he gazed into the fire.

Another adorer was Edward Lytton Bulwer, afterwards Sir Edward, who wrote of Mrs Norton—

"No human beauty ever bore
An aspect thus divine.
The crown, the brows of seraphs wore,
Has left its mark on thine."

It is all the more curious (in view of the great admiration excited by her daughters' beauty) that Mrs Sheridan should have been in such a hurry to dispose of the exceptional wares she had in hand. She was in fact ready to give them to

[1] "I remember," writes Mrs Kemble, "how she used to convulse her friends, *en petit comité*, with a certain absurd song called 'The Widow,' a piece of broad comedy, the whole story of which (the wooing of a disconsolate widow by a rich lover, whom she first rejects and then accepts) was comprised in a few words rather spoken than sung, eked out by a ludicrous refrain of rum-ti-iddy-iddy-iddy-ho, which by dint of her countenance and voice conveyed all the different situations of the little comedy—her lover's fiery declaration, her virtuous indignation and wrathful rejection of him, his cool acquiescence and intimation that his fortune assured him an easy acquiescence in other quarters, her rage and disappointment at his departure, and final relenting and consent at his return, all of which she sang or rather acted with incomparable humour."

the first bidder that offered. Nor was this hurry in order that her young daughters should marry to please themselves. By no means. Helen, the eldest, had the greatest disinclination to accept Captain Blackwood, a rough and ready sailor—an excellent man, but devoid of all the graces that would take a young girl's fancy.

The Norton marriage was still harder to understand. Except that he was brother and heir to Lord Grantly, there was nothing to commend George Chapple Norton. He was a barrister without practice, an unpopular man—the verdict of society being that he was a disagreeable bore. One contemporary describes him as constantly "taking pills and spinning conversation out of his own bowels." Not a man to win the fancy of sweet Caroline Sheridan. He said he had been in love with her six years, so he must have begun the process when she was eleven, for she was barely seventeen when he made his proposal through the medium of the governess—he had not spoken six words to Caroline at this time. Still, although he had nothing to offer her beautiful young daughter, Mrs Sheridan did not refuse him. She allowed him to hang on, exerted her influence to get him some small place, and when Caroline was nineteen bade her marry him. The girl submitted, as girls did, in those days, to parental authority. The marriage, however, turned out a disastrous failure. No two people could be more unsuited to one another—the wife all generous sympathy and warm-heartedness, the husband full of mean ways, and with such a nasty temper as made life with him intolerable to a woman of a high spirit. Money, moreover, that universal disturber of domestic peace, was wanting in the Norton household, and the burden of providing it fell in this instance upon the woman. The talent for writing, inherited from the Sheridans, had shown itself distinctly both in Lady Dufferin and Mrs Norton. With the last named the taste for poetry was innate. Before she could write, she composed in her head. Her mother discouraged rather than incited these juvenile attempts, and resolutely denied her access to her store of pens, ink and paper. The youthful poetess was not to be baulked of her desire, and wrote on the blank pages of her copy books and music books. When she was only eleven years old her first poem appeared in print; this was the *Dandies Rout.*[1] The history of how she came to write it is interesting as the initiatory efforts of all good writers must be.

"In the days when Mrs Norton was a little girl, a favourite gift book for children was called the *Dandies Ball*, a copy of which was given to the Sheridan children by Lady Westmoreland. The perusal of it kindled in the mind of the future poetess a desire to produce a satire upon the exaggerated faults of a class of persons with whom she had nothing in common, and with whom, if she had, it may be supposed, she was not very likely at her age to discover the points most open to ridicule. Be that as it may, she wrote the *Dandies Rout* and carried it herself to Marshall, the publisher of the Dandy books, who agreed to publish it, and to give the young authoress fifty copies for herself. A small number of this supply were given to intimate friends, but the greater portion was changed for other books with a Richmond bookseller. The plates were from her own designs, and the little authoress would have been puzzled to determine whether she were prouder of the offspring of her pen or her pencil. She used to tell a story how, many years later, going into a shop in Regent Street to buy some coloured print book for her little boy, the shopman produced her own *Dandies Rout* as the best thing to please the young gentleman.[2] Her next literary effort was a volume of short poems in conjunction with her sister; this was not so fortunate as the *Dandies Rout*—many ineffectual efforts were made to assure sundry tasteless booksellers that they had an opportunity of putting money into their pockets. It is, however, sometimes utterly impossible to

[1] The word "Dandy" seems to have been applied to children. Lady Morgan wrote to Lady Clarke "How is the young Dandy?"

[2] This must have been the *Emperors Rout.* A little book full of coloured prints of moths and butterflies. The verses are in the Sheridan style—

"Old Colonel Gold Spangle his dancing days past,
Volunteers with good humour the dancers to cast."

The *Athenæum* of 1830 praises this child's story book, which was probably a reproduction of the *Dandies Rout* published by Tilt under another name.

convince men of their own interest, and publishers are notoriously obtuse in this respect. The consequence was these poems never got published; one was a versified version of *Clavis Calendari*, a favourite book with Caroline Sheridan.[1] At seventeen she wrote the *Sorrows of Rosalie* and again encountered the same difficulty in finding a publisher." [2]

Immediately after her marriage, *Rosalie*, with some smaller pieces, was published by Ebers and favourably received, and from this time her pen was the mainstay of the family. Children came rapidly enough and added to the necessity of exertion. Maternal love was strong in Mrs Norton's character, and it is touching to note the pride with which she writes to Mrs Shelley that everything provided for her first baby had been bought out of her earnings. Most men would have been ashamed to live in a great measure on their wife's talent; but Mr Norton not only took everything as his by right, but added the meanness of reproaching and nagging the bread-winner if she did not exert herself sufficiently.

"If Murray will not accept a poem, if Bell does not continue a magazine, if Saunders and Ottley do not buy the MS. of a novel, if Colburn's agreement is not satisfactory and sufficient, if Power delays payment for a set of ballads, if, in short, the wife had no earnings to produce, the husband professed himself quite at a loss to know *how* the difficulty was to be got over." This was only the beginning. Soon the idea came to this chivalrous gentleman that his wife's beauty and charm of manner could be brought to bear in a useful manner upon Lord Melbourne, an old family friend, then in the high position of Prime Minister. He had known Mrs Norton's father and grandfather, and was just the sort of Don Quixote likely to be influenced by the sight of beauty in distress. Mr Norton's idea was a success. He was made a

[1] *Clavis Calendari* was an astrological work.

[2] The above, which is taken from Colburn's *New Monthly* for 1831, does not correspond with Lord Dufferin's statement in his lately-published Memorial of his Mother—"Before she was twenty-one, she and Mrs Norton had been paid £100 for a collection of songs contributed between them."

magistrate, with a salary of seven hundred a year. As a natural result, Lord Melbourne became an intimate friend of the family. "He found a great attraction in Mrs Norton's society. Her literary tastes fell in with his." He met people at her house whom it was interesting to know. It was no wonder that he found pleasure in being a constant visitor. A man of the world, as he was, ought to have been alive to the dangers that lurk in such an intimacy. The whole story, indeed, is one of the saddest on record.

As it is detailed before us, one can read between the lines and see how a high-spirited, beautiful young woman, sought for and admired wherever she went, must have scorned the husband to whom it was her lot to be tied, and how he, seeing her ill-veiled contempt for his meanness and trickeries, girded at her, and at his own impotent attempts to break her spirit.

What led to the final quarrel was not conjugal jealousy but puerile resentment at what Mr Norton chose to fancy an insult offered to him by his wife's family. There was to be a gathering at Frampton, the seat of her eldest brother Brinsley Sheridan, to which Mrs Norton was invited, with her three children. By some unfortunate oversight Mr Norton was omitted from the invitation. He brooded over this until the fancied wrong occupied a large place in his petty mind. He took his revenge by sending the children away (on the very morning they were to go to Frampton). He knew where his wife would feel most keenly. Never was there a woman so full of maternal pride. As Sir John Campbell said, "Notwithstanding her intellectual gifts and the admiration she excited, she was devoted to her babes, and better contented when she showed them to a visitor than if she had been decked out in the most costly jewels." It will be hardly believed that Mr Norton persisted in keeping the whereabouts of the children from their distracted mother, who went about seeking them everywhere. For months she could only see them by stratagem. In hiding them away, and removing them from place to place, Mr Norton was abetted by a woman who played a fiendish part in this domestic drama. There is always some woman ready at hand to put her finger in an ill-assorted matrimonial pie; but on this occasion the "intervener" was an elderly spinster, with no attractions save the one paramount in Mr Norton's eyes—money. Miss Vaughan seems to have hated Mrs Norton, from the mere fact that this young creature was possessed of all the attractions she lacked or had lost (if she ever had enjoyed them). This envy or malice induced her to play the part of an evil genius in the home of the Nortons. She possessed herself of Norton's confidence, and exasperated him against his wife, making the worst of those little imprudences in which the roused and harassed woman sometimes indulged. She fanned the flame of suspicion in his mean, jealous nature. She pointed out the constant visits of Lord Melbourne, and goaded the latent jealousy that is always present in such natures as Mr Norton's. It is probable that only for the influence of this person the Nortons might have been reconciled, but the reconciliation could only have been on the surface, the disagreements would have begun again. Everything, however, seemed to point to the adjustment of the quarrel. Lord Melbourne[1] was always deprecating pushing matters to extremity. On April 10th he wrote the following wise counsel, which it would be well if married ladies inscribed in their private diaries.

"I have often told you that a woman should *never part* from her husband whilst she can remain with him. If this is generally the case, it is particularly so in such a case as yours—that is, in the case of a young, handsome woman of lively imagination, fond of company and conversation, and whose celebrity and superiority have necessarily created many enemies."

[1] William Lamb, Lord Melbourne, is one of the most interesting figures presented on the canvas of the present century. His position in life was enviable. He had fine intellectual qualities, a charming personality and sweet disposition; and yet it may be truly said of him, as of many another, that he made a total shipwreck through want of a good pilot. His first misadventure was his choice of a wife; and yet, as we read the story of his domestic unhappiness, our admiration for him grows. His patience with the extravagant, fitful, hysterical woman, whom he never ceased to love, although her mad freaks were bringing his name into contempt, was admirable, as likewise his gentleness to her in her dying moments, his sorrow for her, only remembering how she had been his first love. All this gives an interest to the reader of Lord Melbourne's life, which is not changed by some spots on the pure surface of a really noble, chivalrous nature.

There is no trace of the co-respondent in this kind, fatherly letter, which was followed by others of a similar character. Sir James Graham[1] and Colonel Stanhope, as well as Mrs Norton's family, tried to settle the terms of mutual agreement, and the husband and wife met. A sort of reconciliation took place, and there was some talk of her returning to live with him. A few days later the whole thing broke out afresh. Society was shaken to its centre when the news leaked out that Mr Norton had brought an action of *crim. con.* against the Prime Minister, and laid the damages at a high figure. It is now universally conceded that the trial was "got up" for political purposes to ruin Lord Melbourne in the opinion of the country. Greville says, "There is no doubt that Lord Wynford is at the bottom of the whole thing, and that he has persuaded Lord Grantley to urge it on Norton," who saw in this a means of humiliating his wife and her family. Again "there is great talk about Lord Melbourne's affair with Mrs Norton, which latter, if not quashed, will be inconvenient. John Bull fancies himself vastly moral, and the Court (of William IV.) is mighty prudish, and between them, our off-hand Premier will find himself in a ticklish position." Greville goes on to say that "people doubt the action coming on." It did, however, and ended in a triumphant acquittal, to the great exultation of the Prime Minister's friends, and the evident disappointment of the mob of Tories, with which the *better sort* had no share.[2]

Lord Chief-Justice Tindal was the judge. Sir William Follett led for the plaintiff, and broke down horribly; the witnesses—discarded servants—were wholly unreliable; the chief male witness was received with shouts of laughter.

[1] Sir James Graham was married to Mrs Sheridan's sister, conse uently was uncle by marriage to Mrs Norton.

[2] Lord Wynford had been guardian to Lord Grantley and Mr Norton, and was supposed to have considerable influence with both his wards. Lord Wynford sent the Duke of Cumberland to Lord Melbourne in one of the lobbies of the House of Commons to say he wished to speak with him, "in order to assure you, upon his honour, he had nothing to do with this affair, nor, indeed," added the Duke, "any of *us*. We would do nothing so ungentlemanlike." Lord Melbourne replied that he never believed rumours, that he had never thought it, and His Royal Highness' declaration was perfecly satifsactory. When Lord Wynford saw Lord Melbourne, he repeated the disclaimer, and added, he had not seen his ward, young Norton, for several years.

The female servants swore as to proofs, but their own characters could not bear inspection. They all had tender relations with those defenders of our hearths and enliveners of our kitchens—Her Majesty's Guards. One of these women expressed such contempt for the idle ceremony of marriage that Sir John Campbell, Lord Melbourne's counsel, compared her to Heloise—

> "Not Cæsar's Empress would I deign to prove;
> No, make me mistress to the man I love."

The verdict was received with shouts of applause, and Sir John Campbell, afterwards Lord Campbell, received an ovation when he entered the House of Commons that evening. No one seems to have thought what all this meant to the unhappy woman who, when this cruel trial came upon her, was in the superb summer of her beauty, with every gift and faculty of her mind at its highest power. Such an experience leaves its traces, and although she quitted the court with no stain on her character, the very fact that she had been dragged there by her unworthy husband clung to her long after the merits of the case had been forgotten. In the early part of this century the social laws as regarded women were far stricter than in our own days of more—perhaps too much—freedom, and the benefit of the doubt would then have been social ostracism.

Mrs Norton, however, had the consolation of having warm sympathisers and generous friends who stood by her during her trial and upheld her socially. In the dedication of one of her poems, the "Dream," she pays a grateful tribute to one of these, the Duchess of Sutherland, who was a warm partisan of the suffering mother.

> "For easy are the alms the rich man spares
> To sons of genius by misfortune bent,
> But *thou* gav'st me what woman seldom dares
> Belief—in spite of many a cold dissent,
> When, slandered and maligned, I stood apart
> From those whose bounded power had wrung, not crushed my heart.

Then, then, when cowards lied away my name,
  And scoffed to see me feebly stem the tide,
When some were kind on whom I had no claim,
  And some forsook on whom my love relied,
And some, who *might* have battled for my sake,
Stood off in doubt, to see what turn the world would take.

Thou gav'st me what the poor do give the poor—
  Kind words and holy wishes, and true tears.
The lov'd, the near of kin could do no more,
  Who changed not with the gloom of varying years,
But clung the closer when I stood forlorn,
And blunted slander's dart with their indignant scorn

For they who credit crime are they who feel
  Their *own* hearts weak to *unresisted* sin ;
Memory, not judgment, prompts the thoughts which steal
  O'er minds like these an easy faith to win ;
And tales of broken truth are still believed
Most readily by those who have *themselves* deceiv'd.

But like a white swan down a troubled stream,
  Whose ruffling pinion hath the power to fling
Aside the turbid drops which darkly gleam
  And mar the freshness of her snowy wing,
So thou with queenly grace and gentle pride
Along the world's dark waters in purity dost glide."

The unworthy persecution of his unfortunate wife by Mr Norton did not cease with this abortive attempt to ruin her character. Although she had left the court without any stain on her conduct as a wife and mother, and had therefore every right to return to her husband's house, and every claim to be with her children, Mr Norton absolutely refused to admit her. In vain did the poor woman (whose strongest passion was her love of her children) humble herself to offer every kind of amends to her persecutor. If she had made any harsh speeches or declarations that she could not stay with Mr Norton, "she repented." She entreated to be allowed to come back "on a year's trial." What torture this must have been to a woman of her high spirit, and still worse the humiliation went for nothing—her request being refused. When all this lowering of her pride failed, she, in desperation, tried a scheme for carrying the children away. She wrote to her friend, Mrs Shelley, how this ended.

"I failed. I saw them all. I carried Brin (Brinsley) to the gate; could not open it, and was afraid they (Miss Vaughan and the servant) would tear him in pieces, they caught him so fiercely, and the elder one was so frightened he did not follow. It may be a sin, but I do curse them and their dogged brutality. *If a strong arm had been with me* I should have done it—"

Then began the old hide-and-seek game. Mr Norton sent the children here, there, everywhere—now in the Highlands, with their Scotch relations: again at the seaside with Miss Vaughan. All this time the harassed woman had to work for her own support. Her mean husband allowed her nothing, and when the tradesmen who supplied her sued him for his wife's debts, he subpœnaed her publishers, and demanded from them an account of her profits. For nearly thirty years this painful struggle went on. Again and again was her name dragged before the public, and the outer world called in to view her domestic canker and decide upon the merits of the case. The last time Mrs Norton appeared in court it was to answer a second accusation as to the old scandal anent Lord Melbourne, who was now dead, but whose sister, Lady Palmerston, allowed Mrs Norton an annuity of five hundred a-year. The brutality of Mr Norton and his counsel on this occasion roused the indignation of everyone in the court, including the judge and jury. Mr Norton chose to sit upon the bench occupied by his wife, and his efforts to browbeat and embarrass were of the most ungentlemanly character: so, too, with the questions put by his counsel. The result was a verdict for Mrs Norton; but this triumph did not counterbalance the torture she had undergone. It roused her to break the silence she had hitherto kept, and which it would have been wiser to have maintained to the end. Under the circumstances, with her life utterly wrecked by the man who had married her to further his own advancement, it is hard to blame Mrs Norton for writing the story of her husband's cruelty and meanness in a pamphlet entitled *English*

*Laws for English Women*, which appeared in 1855, and was dedicated to the Queen. This narrative, which bears the impress of truth, was answered by a feeble letter from Mr Norton to the *Times*. It is doubtful whether the airing of her matrimonial troubles in public improved Mrs Norton's position. Her own family disapproved of the indelicacy of this public appeal, which undoubtedly attracted attention to her position, and gave an unenviable notoriety to her name. In such cases as hers, publicity is always a doubtful good, whereas dignified silence leaves nothing to regret. A story such as this, once known to the general public, is never allowed to die; it clings to the unfortunate hero or heroine like the shirt of Dejanira. The ominous whisper goes round when he or she enters or leaves the room, "Don't you know—the celebrated trial? Ah, just so—dear me—" In this way we find constant allusions to Mrs Norton's unfortunate episode, more or less malicious, according to the nature of the writer.

"In 1845," writes Crabb Robinson, "I dined with Rogers, an interesting party of eight—Moxon, Mr and Mrs Kenny, Spedding, Lushington, Alfred Tennyson and a lady, who, Rogers said, was coming on purpose to see Tennyson. He made a mystery of this fair devotee, and would give no name. It was not till dinner was half over that he was called out of the room, and returned with a lady on his arm—a lady neither splendidly dressed nor strikingly beautiful. A whisper ran along the company, which I could not make out. She instantly joined our conversation with an ease and spirit that showed her quite used to society. She stepped a little too near my prejudices by a harsh sentence about Goethe, which I resented. And we had exchanged a few sentences when she named herself, and I then recognised the much-eulogised and calumniated Mrs Norton, who, you may recollect, was purged by a jury finding for the defendant in a *crim. con.* action by her husband against Lord Melbourne. When I knew who she was, I felt that I ought to have distinguished her beauty and grace by my own discernment, and not waited for a formal announcement. You are aware that her position in society was to a great degree imperilled."

Her own sex, unfortunately, were not always so lenient as the writer just quoted. In Lady Granville's and Lady Eastlake's recently-published memoirs, there are a good many cutting remarks levelled at Mrs Norton. Lady Granville does not disguise her dislike of anyone who ventured to be original. She also finds fault with her for not being in keeping with her own opinions and writings. It is impossible, she says, to bind her up with her own stories![1] This is very smart, but surely it is unfair. No man, or woman either, can always correspond to their written testimony. It is, as we all know, far easier to preach than to practise. Lady Eastlake, who was the essence of propriety, is shocked at Mrs Norton's using her black eyes so wickedly; and whether on this account, or from closer observations, arrives at the conclusion that this clever writer has neither genius nor simplicity, nor even pathos. "No," she says emphatically, "she is an actress—a consummate actress—who studies the part she plays, and that part is always an attempt to fascinate, she cares not whom." One cannot help thinking the wicked, black eyes may have fascinated the excellent President of the Academy, and hence this virtuous denunciation. Sweet Caroline Norton what a singular power of fascination you possessed! Even the coldest of reviewers fell under your influence, and had a kind word for your literary efforts, and were nearly always in your favour. Some of them, indeed, wrote of her in terms that would affront more than gratify writers who would rather be judged by the merit of their work than their personal attractions. Still, after all, a reviewer is but a man; and when we find the brutal Gifford talking of "the beautiful daughter of our old friend, Tom Sheridan," we must think the glamour of that beautiful daughter's "wicked eyes" was on the writer, who goes on to talk of her "pouting, vermilion lips" before he raises his tomahawk, which comes down gently "for the sake of poor Tom."

Another critic (Lockhart) makes no flimsy pretence of old

[1] Lady Granville's testimony is valuable as a contemporary, and although she does not conceal her dislike to Mrs Norton, she throws no stone against her character. She had her daughter and her husband staying with her at the time of the trial, and remarks that they (the Fullartons) are very curious how it will go; and then she adds, "The great thing that will go against Mr Norton is, that he *swal-*

friendship for "papa," but avows his passion boldly for "fair Mrs Norton, beautiful Buddhist, as *Bedlam* Bulwer baptises you, passionately enamoured as we are of L. E. L., soul-struck by the wonders of Mrs Hemans's muse, in no slight degree smitten by Mary Ann Browne, pitying, venerating such relics of antiquity as Miss Edgeworth and Lady Morgan, yet we must make Mrs Norton *the leader* of *the* female band."

On one occasion only do we find sweet Caroline treated with something bordering on impertinence, and yet it was in all good humour, so that the rudeness hardly counts. The occasion was in 1831, when a ludicrous hoax was perpetrated upon well-known literary personages. The hoax was stated to have been originated by a clergyman called Miller, who had a craze (very general even in the present day) for collecting the autographs of the eminent, and hit upon the cunning device of applying for the character of an imaginary domestic servant, a bait to which these clever individuals at once rose.

It has been suggested that the inventor of this very transparent scheme was the editor of *Fraser's Magazine*, who published the Miller correspondence—500 letters. His having done so lends colour to the idea. It does not, however, detract from the fun of the situation, which is greatly enhanced by the gravity of some of the replies. One cannot help smiling at Miss Edgeworth's voluminous and decidedly old-maidish letter, which must have convulsed with laughter the perpetrator of the hoax.

The general tenor of the replies is most courteous, and they show a curious uncertainty as to whether the man or woman did fill the situation for which the reference is required. Lady Charlotte Bury has great doubts as to Sarah Deacon, "but would be sorry to hurt anybody's character by an unjust suspicion." Sir Edward Lytton Bulwer has not the slightest recollection of William Jeffries, and thinks the man has made a mistake. "He may probably have lived with my brother,

*lowed* any titled or rich admirer of his wife, but was severity itself to *a poor man like* Captain Trelawny." [Captain Trelawny was not an admirer of Mrs Norton, but of her friend, Fanny Kemble.]

Mr Henry Bulwer, 38 Hill Street." Gentle Sir Walter Scott is the only one who seems to have detected that some trick was at the bottom of the inquiry.

"I regret my name has been used to mislead your benevolence. I know no such person as Duncan Campbell, nor has a man of that name ever lived as servant to me. The fellow has imposed upon you, and deserves punishment: and for the sake of others, I hope you will inflict it."

Sweet Caroline Norton walked blindfold into the net, and writes quite a long letter about Amelia Deacon, "who never lived with me as lady's-maid, or, so far as my recollection serves, in any capacity. It is, at any rate, impossible she could have lived with me two years, as it is but three since I commenced housekeeping, and my present establishment has undergone no alteration for the last twelve months or more."

This letter was honoured by special attention. "The future antiquary," says Morgan Rattler, "when the time comes that even you will be antiquity, when to you will be applied the song sung with such gusto by your glorious and Gillrayed grandfather—

"'Though her lightness and her brightness
Do shine with such splendour,
That nought but the stars
Are thought fit to attend her;
Though now she is fragrant
And soft to the sense,
She'll be damnably mouldy
A hundred years hence.'

In that unhappy time," continues the uncivil writer, "it will be known that in January 1831 you had commenced housekeeping but three years, and that your then actual establishment, or, as you call it, 'your present establishment,' had not undergone alteration for twelve months or more."

Among those hoaxed were—

Thomas Haynes Bayly. Theodore Hook.
Edward Lytton Bulwer. Letitia Landon.
Lady Charlotte Bury. William Maginn, LL.D.
S. T. Coleridge. Thomas Moore.

| | |
|---|---|
| John Wilson Croker. | Caroline Norton. |
| Maria Edgeworth. | Anna Maria Porter. |
| Lord Eldon. | Bryan W. Procter (Barry Cornwall). |
| Henry Hallam. | |
| James Hogg. | Samuel Rogers. |

Like all the fashionable writers of the day, Mrs Norton contributed abundantly to the army of annuals—keepsakes, forget-me-nots and books of beauty, which flooded the booksellers' shops. She was at one time editor of the *Book of Beauty*, and likewise of *Fisher's Scrapbook*.[1] A woman of fashion was all-important in the position of editor, as her connection with persons "in society" enabled her to procure any amount of indifferent compositions, the contributors being sufficiently repaid by their names appearing in print, while the publisher found his advantage in the sale the noble author's feeble productions commanded. No house that respected itself was without some one or other of the silk-bound annuals; the *Book of Beauty* was the most popular; it was to be seen on the round table, which in those days occupied the centre of the drawing-room—a fine, solid piece of furniture with a claw-foot. A cornucopia for flowers was the centre ornament, large volumes of scrap-books, *Finden's Tableaux* and books of foreign scenery, together with the inevitable annuals, were arranged symmetrically (in careful families, they had silk or cashmere covers), and were supposed to give a literary "*ton*" to the house. The expense of producing these elegantly got-up books was not sufficiently remunerated by their sale, large though it was, and in the end every publisher who had to do with such ventures lost heavily. Heath, the publisher of the *Book of Beauty*, and *Finden's Tableaux*, died a bankrupt. The present generation sees a revival of this taste for "picture-books," which is growing every day until the appetite for illustration seems to have arrived at an almost unhealthy stage: the process production, however, is not so

[1] *Fisher's Drawing-Room Scrapbook* was a most artistic production: it had several lady editors. Miss Landon's reign was remarkable for delicacy and extreme finish; Mrs Norton's for the large number of poems contributed by Lady Dufferin and other members of her family. There are some beautiful portraits.

expensive as the almost obsolete but far more beautiful steel engraving.

Mrs Norton cannot be classed with the ordinary contributor to the annuals: her poetry was thoroughly artistic, and, as one critic remarks, possesses "a breadth and finish almost masculine," differing widely from the fashionable literary lady of her period. This he ascribes to her "association with prominent literary and political characters, which contact gave to her poetry an earnestness of feeling and a masculine cast of thought" Another critic says her poems are the genuine product of a cultivated mind, a rich fancy and a warm, well-regulated heart; it is evident, he adds, that she wrote because she wished to express her own feeling, and not from a dilettante desire to figure in print. Lockhart, in the *Quarterly*, goes even further, and compared her to Byron. "It is not," he says, "an artificial imitation, but a natural parallel. She has much of that intense personal passion by which Byron's poetry is distinguished from the larger growth and deeper communion with man and nature of Wordsworth. She has also Byron's beautiful intervals of tenderness, his strong, practical thought and his forcible expression." "The Undying One," a sort of Vanderdecken legend that came out in 1830, was slightly jeered at by the *Edinburgh Review*, which nevertheless draws attention to the touching lines which are put into the mouth of a woman mourning her husband,—

"My early and my only love, why silent dost thou lie,
When heavy grief is in my heart and tear-drops in mine eye?
I call thee, but thou answerest not, all lonely though I be:
Wilt thou not burst the bonds of sleep and rise to comfort me?

O, wake thee! wake thee from thy rest upon the tented field,
This faithful breast shall be at once thy pillow and thy shield.
If thou hast doubted of its truth and constancy before,
O, wake thee now, and it will strive to love thee more.

If ever we have parted and I wept thee not as now,
If ever I have seen thee come and worn a cloudy brow,
If ever harsh and careless words have caused thee pain and woe,
Then sleep, in silence sleep, and I will bow my head and go.

MRS. NORTON.

[*From Maclise's Sketch in the Fraserian Gallery.*

But if through all the vanished years whose shadowy joys are gone,
Through all the changing scenes of life, I thought of thee alone,
If I have mourned for thee when far, and worshipped thee when near,
Then wake thee up, my early love, this weary heart to cheer."

In spite of these really pathetic lines and many others of equal beauty, "The Undying One" was very dreary, and no one could read it twice; it was followed by "The Dream," and later on by "The Child of the Islands," dedicated to the Queen on the birth of the Prince of Wales. An effort has been made of late to bring forward Lady Dufferin's poems, and place them on a higher platform than Mrs Norton's. In her own generation they were not considered in the same category. Lady Dufferin had a pretty turn for rhyming and a natural grace of expression, but no one could take seriously her little ballads such as "Katey's Letter," "Miss Myrtle," or the "Emigrant's Farewell."[1] She had neither the strength nor the pathos of Mrs Norton, and was incapable of a sustained effort such as the "Lady of La Garaye," the best of Mrs Norton's longer poems. The subject is taken from a Breton legend, and the treatment is so tender, the rhythm so flowing, that it should keep the memory of the writer ever green; it seems, however, to have fallen out of recollection. One of Mrs Norton's most charming short compositions is "The Careless Word." It is full of pathos. As it is quite unknown to the present generation, and probably forgotten by the last, I make no apology for introducing here—

### THE CARELESS WORD.

A word is ringing through my brain,
It was not meant to give me pain,
It had not one to bid it stay
When other things had passed away.

[1] Lady Dufferin's "Emigrant's Farewell" has had a certain success, but neither she nor Mrs Norton were successful in their Irish efforts. As a competent critic said, they have not the true *ring of the potato* (such as can be found in "Father O'Flynn," for instance). This want is easily accounted for. Although of Irish descent, the daughters of Tom Sheridan lived very little in Ireland (Mrs Norton only occasionally on visits), and it requires an Irish education to get the true ring. Its absence is easily detected by the natives—the imitation may pass muster in England.

It had no meaning more than all
Which in an idle hour fall.
It was when *first the sound* I heard—
A lightly-uttered, careless word.

That word—oh, it doth haunt me now
In scenes of joy—in scenes of woe,
By night by day—in sun or shade,
With the half smile that gently play'd
Reproachfully, and gave the sound
Eternal power through life to wound,
There is no voice I ever heard
So deeply fixed as that one word.

. . . . . . . . . . . .

When dreams bring back the days of old,
With all that wishes could not hold,
And from my feverish couch I start
To press a shadow to my heart—
Amid its beating echoes clear,
That little word I seem to hear.
In vain I say while it is heard,
Why weep! 'twas but a foolish word.

It comes, and with it come the tears,
The hopes, the joys of former years,
Forgotten smiles—forgotten looks—
Thick as dead leaves on autumn brooks,
And all as joyless, though they were
The brightest things life's spring could share.
Oh, would to God I ne'er had heard
That lightly-uttered, careless word!

It was the first—the only one
Of those, which lips, for ever gone,
Breathed in their love—which had for me
Rebuke of harshness at my glee.
And if those lips were here to say
"Beloved—let it pass away,"
Ah! then, perchance—but I have heard
The last dear tone—the careless word.

Oh ye who, meeting, sigh to part,
Whose words are treasures to some heart,
Deal gently, ere the dark days come,
When earth hath but for *one* a home;

Lest, musing o'er the past, like me,
They feel their hearts wrung bitterly,
And, heeding not what else they heard,
Dwell weeping on a careless word.

The simple pathos of these lines must, it seems to me, appeal to all who have suffered from the careless utterances of those who would not have inflicted pain, but from mere thoughtlessness did so, and who now can no longer soothe the bitter pang left by their words. Mrs Norton excelled in touching those inner wells of feeling which lie deep down in every heart. There are several equally beautiful passages in the "Lady of La Garaye." I would not, however, for a moment pretend that all her poems have this rare gift. As one of her critics remarked, "Mrs Norton indulges in too much twaddle; we would, if we could, advise her to think more and write less."

This advice, which is often given to writers, is not always so easy to follow. Mrs Norton, in her early married life, was making close on fourteen hundred a year by her poems and contributions to magazines, daily papers, etc., and after her separation from her husband, she had to keep herself, and to help in the education and maintenance of her children, besides having other calls upon her purse. Under these circumstances, continued work was a necessity, and as her popularity was ever on the increase, she found no difficulty in placing everything she wrote. Her prose writings were as successful as her poetry. The present generation knows little of either. In their day, however, "Lost and Saved," "Old Sir Douglas," and "Stuart of Dunleath" made a distinct mark.

Her ballads, likewise, were the rage, and were set to music by the best musical composers. One of these was "Love Not;" another, "The Blind Man's Bride," one that is little known, might well deserve the attention of some of the fervid school of present-day composers—

"Oh, then, lady, how lowly I am
In the blaze of thy beauty to dwell;
My pride has outspoken at last,
And the answer shall be my farewell.

Then, careless and proud as thine own,
  The words of that parting shall be ;
For I hold it a dream of the past
  That thou once wert beloved by *me*.

When the name that has made thee so proud,
  And has tarnished thy nature like sin,
Shall be lost to the world's hollow crowd
  As compared to the name I shall win !
Then the anguish I suffer to-day
  Thy vain heart's proud glory shall be ;
And the boast of thy desolate age
  That *thou once* wert beloved *by me*."

Mrs Norton had all the Sheridan wit and readiness. On one occasion she was taken in to dinner by a stupid Russian prince, who at last ventured on a compliment, saying, with an air of ineffable conceit, "*Eh bien, belle Muse, comment trouvez vous Paris?*" Mrs Norton's brilliant eyes measured him coolly, as she answered, "*Comment, Monsieur, vous savez qu'il y a des Muses!*" To account for the extraordinary fascination she exercised over old and young, even after she had attained the age when most women cease to exert an influence upon the mind masculine, we must remember that her magic was quite as much due to her mental as to her personal gifts. She had acquired the art, without using any so-called art, of looking half her age, and was sometimes mistaken for her son's wife.

Her later years, although more peaceful as regarded the persecutions of her husband, were shadowed by other, and perhaps deeper, sorrows. The sons for whom she had suffered so much were taken from her one after the other. The youngest, Willie, died when a boy ; Fletcher, a most promising young man, lived to be *attaché* at the Embassy at Paris, where he died October 1859. Mrs Norton wrote to her cousin Mr William Lefanu, an account of his last moments. "We could scarcely tell *when* he died, but the restlessness, the sadness, the ecstacy all passed out of his face, and there was nothing but peace ; and we had only to close his beautiful soft eyes that, from the hour they opened on this world, had never looked hardly, scornfully, or unkindly on any human being." [1]

The poor mother's love was now concentrated on her eldest boy, Charles. "He was handsome, clever, kindly, but wild." He it was who married the peasant girl in Capri. He sent over his children—a boy and girl—to his mother's care, a trust she fulfilled loyally, although it involved more exertion and many anxieties."

In 1876 Mr Norton died. "It was a curious retribution that he should have been on the eve of succeeding to the title and estates of his brother, Lord Grantley." It is pleasant to think that his death gave to his long-tried wife a gleam of the sunshine and prosperity which, to such natures as hers are a necessity of existence. She had long been acquainted with Sir W. Stirling-Maxwell of Keir, an accomplished and elegant scholar, an amiable and excellent man—in every way the reverse of Mr Norton.

Their marriage was an ideal one, but happiness, which is often a treacherous friend, came too late. Mrs Norton's health was already seriously impaired, and she had hardly realised what it was to be loved and cared for, when the gleam of sunshine vanished in the darkness of the grave. Her death took place in 1877, the same year as that of her son Charles, who had not long enjoyed the title and fortune of Lord Grantley.

Sir William Stirling-Maxwell did not long survive his wife. He was seized with typhoid fever at Venice in 1878, and died amongst strangers. Mrs Lewis Wingfield, Lord Castletown's sister, happened to be in Venice at the time, and hearing that an Englishman was alone and dying, did all in her power for him.

The portraits of Mrs Norton are numerous. The one selected here, which is after Landseer's picture, is not so well known as the one after Hayter, which gives an idea of a Spanish dancer more than of an English lady. I imagine my readers will appreciate the spirited sketch of her by Maclise

[1] *Lives of the Sheridans*, Vol. II., page 444. Letter from Mr William Lefanu to the author, Percy Fitzgerald.

which is singularly piquant and attractive. There is another of her by the same artist, showing her in a more stately and imposing mood, seated amongst the Fraserian lady contributors, near Lady Morgan and L. E. L.[1]

[1] These ladies, amongst others, were called "*Regina's* Maids of Honour," and in the letterpress there is a gushing allusion to Mrs Norton.

"Full the face that flashes near her; can we draw away our gaze?
Vision nobler, brighter, dearer, did ne'er on human eyeball blaze!
Front sublime and orb of splendour, glance that every thought can speak,
Feeling proud, or pathos tender, the lid to wet, to burn the cheek,
Or, my halting rhyme to shorten, can't I say, 'tis Mrs Norton?
Heiress of a race to whom Genius his constant boon has given,
Through long-descended lines to bloom, in wit of earth or strains of Heaven.
Oh, if thy Wandering Jew had seen those sunny eyes, those locks of jet,
How vain, how trifling would have been the agony of fond regret
Which, in thy strains, he's made to feel for the creations of thy brain—
Those wounds, thou say'st, he lived to heal—thee lost, he ne'er had loved again!"

MISS O'NEIL (LADY WRIXON BECHER) IN THE CHARACTER OF "JULIET."

*(From Thomson's Picture.)*

# ELIZA O'NEILL, LADY WRIXON BECHER

(*Born* 1791—*Died* 1872)

In comparison with other actresses of equal note, we have very scant information concerning Miss O'Neill, who, nevertheless, was not only an artist of the highest merit, but likewise a beautiful woman of unblemished reputation. Her career in this regard may be likened to that of Miss Farren, with this difference, that whereas Miss Farren's propriety was the outcome of a cold, calculating nature, Miss O'Neill's seems to have proceeded from a higher and purer source. Both women had the advantage (denied to many of their dangerous profession) of a watchful mother. There are other points of resemblance between the two actresses. Eliza O'Neill, like Elizabeth Farren, was the daughter of an Irish manager, or stage manager, of a strolling company which oscillated between Drogheda and Dundalk.[1]

Mr John O'Neill was not a favourite of fortune. The sole blessing that the fickle jade presented him was an excellent wife. Mrs O'Neill, *née* Featherstone, was a handsome, sensible woman, who kept her vapouring husband in order, and when she was not occupied with the cares of her family, took her part in melodrama. Her histrionic talents may not have been of the first order, but they sufficed for the audience to which she played, and she was probably a better actress than

[1] The Drogheda theatre, so called by courtesy, was a disused and broken-down building outside that picturesque town. The theatre, so called, in Dundalk was in the Brewhouse. The son of a gentleman residing in the neighbourhood of Dundalk often heard his father describe the extreme poverty of the O'Neill family. Eliza was not much considered as an actress; later, when she had made her success in Dublin, he went to see her, and could hardly get standing room in the house.

her husband was an actor. Mr O'Neill was a thorough Milesian, with what can only be described as "a thundering brogue" and an immense amount of swagger as to the ancient clan of O'Neill (Shaun of the Red Head and others), from which he claimed descent. In virtue of these claims he was treated "as a gentleman" by the residents round Drogheda, with whom he was a favourite; and when he went to demand "a bespeak" he was invited to sit down and take a glass of wine or spirits.[1] On these occasions he was sometimes accompanied by his little daughter Eliza, who already was somewhat of an infant phenomenon. She was a child of very tender years when she first trod, or in strict truth was carried on the boards in her father's arms, and with every year she made an advance.[2] She was ten years old when she played the young Duke of York to her father's delineation of the crookbacked Duke of Gloucester. Even at so young an age she showed considerable talent in the part, and attracted large audiences, who undoubtedly did not come to hear Mr O'Neill's mouthings and contortions, or to see the other members of the O'Neill family who, like the "Daggerwoods of Dunstable," were numerically strong, but theatrically weak. There was an extraordinary strength, however, in their family tie, as Mr Talbot was to find out presently. This gentleman, who was an important personage, as lessee of the Belfast, Londonderry and Newry theatres, chanced

[1] Mr O'Neill was oftentimes much exercised in his mind by the plays his patrons bespoke, which required all manner of scenery, machinery and equipments, which his slender resources were inadequate to supply. On one occasion a lady of importance residing near Dundalk had commanded the play of "Pizarro," and a star actor was engaged to come down from Dublin to fill the principal part. At the rehearsal, the actor frequently asked, "Where is so-and-so?" and the reply was always, "It will be all right on the night of performance," but when the night came scarcely anything *was right*. Amongst other deficiencies there were no supernumerary soldiers, for if the manager could have found the men he could not have supplied them with clothes. In this position he had thought it best that one Peruvian soldier should represent the tumultuous army of the renowned *Inca*. The Dublin star, not being apprised of this, was just commencing his address to the assembled warriors when he suddenly stopped short. Then, with much presence of mind changed the plural to the singular tense, "What, all slain but thee; come, then, my brave *associate*, partner of my toil."

—"*Actresses of Our Time*," Mrs C. Baron Wilson.

[2] The preceding anecdote will account for Mr O'Neill impressing *all* his family into the *service* of the stage. It will be remembered that the famous Crummles did the same.

to see Eliza on the humble boards of the Drogheda barn, and being much struck with her youthful promise, offered her an engagement at Belfast. This was a stepping-stone to further greatness, as he pointed out she might in time get promoted even to Dublin. To his surprise, Eliza, who was of the calmest temperament, received his approbation pleasantly, but refused the engagement unless the whole of the Daggerwoods of Dunstable were likewise engaged. It was rather a cool demand. There were, besides the prima donna, her father and three brothers, her sister and sister-in-law. It was true that their salaries did not amount to much, also, that as they had been all their life accustomed to stage business, they could be utilised for minor parts and occasional stop-gaps. Mr Talbot agreed to the actress's terms, and her success justified his judgment of her abilities. The Belfast press was enthusiastic as to the young actress, and its notices chancing (probably there was little chance in the matter, as Mr O'Neill had not been stage manager all those years without understanding the art of puffing his wares) to catch the eye of Jones, the lessee of Crow Street Theatre, Dublin, the event prophesied by Mr Talbot took place. A liberal salary was offered for *the actress*, but the tail (as the O'Neill family were designated), was refused. But here again Miss O'Neill's calm determination not to be separated from the other members prevailed, and the tail accompanied her to Dublin.

This engagement, although a decided advance, did not at first bring the new actress as much before the public as her merits gave her every right to expect—the principal *rôles* being all occupied by an actress of considerable talent and remarkable beauty. This was Miss Walstein. She had a number of admirers and friends, and being called the Hibernian Siddons gave herself the airs of a superior being, and allowed no rival near her throne. It was in vain that Mr O'Neill blustered and talked of the "onfairness with which me daughter Eloiza is treated." Mr Jones only shrugged his shoulders and suggested with a half smile that "me daughter's" extreme propriety stood a little in her way. If she had powerful protectors like

Miss Walstein—men of fashion and position, that no manager could refuse—her advance would be more rapid. Virtue, however, brings its own reward. A lucky chance procured Miss O'Neill the desired opening, and, singular to say, this chance was due to the "airs" Miss Walstein gave herself. It was during the course of Miss O'Neill's first season in Dublin that a celebrated equestrian company, which had disgraced the time-honoured boards of Covent Garden by performing "Timour the Tartar," was engaged by Mr Jones for a short run: the principal part, Zobeida, was assigned by right of custom to Miss Walstein. But whether the lady thought it beneath her dignity to emulate a circus rider, or was too timorous to trust herself on a barebacked steed, she threw up the part, secure in her own popularity to risk nothing from disappointing the public. The part was given to Miss O'Neill, who accepted it reluctantly; she, too, feeling that it was *hors ligne* for an actress who aspired to be in the front rank of the profession. Miss O'Neill, however, had no choice, as her agreement bound her to accept any part vacated by Miss Walstein, and in addition she knew she was not sufficiently strong to risk a quarrel with managers and public. It was said in the green-room that Miss Walstein, whose jealousy was quick to take alarm, had laid this trap to get rid of a possible rival. If this were so, her scheme recoiled on her own head, for Miss O'Neill scored a triumph. She rode splendidly. She fought heroically. She declaimed melodiously. She forced the iron of jealousy into Miss Walstein's very soul, and made her curse her own folly for indulging her envious humour.

It was too late now. The new actress had caught the public, and the manager was too wise to baulk their fancy. The papers followed suit. In her first season they had talked of her as a tolerable substitute for Miss Walstein, but deficient in power and conception. This was now to change. She divided the business with the popular Walstein. "The Lady of the Lake" made a tremendous success. Walstein, who still had a large following, was an admirable Blanche, and Miss O'Neill a captivating Ellen. The critics were full of comparisons between the two actresses, for the Walstein still retained her popularity.

> "Walstein is dignified in every scene,
> She looks a goddess and she moves a queen,
> While poor O'Neill does nothing more than human,
> A lovely, sensible and feeling woman.
> Walstein can ease and majesty impart,
> O'Neill's content if she can touch the heart;
> She leaves to Walstein admiration's glare,
> And having touched the heart she nestles there."

Another writer described the rivals as the eagle and the dove—"Walstein, the eagle, swept on the boards, filling the mind with images of vigorous, noble power; the dove, suppliant, fluttering into the bosom and resting there with a fondness that is more than equivalent to the terrors of the beak and the lightning of the eye."

It was this gentle timidity, this dove-like sweetness, that proved Miss O'Neill's principal attraction both on and off the stage, and attracted men to her, perhaps more than did her actual beauty, which was of the classical order. Her features had a Grecian outline, her voice was deep and mellow, her figure of middle size and she had a slight stoop which does not seem to have detracted from her grace. She had many lovers, amongst them Richard Sheil,[1] who wished to make her his wife, but her affections were already given to her future husband, Mr Wrixon Becher, who belonged to a highly respected family in Cork. Miss O'Neill had made his acquaintance at Kilkenny, where she was invited to play for some charity with the Kilkenny amateurs.[2] Allusion has before been

[1] Richard Sheil was much attached to Miss O'Neill. She played the heroine in his tragedy "Adelaide; or, the Emigrants," and to her beautiful delineation was due the success it obtained. Mr Sheil used to relate how he wrote for her a refusal of an offer of marriage from Lord Normanby.

[2] Thackeray, who has introduced Miss O'Neill into *Pendennis* as the Fotheringay, alludes in his charming description of her to her singular and bewitching sweetness. "Those who have only seen Miss Fotheringay in later days since her marriage and introduction into London life, have little idea how beautiful a creature she was. . . . Her forehead was vast, and her black hair waved over it with a natural ripple [that beauties of late have tried to imitate], and was confined in shining and voluminous braids at the back of a neck such as you see on the

made to the passion for amateur acting that has always been a salient feature in the Irish character. The *dramatis personæ* who had strutted their brief hour upon the mimic stage at Carton [1] or Leixlip [2]—the beautiful Montgomerys,[3] Lord Mountjoy, Captain Jephson, Dean Marlay and Sam Whyte—had long since passed away, but their successors were as keen and perhaps better Thespians than they had been. Lords Barrymore and Blessington, the Powers, Burkes and Richard Sheil were more in the ranks of the professional than the amateur actor. Their great gatherings were held at Kilkenny in the race week or at Christmas. The theatre that had been built by Lord Waterford for his stage-struck son Tyrone, and which had proved so disastrous to Mr Owenson, was still unoccupied and could be hired for a small sum.

What pleasant flashes come back as one reads of the fun and jollity of these Kilkenny meetings, of the brilliant array of talent and beauty and wit that congregated from time to time. Grattan and Bushe,[4] Sir Hercules Langrishe, Philpot Curran, Chancellor Fitzgibbon and James and John Ponsonby, Lords Clonbrock, Blessington and Barrymore, the ever-

shoulders of the Louvre Venus (that delight of gods and men). Her eyes, when she lifted them up to gaze on you, and ere she dropped their purple, deep-fringed lids, shone with tenderness and mystery unfathomable. . . . She never laughed (indeed, her teeth were not good), but a smile of endless tenderness and sweetness played round her beautiful lips and in the dimples of her cheeks and her lovely chin; her nose defied description in those days. Her ears were like two little pearl shells which the earrings she wore, though the handsomest properties in the theatre, only insulted. But it was her hand and arm that this magnificent creature most excelled in . . . they surrounded her. When she folded them over her bosom in resignation; when she dropped them in mute agony or raised them in superb command, when in sportive gaiety her hands fluttered and waved before her like—what shall we say—like the snowy doves before the chariot of Venus—it was with these arms and hands that she beckoned, repelled, entreated, embraced her admirers—no single one, for she was armed with her own virtue and with her father's valour."—*Pendennis*, Vol. I., Chapter IV.

[1] Carton, the seat of the Duke of Leinster in Kildare.

[2] Leixlip, the summer residence of the viceroys in the last century.

[3] See *Some Celebrated Irish Beauties of the Last Century*.

[4] Bushe was a great wit. On one occasion, when the Kilkenny amateurs were performing, he, being an intimate friend, was requested to give his opinion of the performance, and the respective merits of the performers. "My dear friends," he said, "comparisons are at best but invidious. Besides, how can I give a preference where *all* are perfect!" Nothing, however, would satisfy the actors. "We are amateurs and friends," they said. "Jealousy, therefore, is out of the question; your opinion we must have." "Well, well," gravely replied Bushe "I give it most reluctantly, I protest to you I prefer the prompter, for I *heard* the most and *saw* the least of him."

popular Richard Power of Kilfane,[1] and a host of others. Amongst them we find Mr Wrixon Becher as one of the *corps dramatique.* He evidently made the most of his opportunities. But nothing definite then took place. Both were too young to think of matrimony, and the actress was heavily weighted with the support of her family, who were at that time almost entirely depending on her exertions. No better daughter and sister could be imagined. A great change was, however, at hand.

Towards the close of 1813, or beginning of 1814, Mr John Kemble was engaged as a star to play at Dublin, Limerick and Cork. Miss O'Neill acted with him, and he at once recognised her dove-like attraction. He wrote to his partner in London—

"There is a very pretty girl, with a small touch of the brogue on her tongue. She has great talent and some genius; with a little expense and some trouble we might make her an object for John Bull's admiration in juvenile tragedy. They call her here—'tis in verse, for they are all poets, all Tom Moores—the 'Dove,' in contradistinction to her rival, Miss Walstein, whom they designate the 'Eagle.' I recommend the 'Dove' to you as more likely to please John Bull than the Irish 'Eagle,' who is only a Siddons diluted, and would only be tolerated when Siddons is forgotten. I have sounded the fair lady on the subject of a London engagement. She proposes to append a very long family, a whole clan of O'Neills, to her engagement, to which I have given a decided negative. If she accept the offered terms I shall sign, seal, and ship herself and clan off from Cork Street. She is very pretty, and so, in fact, is her brogue, which, by-the-bye, she only uses in conversation, and totally forgets when with Shakespeare and other illustrious companions."

[1] The Powers of Kilfane were all highly respected and most popular; a ballad called "The Joys of Kilfane" sings their praises from one generation to the other.

"May the son, like his sire, be beloved and respected,
May he live to see Erin great, glorious and free;
May his wisdom increase, by kind heaven directed,
And may, oh yet may he still happier be."

This letter gives a pleasing idea of the very pretty girl with the touch of soft brogue always pleasant to English ears. Her desire to include *the clan* is a good touch. She gave way, however, on that point, as the salary offered was so much higher than any she had previously received as to make it unnecessary to enforce the condition. She compounded for one brother, Robert O'Neill, who was to be her personal protector, and in this capacity to have free access to the green-room and wings, and, occasionally, a walking gentleman's part.

Under these conditions she signed the agreement for three years, at a salary of from £15 to £17 a week. When the news was known in Dublin, there was great excitement. The friends of Miss Walstein were indignant that the "Dove" should have stolen such a march upon the "Eagle." There is, however, always truth in the old adage that one is never a prophet in one's own country. No sooner had the seal of fashion been placed upon the actress by the approbation of the great London manager than those who had not thought much of her before this event were seized with a tumult of admiration. Ladies had to be carried out every evening in a fainting condition, and one became insane from seeing the performance of Belvidera. Miss O'Neill left her own country with every mark of appreciation.

Her first appearance was fixed for October the 6th, in the part of *Juliet* to Conway's "Romeo." There was not much expected from the *débutante*, but after the first act her success was assured, and as the play proceeded the audience began to see they were the spectators of an almost ideal performance.

"At first she was sportive and natural, a joyous, caressing child. Then when the first touch of love came to her she changed subtly, in an almost imperceptible manner. Her movements became more voluptuous, her face seemed to alter its expression, and breathed a secret happiness: this expanded until, like a beautiful flower, she burst into full bloom. By degrees, when sorrow added its crowning and sacred imprint to her passion, she managed to convey to the spectator the most exquisite tenderness—her despair was heart-breaking. In her death scene she almost touched the ridiculous—at least, what would have been the ridiculous in any other actress, but seemed with her sublime. Her scream was like an electric shock."

The whole performance produced a profound sensation, Conway making a romantic *Romeo*, so that playgoers for the first time saw the true "Romeo and Juliet." The applause was enthusiastic, and when the curtain fell and "The Merry Wives of Windsor" was announced for the succeeding night, there was a universal cry for "Juliet," which was accordingly substituted.

Macready, speaking of Miss O'Neill's *début*, says,—"Her beauty, grace, simplicity and tenderness were the theme of every tongue. In her Siddons had a worthy successor, in her native elegance, unaffected earnestness and gushing passion."

Reynolds, on the other hand, who witnessed her performance, and was present at the rehearsal, was not so enthusiastic. "This young lady," he says, "in addition to having a very pleasing person and a good voice, possessed no inconsiderable portion of feeling, but which, in my opinion, was of too boisterous and vehement a nature." He frankly owns that he is in the minority, for the verdict of the million pronounced Miss O'Neill a younger and better Mrs Siddons.

Hazlitt gives her most discriminating praise. "Her excellence," he says, "consisted in truth of nature and force of passion. Her success as *Juliet* has never been equalled by any succeeding actress up to the present time, for it may be frankly said that a convincing *Juliet* has not yet been born. She scored, however, other triumphs. Her *Belvidera* was an exquisite performance, so also *Evadne* and *Mrs Haller*, which was so unspeakably touching as to become almost too painful. Her pathos was at all times effective. She cried more naturally than any actress, the tears seeming to come from her very heart. On the other hand, her laugh was strained and artificial, not fun-provoking like Mrs Jordan's.

Her comedy was altogether a failure. She never enlivened the spirits, and her whole air and manner were

"Rather like tragedy going a-rout.'

After essaying *Lady Teazle* and *Lady Townly*, the management withdrew her altogether from comic parts, and she only appeared in tragedy, in which she was unrivalled. "There was this difference between her and Mrs Siddons, for whom we felt awe, veneration and a sort of holy love. She was so great in her sufferings, her soul never seemed subdued. We almost feared to offend by comparison. Miss O'Neill twined herself round our hearts and into our affections; still, Mrs Siddons made an impression upon our minds that time never eradicated. The two ladies were excellent friends, and Mrs Siddons always declared her high opinion of Miss O'Neill's talents."

The stage, however, had not the attractions for her that it has for other artists. She preferred the tranquillity and security of domestic life, and in this she resembled one of our own time, who also withdrew from the public gaze into retirement when her fame was at its full height. That both artists acted well for their own happiness there can be no doubt, but this preference of sterling gold to tinsel shows a superior mind, well balanced, for admiration is so dear to a woman's heart that to voluntarily resign the homage of the world at large for the love of only one man is a proof of affection he, at all events, should value at its true price.

Miss O'Neill left the stage without a blemish on her character. Without being such a statue of cold propriety as Miss Farren, she had never allowed malice to have the chance of convicting her of the slightest indiscretion — the worst accusation that could be brought against her being that she was rather avaricious. If this were true, she was amply justified by the reason.

True to her fidelity to her family, Miss O'Neill did not allow herself to think of her own happiness until she could leave those for whose benefit she had worked so hard in comparative comfort. During the five years she spent in London she amassed a good sum of money. This was settled altogether on her parents and only sister. Her brothers were all able, through her means, to provide for themselves.

John had a colonial appointment, Robert was a surgeon, Charles an officer in the navy. These affairs being all settled, Miss O'Neill quietly withdrew from the stage without any leavetaking. The last the public knew of their favourite was the following announcement,—

"Miss Eliza O'Neill was married on December 18th, 1819, to William Wrixon Becher, Esq., M.P. for Mallow, and one of the most celebrated and accomplished of our theatrical amateurs. The ceremony was performed at Kilfane Church by the Dean of Ossory. The whole of Miss O'Neill's fortune (thirty thousand pounds) is settled on her family; her loss to the public is much regretted."

A few years after the marriage Mr Becher succeeded his uncle as Sir Wrixon Becher. Lady Becher was as popular in private life as she had been in public. The writer remembers seeing her when, in her old age, there was not much trace of the beauty which had charmed her contemporaries. She still retained, however, a singular gentleness of manner.

She died, in 1872, at the advanced age of eighty-one.

The portraits of Miss O'Neill are numerous—as *Belvidera* by Dawes, R.A., as *Juliet* by both Dawes and Thomson. The one produced here is by the first-named artist. Sir Charles Dilke has a pretty girlish portrait of her, and at the Garrick Club there is a full length by G. F. Joseph, A.R.A., of her as the tragic muse which gives a better idea of her beauty than any of her pictures. In connection with this portrait, Mrs Bancroft relates a touching incident. When quite an old lady, Lady Becher asked to be taken to the Garrick Club to see this picture, which now adorns the staircase. As she stood in front of the beautiful representation of herself as she was in the days of long ago, her mind seemed to go back to past scenes, and covering her face with her hands, she burst into a passion of tears.

# MARIE DOLORES GILBERT, LOLA MONTEZ

(1818-1861)

As in all lives there are shadows, so in all biographies there is an occasional development of the worst or seamiest side of human nature, and although such histories are neither pleasant to write nor to read, still in a volume of biographies it is necessary to show the reader these shadows as a relief to the higher lights. In this sense we cannot have a greater contrast than the one presented by the sedate and virtuous career of Miss O'Neill and the disorderly, riotous chronicle we are about to enter upon. Nevertheless, the life of Lola Montez is not without deep interest and a certain amount of profit. This is my excuse for reproducing her now forgotten story, which, in its time, excited the attention of Europe.

As a contemporary writer remarked, "A woman who, in the full light of the nineteenth century, renewed all the scandals that disgraced the Middle Ages, and, with an audacity that is almost unparalleled, seated herself upon the steps of a throne, is worthy of mention, if even to show to what an extent vice can sometimes triumph, and to what a fall it can eventually come."

In spite of her Spanish name, Lola Montez was of Irish descent, her father being the son of Sir Edward Gilbert, whose ancestors were of English planting but had lived long enough in their adopted country to be "more Irish than the Irish." [1]

[1] Lola Montez has had no less than twenty-four biographers, a proof of the attraction that underlies such seamy lives. Amongst these twenty-four writers a great diversity of opinion exists as to her nationality: one brings her into the world in Spain, another in India, a third in Turkey, a fourth names Geneva, a fifth Cuba; again it is said she was the child of Spanish gipsies, the daughter of a Scotch washerwoman, and one very daring biographer gives her Lord Byron for a father. The truth was more prosaic than these fantastic pedigrees.

LOLA MONTEZ.

*From the Original Picture in the Munich Gallery.*

The Gilberts were well considered, tolerably rich, and Lady Gilbert had the reputation of a beauty. It was a sore distress to father and mother when their son, a young officer on leave, fell in love with and married a Creole dancer Lola Oliver. (She called herself Oliverres de Montalva.)

Finding that his parents would do nothing for him, Gilbert, on the expiration of his leave, returned to India, taking his young wife (she was seventeen) with him. He had only been a few months with his regiment when he died of cholera, leaving his widow penniless, with a baby—Dolores, or Lola, our heroine, born in 1818.

There is a special providence for officers' widows, who are almost sure to find a vacant heart amongst their deceased husbands' friends. In some cases the stronghold has been captured *du vivant du feu le Mari.* However that may be, Mrs Gilbert was singularly lucky. No braver officer or more honourable, kindhearted man could be found than Colonel Craigie, who, Dobbin-like, took upon himself the care of the widow and her child. He was a man of distinguished service, and soon after his marriage was made deputy-adjutant-general of the forces in India. On her side, to do Mrs Craigie justice, she lived up to her exalted position, and never did anything (so far as we know) to forfeit her husband's affection and the esteem of society.

Lola, who made part of the new household, was a veritable thorn in the flesh of mother and nurse. She had all the agility of a monkey, and was as full of tricks—climbing trees, getting on the roof, dropping into the balcony, and speaking a language of her own manufacture, an extraordinary jumble of Hindustani, Bengalese, Spanish and English. No one took any trouble with the child; she was taught nothing except by the Hindoos, who showed her how to dance in their own voluptuous manner. At last the attention of her excellent stepfather was attracted to the development of this precocious infant and he lost no time in sending her home to his own father in Scotland. From there she was placed in a school at Bath, where, amongst other *diableries* she got up a flirtation with the music master.

When she was sixteen, her mother came to England for a short time, and took Lola away from school, her intention being to take her back with her to India, where she had arranged to marry her to an Indian judge, Sir Abraham Lumley.

Lola managed not only to ferret out this scheme, but to completely upset it by eloping with a young officer who had come over in the same vessel as Mrs Craigie, and was on intimate terms with the family. Captain James of the 21st Bengal Infantry took her to Ireland, where they found great difficulty in getting anyone to marry so young a girl without her mother's consent. After some delay, Mrs Craigie was persuaded by Captain James's sister to give it, and the lovers were married in 1837 by Captain James's brother, a Calvinist minister.

The young couple then went to Dublin, where Lola's beauty and romantic story aroused the greatest interest.

Lord Normanby, who was then Viceroy, was an admirer of pretty women, and singled out Mrs James for much attention. "Women of your age," he would say, "are the queens of society." These compliments and attentions were by no means pleasing to the young husband, who was really in love with his worthless wife; and he took the first opportunity to remove her out of harm's way into the safe harbour of his father's country house in Westmeath, than which nothing could be duller.

Lola describes with some humour the insupportable weariness of life in the country parts of Ireland, the two occupations being hunting and eating, which, she says, "alternate with monotonous fidelity, only broken by innumerable cups of tea (medicinal baths for the inside) taken with the most imperturbable gravity at regular times of the day. This existence," she goes on, "was so wearisome that I should have shot myself only that, fortunately, my husband got the order to join his regiment in India."

On her passage out she amused the dulness of a sea voyage by flirting with three admirers, one of whom was the captain of the ship, a profound thinker, who defined love as a pipe which is filled at eighteen, smoked until forty, and the ashes of which are collected until the latest moment of life—an original thought which is not unlike some of Henri Murger's sayings.

While his wife was the centre of attraction, Captain James, who bears a strong likeness to Rawdon Crawley, spent his time drinking porter and "sleeping like a boa-constrictor."

When they arrived in India, Captain James had to take part in the Afghan campaign, and not daring to leave his volatile wife alone, he was obliged to take her with him at great expense, hiring a palanquin and native bearers to carry her.[1] She, however, enjoyed the expedition and seems to have seen many curious things. Her Indian stories are strange, and bear a certain stamp of truth, as when she relates the ball given by the Rajah of Lahore to the English officers, and the present he made to each officer of a Georgian or Circassian slave, which Lord Auckland (the Governor-General) took upon himself to decline.

By the time the campaign was over the domestic happiness of the James couple was utterly wrecked. According to

[1] There are generally eight bearers to each palanquin, four employed at one time the others relieving in turn. It is extraordinary the amount of fatigue these human horses will endure. They lighten their labour by chanting as they walk, the subject of their chant being relative to the burden they carry. When carrying an English clergyman, who weighed not less than two hundred pounds, the men sang :—

"Oh, what a heavy bag,
No, it is an elephant.
He is an awful weight,
Let's throw his palkan down,
Let's set him in the mud,
Let's leave him to his fate ;
No—for he'll be angry then—
Ay, and he'll beat us then
With a thick stick.
Then let's make haste and get along,
Jump along quick."

When carrying Lola (according to her own accounts) they sang the most flattering description of their lovely burden

"She's not heavy,
Cabbada.
Little barta,
Cabbada.
Carry her swiftly,
Cabbada.
Pretty barta,
Cabbada."

Lola's statement, he left her, but as he instituted divorce proceedings in England and obtained his suit, one must disbelieve this story. Neither would her mother, Mrs Craigie, receive her when she took refuge with her in Calcutta. Her stepfather was, however, more merciful. He gave her one thousand pounds, and put her on board the ship that was to take her to England, placing her under the care of a Mr and Mrs Sturgis, American friends of his who were going to Europe. This excellent man also wrote to his brother, who lived in London, to meet her on her arrival, and, after giving her time to rest, to despatch her to Perth, where she was to reside with Colonel Craigie's father until some arrangement could be made with her husband. Lola, however, had no idea of spending any more dreary days, neither did she want any reconciliation with Captain James. While on the voyage, she got on terms of great intimacy with an American lady, who encouraged her ideas of independence, and by the advice of this new friend she resolved to go on the stage. Mr Craigie's kind offers were therefore politely declined, and Lola, on her arrival in London, lost no time in placing herself in the hands of Miss Fanny Kelly, then very well known as a trainer of *débutantes* for the theatre. This lady's professional experience soon discovered that beyond her youth and beauty the new actress had no talent that could ensure success. She therefore counselled her to give up the idea and adopt that of *danseuse*, as more suited to her abilities. This advice Lola followed, and studied under a Spanish dancing mistress in Madrid for six months, when she was considered fit to appear. She then returned to London and was engaged by Lumley, manager of Her Majesty's Theatre. Her *début* was to be in "The Tarantula."

That Lumley, who was an experienced caterer and understood his patrons well, should have engaged so inexperienced a dancer was a proof that, in spite of a certain want of finish, Lola possessed some elements of success — principally her beauty and abundant audacity. These attractions would undoubtedly have carried weight, had there not arisen an unlucky *contretemps*.

Those who can look back so far as 1843 will remember that the ballet was the principal attraction of Her Majesty's Theatre. It was not so much the singing of Grisi or Persiani that filled the house as the dreamy grace of Taglioni and her rivals, Fanny Ellsler, Cerito and Dumilâtre. The *jeunesse dorée*, who had no music halls wherein to amuse themselves, came in force to see their favourites, and stalked out when the dance was over. It was the *chic* thing for men of fashion to club together to hire the omnibus boxes on each side of the stage, and these, on special occasions, were filled by Lumley's patrons, whose word was law as to the success or condemnation of a *débutante*.

On the night of Lola's *début*, Saturday, June 10th, 1843, the omnibus box on the right-hand of the stage was occupied by a well-known dilettante nobleman, Lord Ranelagh[1] with his friends, all eager to see the new dancer, of whom little was known—Lumley, keeping silent, but smiling significantly, as if to say, "I have a surprise in store, *you shall see*." The whole incident is highly dramatic. The house was crowded . . . opera glasses raised in expectation. When the curtain drew up, an undoubtedly beautiful dancer bounded on to the stage; but she had hardly executed one of her steps when an ominous hiss was heard from Lord Ranelagh's box, and a voice called out, "Why, it's Betty James." The hiss

[1] Twenty-five years later the name of this nobleman came before the public in connection with the famous trial of Madame Rachel for promising a certain widow that she would not only make her beautiful for ever, but a Countess into the bargain. She stripped her silly dupe of everything she possessed, and never even introduced her to Lord Ranelagh, who was personated by a man called William. The maiden name of Madame Rachel was Russell. She was born in 1806. Her father was much respected. She first married Jacob Moses who was lost in the *Royal Charter*, which foundered on the Welsh coast, homeward bound from Australia. This was in 1859. The widow married Mr Philip Leverson. After her marriage she had a bad fever. Her hair, which was luxuriant, fell off, which distressed her extremely. She got a recipe from a physician, which he said would make her hair more beautiful than ever and so it did. This gave her the idea of making a living by colouring hair and finding she succeeded in this, she made a trade of cosmetics, and published a list, which to read over is truly wonderful—fifty different ways of improving a drab, freckled or pimply complexion. Such delightful creams and washes, youth and beauty creams, and senses of peace, also a royal bath preparation which only cost £2, 2s.! Jordan's water was a little expensive—£20—especially as Venus's complete toilet could be had for the same money. She had, however, hosts of clients, for since the days of Cleopatra women love to add to Nature's charms, and even the Vicar of Wakefield's well-brought-up daughters dabbled in face washes.

was taken up and sustained by the box on the left, and gradually spread through the house. The dancer, whose nerves were not easily shaken, continued her pirouettes, but the curtain quickly descended, and with it ended Lola Montez's engagement at Her Majesty's Theatre.

That it should have been so seems to have been somewhat unjust. The papers[1] more than hinted the beautiful señorita had been sacrificed to a jealous cabal, while other sources have ascribed the incident to a previous quarrel with Lord Ranelagh. It was, however, the age when the patron was all powerful, and in face of the hostility of Lord Ranelagh and his set it would have been impossible again to put forward the unfortunate Lola. So the angry manager told the indignant *danseuse*, who had nothing for it but to pack up her dresses and return whence she came. Lola, however, despite her feigned indignation, was probably well aware of the cause of this apparently enigmatical attack upon her. Although her years numbered little more than two decades, she had seen a good deal of life, and it is not unlikely that Lord Ranelagh had played *jeune premier* in some of the scenes of her varied career. The remark, "Why it's Betty James," was significant of some previous knowledge (on his side) of her antecedents.

Finding the road to fame closed to her in London, Lola proceeded to Paris, where she appeared at the Porte St Martin, and was again hissed off the stage, her incomplete performance not being likely to find favour with the fastidious Parisians. At this second rebuff her temper, which was quite uncontrolled, displayed itself. She made grimaces at the audience, and, De Mirecourt says, took off her garters and threw them at the pit. When she went behind the scenes she used her whip to the attendants. Such exhibitions of temper on her part were like fits of insanity, and all through her life she was liable to such sudden outbursts of rage. After this second failure she undertook a European tour, which was

[1] The *Illustrated London News*, 1843, was loud in its regret at not seeing again "a dancer who excited a novel and delightful sensation, and who has not been heard of since. She was decidedly successful, but perhaps the votaries of *the classical school* have set their faces against national dances."

brimful of excitement. As we read we live in a glittering circle and breathe a perfumed air. No voice breaks the silence save that of a royal personage. Amidst much that is pure invention, some of the stories have an unmistakable ring of truth, as that when she was at Berlin she got an engagement to dance at a *fête* given by the King (afterwards Emperor), Frederick William. Before her turn came, Lola was seized by the most extraordinary dryness in her throat, which she felt should be assuaged before she began her performance. When, however, she asked for a drink of water, her request, simple as it seemed, was politely refused, it being against all rules of etiquette that an artist or actor should eat or drink in the presence of royalty. On this Lola's quick temper flared up, and in her turn she flatly refused to go on until the water was got for her. In this difficulty the Grand Duke Michael came to the rescue. He went to the King and told him the condition of affairs, whereupon Frederick William, who was of a kindly nature, sent for a goblet of water, and having put it to his lips presented it to her with his own hand, thus satisfying at the same time the strict rules of etiquette prevailing at the German court and his own kindness of heart.

From Berlin the adventuress returned to Paris, where she found an admirer who considerably influenced her future career. Dujarrier, the editor of *La Presse*, was a man of a different calibre from the *flaneurs* who clustered round the dancer. He saw that if properly educated, and her undoubted talents developed, she would be invaluable, by reason of her beauty and fascination, as a political spy. He set himself the task of educating her, and to him was due her extraordinary mastery of politics and the development of her great intellectual gifts. As a test of her powers, Dujarrier entrusted her with a secret service expedition to St Petersburg, to arrange some matters connected with the Caucasus.[1]

[1] While on this secret service engagement she was, she states, "on one occasion in conclave with the Emperor Nicholas and Count Beckendorf, when it was suddenly announced that the chief of the Caucasian army was without desiring an audience. Lola was, on this, unceremoniously thrust into a closet and the door locked upon her. A grand quarrel ensued between the Emperor and the chief, in the midst of which Nicholas and his suite left the room, completely forgetting that Lola was locked up. A whole hour passed; when, accord-

Nothing, however, came of it. This did not shake the master's confidence in his pupil, and having mutually fallen in love, they were engaged to be married, when again Lola's evil destiny interfered. The editor of *La Presse* was very unpopular with a certain section of politicians, and politics were the ostensible reason for his duel with Beauvallon, a rival editor, in which Lola's lover lost his life. On the morning of the meeting he wrote to her in the heroic style of a Frenchman—

"I am going out to fight with pistols. This explains why I did not come to you. I have need of all my calmness. At 2 o'clock all will be over. A thousand adieux, my dear love, whom I love so much, and the thoughts of whom will never leave me."

Lola evidently had a poor opinion of Dujarrier as a shot, for her first idea was to rush off to fight Beauvallon herself, for, as she said later on at the trial, I was a better shot than Dujarrier, and if Beauvallon wanted satisfaction I could have given it to him. As it was, she met the dead body of her lover coming back. The easily-excited Parisian mob made a heroine of her for a few days, and when she appeared at the trial, which took place at Rouen, clothed in the deepest mourning, she received a public ovation.

We come now to the turning-point of our heroine's career, and from this point her story reads like some fairy-tale, so strangely did the events crowd upon one another. It was in 1847 that Lola Montez appeared at the Munich Opera House as a dancer. That she should have obtained an engagement at this very exclusive theatre was due, undoubtedly, to the influence of those who sent her to the Bavarian Capital as a political agent. It was said that she was paid by the party of Reform, who had long been looking out for someone

ing to this wonderful narrator, the Emperor came running back and unlocked the door, not only begging pardon for his forgetfulness in a manner that only a man of his accomplished address could do, but adding to his apologies the gift of fifty roubles. This story seems highly improbable. Russian Emperors do not run about unlocking doors for political spies! Nicholas was every inch the Czar, and could have sent Beckendorff, as no doubt he did. A lie cost Lola very little.

fitted for the post, and now found what they wanted in this apparently frivolous dancer, who in reality was an astute politician. As luck would have it, Lola, on the first night of her appearance at the Opera House, captivated the King by her personal attractions. She was then in the very zenith of her singular beauty, a beauty which owed more to its intellectual qualities than to its mere outward attraction. Seen in repose, she hardly merited the name of a great beauty; when she spoke, however, the vivacity and the expressiveness which lit up her mobile features and magnificent eyes made her undeniably and dangerously fascinating. She was eminently suited to attract Ludwig of Bavaria, that singular personality whose character presents a mixture of Haroun-al-Raschid and Henry IV. of France. In spite of his many weaknesses, there is a certain interest attaching to the extraordinary simplicity with which he imagined he could lay down at will his royalty and act as a private gentleman. "Such a habit of mind may survive intact while supported by the vigour and elasticity of youth, but as age creeps on it transmutes violations of established forms into confirmed eccentricities, which appear ridiculous to those persons who have not the power of seeing the true character under the motley garb of oddity."[1] Hence the people, for whom the King

[1] One of the King's eccentricities took the form of rambling at all hours alone on foot, *à la* Haroun-al-Raschid through the city, even late at night. "It is impossible," writes a visitor to Munich in 1847, "not to be conscious of his approach, even at a considerable distance, as you see a long line of pedestrians suddenly arrested in their progress to and fro, and standing with their hats off ready to greet him as he passes. A stranger, not knowing the rank of the remarkable personage approaching, is considerably puzzled. He sees advancing a tall, well-proportioned personage, who is, evidently, utterly indifferent to what is going on around—who walks not in a straight line but zig-zag, with a confidence as though would he go against a wall it would crumble at his approach. His costume is that of a fox-hunting country gentleman of the fine old sort: absorbed in thought, he bows mechanically, yet courteously, even affectionately, to the spectators That he saw far more than is supposed was made plain by an incident that was much talked about at the time it happened. One evening the King was passing through the Ludwig Strasse amidst a serried line of his loving subjects, all hat in hand. One of them, either a stranger or a malcontent, stood erect and covered in the midst of the loyal Bavarians. Probably he calculated on the King's preoccupation to escape notice. He reckoned, however, without his host. The King's keen eye at once detected the rudeness, and without stopping in his course, or apparently even glancing at the offender, he simply raised his hand, and as he passed knocked the man's hat off." This story was often told by the burghers of Munich, who highly approved the King's action.—*Fraser's Magazine.*

did much, thought poorly of him, because he had odd ways that made them laugh. The good he did was marvellous; especially on Munich he lavished his munificent gifts. In one thing only he restricted his subjects—allowing them no political freedom, and even personal liberty was hedged in with all manner of petty laws. All this was, however, now to change From the night when Lola danced before the Bavarian Monarch, a new era set in. Five days later she was formally introduced at Court as *maîtresse en titre*, the King saying, "Gentlemen, I present you my best friend." She was created Baronne de Rosenthal and Comtesse de Landsfeld, and the King gave her large appointments, and a fine residence on the Rue Thérésienne was splendidly furnished for her. Lola played her part with considerable ability. She had a strong will, and exercised the most wonderful fascination not only over the doting old king, but over his ministers; never has Phryne played so bold, so strong a part. What she did is matter of history. "For more than a year this adventurous little Irishwoman was a power in Europe. She overthrew a ministry of twenty-five years; she drove out Austrian influence; a new system began to grow up, and the influence was not *all evil:* there was much that was liberal and intelligent." That this last did not originate with Lola we can be fairly certain: she was only a puppet in the hands of those who employed and paid her. Her success, however, surpassed all expectations, and no one can deny that, as a political character, Lola Montez held an important position in Bavaria, besides having agents and correspondents in all parts of Europe. She brought to bear upon her new position the insight she had acquired into the manœuvres of diplomacy during her intimacy with Dujarrier, and she was clever enough to turn this knowledge to advantage in her new sphere. Her ideas were original, and her novel manner of expressing them had a charm for the King, who had a comprehensive mind. Whatever other indiscretion could be laid to her charge, no one could accuse her of betraying State secrets, and in the internal affairs of Bavaria she had the good sense to be guided by those who were competent to direct the puppet who played the part for them. For the rest, she was a charming and eloquent talker, and displayed in her conversation a wide and keen intelligence, and a mental grasp unusual in a woman. Her manners were distinguished, and she was a graceful hostess, understanding the art of dressing to perfection. For a year or more she held high state as a sort of vice-queen, while all Europe looked on in astonishment at the infatuation of the old King, and the success that attended the Reform party, which she supported. She turned out the head of the University, Lasoults; Döllinger also, then the mainstay of the Ultramontanes, had to resign his post. The task, however, of reorganising an entire nation was a little too much for "Betty James." She might have accomplished more if she could have controlled her fiery temper, which prompted her occasionally to throw a waiter out of the window,[1] and to bestow upon an officer a box on the ear. She was known to horsewhip her coachman.

These excesses might have been passed over, but all right-minded people of all classes joined in condemning the spectacle daily displayed before the whole city of the infatuation of the King for this adventuress. He forced his wife and daughter to receive her, and the Queen had to present her rival with the Order of the Chanoines of St Teresa, an order she had created, and which bore her name. The honest citizens refused to be led by such a leader, and when she took her daily drive with the King she was loudly hissed. On the other hand, the whole Court, to its everlasting shame, bowed down before the new idol he had set up. She was courted, flattered, and received large bribes to secure her interest with the senile Monarch. It was, in fact, the old story of Louis XIV. and his mistresses played over again in this nineteenth century.

A storm, however, was gathering, and soon burst over Lola's head. The first astonishment excited by her success had begun to subside, and the Ultramontane party to re-

[1] The infatuated monarch admired this display of spirit on the part of his Lolotte, and on one occasion, when she failed in her laudable desire to punish some one who had offended her, he wrote her a string of amatory verses. He indulged much in poetry when troubles came.

cover from the paralysis that had seized upon them; a determined opposition took the place of the inaction that had hitherto prevailed. The Jesuit order, which was all-powerful in Bavaria, bore down upon her, and although she held on for some months, fighting against heavy odds, she was finally crushed. The revolution was brought about by the German students who, in those days, were divided into associations, each being distinguished by a particular colour and a remarkable head-dress. The Munich students were named after the five principal provinces of Bavaria—Franconia, Istria Palatinate, Bavaria and Suabia. The favourite wished to add a sixth, to which she gave the name of Allemania. The Allemannen numbered from sixteen to twenty youths of the first nobility, and were altogether under her protection: they wore caps of bright red, trimmed with parti-coloured gauze. The other and older associations of students utterly refused to receive these new colleagues, and looked upon them as do the rooks when a crow intrudes into the family councils. The fights between them were of everyday occurrence. Things were in this position when, in February 1848, the academical course began. The Allemannen presented themselves with the other students at the lectures given by Herr Seiter, and were received with hisses and demonstrations of dislike. The Countess Landsfeld felt this to be a personal insult to her, and the heads of the University were informed that an inquiry should take place as to who was in fault. The students snapped their fingers at the inquiry, which, however, did not take place, and, growing bolder by this impunity, in a few weeks they made a more organised attack upon the wearers of the red caps. It was in vain that the heads of the different colleges tried to establish order. Prince Wallenstein, one of the ministers, came to harangue the rioters, but his intervention was of no use. On leaving the University, the Allemannen were pursued by a crowd of students, jeering and crying out a saying of their patroness, Countess Landsfeld, "*Mauvais cheval peut broncher, mais non toute une écurie.*" This insult exasperated the others to fury. As they entered the *café* of a man called

Rothmauer, one of them, the Graf von Hirschberg, drew his dagger and precipitated himself upon his tormentors. The dagger was quickly taken from him, but the police dared not arrest one of Lola's Allemannen, who sent a message to their patroness to demand protection. She responded at once to their appeal, arriving on foot, and without any escort, being firmly convinced her presence was sufficient to quell any tumult. Here she reckoned without her host, for, being recognised, she was hissed, hustled, ill-treated, and although she applied at different houses for shelter, none would let her in. The Austrian Legation shut its doors in her face.

The King, who was entertaining a party at the palace, hearing of the dangerous predicament his Lolotte was in, arrived in the midst of the uproar, and, with the most chivalrous courtesy, gave her his arm to conduct her home. Her last act was to turn round and fire a pistol at the mob. It hurt no one. A company of cavalry now appeared on the scene, and the crowd was quickly scattered. The following week a royal proclamation declared the University of Munich closed for a year.

This arbitrary act caused a crisis. The whole populace joined the students, and the entire municipality of Munich demanded the banishment of the favourite, and what had been only a college riot turned into a revolution. Ludwig was inflexible: he would rather lose his crown than part with his beloved Lolotte. The Chamber of Peers, however, alarmed at the height to which the public exasperation had attained, were determined, and, after hours spent in argument and persuasion, wrung from the miserable old man an order for the expatriation of the Countess. She, meantime, had very nearly scored a triumph by the courage she showed in suddenly appearing amongst the mob who were howling for her life. A hundred guns were pointed at her, a hundred fat, apoplectic voices fiercely demanded that she should cause the repeal of what she had done. Lola had the courage to face her adversaries and tell them it was impossible to accede to their request; they could take her life if they would, but that would never mend their cause or prove they were in the right. In the midst of this imprudent speech she was dragged back within her house by her friends, and soon after, seeing that preparations were being made to burn it down, she yielded to the force of circumstances, and made her escape, disguised as a peasant girl.

The King abdicated in February, 1848. His consent to this step has been, by some writers, ascribed to the influence of Lola Montez, who, according to this view, returned to Munich disguised as a boy, and never left until she had wrung from the monarch his consent to the step desired by the nation. If this story be true, one may conclude that it was from no spirit of magnanimity that the beaten favourite urged the King to gratify his people, but that she was again a political agent engaged this time on the opposite side. The King imagined that, having done her bidding, his fair inamorata would be content to spend the remainder of her days in his society. Lola, however, did not see the advantage of such a sacrifice, and coolly dismissed a royal lover who had no royal wealth wherewith to endow her.

Another version of the incident states that she was conducted out of the country by an escort of police, some of them sitting inside the carriage, and that no sooner was it known that she had left the city than the mob vented their fury on her house, sacking it from top to bottom.[1] It is, however, agreed on all sides that the king expected that, after his abdication, she would return to him, and that he was disdainfully dismissed.[2]

The sole interest that Lola Montez's story possesses ceases

[1] It was currently reported that one of the most interested spectators was the old King, who seemed to enjoy the sight, but, being recognised, stones were thrown at him, one of which struck him on the forehead and wounded him severely.

[2] Whichever version is true, it is pretty certain that, in the first instance, Lola did not go very far, and that at first she entertained the hope of returning. The King wrote her constantly, and sent her lovesick verses, some of which are not destitute of pathos.

TO THE ABSENT LOLOTTE.

The world hates and persecutes
That heart which gave itself to me

after we have reached this point. The rest of her career presents the usual downward course of women of her class. In the summer of 1849 she was once more in London, engaged by the manager of Covent Garden to appear as the heroine of her own adventures in a drama called "Lolez Montez," or "La Comtesse pour une Heure." This was, however, withdrawn by order of the Chamberlain. Meantime, she had managed to get a young officer of the Life Guards, of good family, and rich, into her toils. George Trafford Heald married her at St George's, Hanover Square, in 1849. His family, finding out that some legal formality was wanting in the divorce from Captain James, brought an action of bigamy against her, and she and her young husband escaped to Spain, where they lived for two or three years a sort of cat-and-dog life. There were perpetual quarrels, in one of which she stabbed him. He ran away, but, curiously enough, returned to her, but the fights began again. Finally, Heald was drowned at Lisbon – it was said, accidentally.

After this Lola proceeded to America, where she appeared at New York in a piece written expressly for her, which represented the principal adventures of her career in Bavaria. She made an enormous pile of money, but spent it quickly. She then arranged to give audiences for a quarter of an hour, when persons provided with a ticket could converse with her and hear her adventures. When she went to California, she hit upon a novel expedient to draw the public. The newspapers announced that all the profits of her audiences were to go to the poor of the town, as the Countess was about to enter a religious order, and this last appearance was a sort of *amende* for her former life. This was another lie. At San Francisco she again entered the bonds of matrimony with F. P. Hull. the wealthy proprietor of the *San Francisco Whig*,

But however much they strive to estrange us,
My heart will cling the more fondly to thee ;
The more they hate, the more thou art beloved.
And more and more is given to thee
Of that of which they yearn to deprive thee.
I shall never be torn from thee,
My Lolotte.

a newspaper of importance; but this marriage was dissolved in a few weeks.

We next find her, 1856, in Australia, in company with a bear and a donkey. She was engaged at the Victoria Theatre, where she distinguished herself by horsewhipping an editor, named Seekampf, who had said something disparaging of her. This adventure made her highly popular with an audience in the far West, and when she appeared on the stage she received an ovation. She returned thanks for this kind reception, and regretted she had to allude to Mr Seekampf (but she added ingenuously), "it is not my fault; this very morning he has renewed his ungentlemanly attacks. I offered at once to fight a duel with pistols, but the coward, who does not fear to attack a woman behind her back, has run away when she is in front of him." At Ballarat she made another scene and there was more horsewhipping. This time, however, she was worsted by a woman, who was more than her match. This was the wife of the manager of the theatre, Mrs Crosby, and when Lola, who imagined the manager wanted to cheat her, raised her whip to beat him, this athletic woman fell upon her, and, her strength being enormous, she in a few minutes broke Lola's wrist, and left her in a fainting condition. In the September of this same year we find her in France, addressing the following curious letter to the French and Belgian papers from St Jean de Luz:—

"As the French and Belgian newspapers are publishing as a fact that the suicide of the artist Manclerc, who précipitated himself from the Pic du Midi, was due to the trouble I had occasioned him, this calumny Mons. Manclerc would, if he were alive, contradict himself. It is true we were married, but, after eight days, finding that the union was not likely to be a happy one, we separated by mutual consent. Perhaps the story of the Pic du Midi has only existence in the brain of some journalist, who revels in tragic details. Anyhow, I count upon your sympathy, Mr Editor, to exculpate me from any share in the event.—Yours, LOLA MONTEZ."

Girardin, the editor of the *Presse*, who was at the moment

stranded for copy, reproduced the above letter, which happening to fall into the hands of Manclerc, who was then at Bayonne, produced the following denial of the whole occurrence :—

"SIR,—I have just seen in the number of the *Presse* for September a letter from Lola Montez, in which there is mention of a fall and of a marriage: in both of these events I am said to have been the principal actor. I can only say I know nothing of either of these important occurrences. During my life I have never felt the least desire to precipitate myself from the Pic du Midi or any other height, neither have I had the honour of being, for even eight days, the husband of the Countess of Landsfeld, etc., etc., etc.

"MANCLERC."

After one or two more compromising adventures, Lola returned to New York, where she gave "Lectures on the Art of Beauty," which were afterwards published in a volume.[1] Here her natural cleverness asserted itself, and some of her remarks are not without interest.

"On the whole," she says, "I must give the preference to the English nobility for the most beautiful women I have ever seen, beginning with the late Duchess of Sutherland, who might be considered the very type of the beautiful aristocracy of England. I next think of Lady Blessington. In Italy they called her the Goddess; she was a far more intellectual type than the Duchess of Sutherland. The present Duchess of Wellington is a remarkably beautiful woman, with no animation, as cold as a piece of marble." She winds up with the Sheridans—"the most beautiful family in England." "France," she graciously remarks, "is not *without* its beautiful women. La Marquise de la Grange was a grand study for an artist. The Empress Eugenie, when I last saw her, was one of the most vivacious, witty and sprightly conversationalists." She then makes the rather startling statement that the Empress "is a small woman, all her portraits exaggerating her size." The Grand Duchess Olga of Russia, was "so

[1] The lectures were written for her by the Rev. Chauncey Burr.

lovely that when she appeared in public the whole audience rose and greeted her with shouts of applause." In the *Art of Beauty* there are some curious lessons as to the means of preserving and adorning beauty, the writer insisting largely upon the advantages of the Tepid, not the Cold, bath, which she styles "the purest exercise of health, the sweet refresher of the summer heats."

The lectures, however, ceased to attract, and "the sweet refresher" did not preserve the unfortunate Lola from the consequences of her ill-spent life. Shattered in health, deserted by her gay associates, she was fast sinking into the extremity of poverty when she was met in New York by Mrs Buchanan who had known and loved her in her school days at Bath. This good Samaritan did not shun her fallen sister, but at once spoke to her, and never ceased her charitable efforts until she succeeded in rescuing her from the depths into which she had fallen. Lola's conversion from her evil ways seems to have been sincere. How long it would have lasted, with an erratic nature such as hers, would be hard to say. She had thrown herself, with all the energy of her nature, into the work of rescuing those who, like herself, were homeless and sinful when she was mercifully struck down with a fit of paralysis. She lingered only a short time, and died sincerely penitent January 1861, and was buried in Greenwood Cemetery, New York.

# AUTHORITIES

| | |
|---|---|
| MRS JORDAN | Life of Mrs Jordan, by James Boaden—Private Life, by a Confidential Friend—Jordan's Elixir of Life, 1789—The Wandering Patentee, by Tate Wilkinson—Personal Sketches of His Own Time, by Sir Jonah Barrington—Personal Memoirs, by P. L. Gordon—Their Majesties' Servants, by Dr Doran—Horace Walpole's Letters, edited by P. Cunningham—Account of the English Stage, by P. Genest—Journal and Correspondence of Miss Barry—Celebrities I have Known, by Lord W. Lennox—Contemporary Criticisms—Private Letter from Members of the Bland Family—Dictionary of National Biography, Vol. XXX., page 192. |
| LADY ANNE AND LADY GERTRUDE FITZPATRICK. | Letters addressed to the Countess of Ossory, by Horace Walpole—Life and Times of Sir Joshua Reynolds, by C. R. Leslie and Tom Taylor—Sir Joshua Reynolds and His Works, Gleanings from his Diary, by W. Cotton—Engraved Works of Sir Joshua Reynolds, by Graves—Catalogues of Algernon Graves—Private Information. |
| MARY BIRMINGHAM, COUNTESS OF LEITRIM; ANNE, COUNTESS OF CHARLEMONT. | Autobiography and Correspondence of Mrs Delany, edited by Lady Llanover, Vol. I.—Memoirs, Journal and Correspondence of Thomas Moore—Life of James, First Earl of Charlemont, by F. Hardy—Life of Alfieri—Life, Letters and Journal of Lord Byron—Memoirs of Sir N. W. Wraxall—Family Letters—Private Information. |
| SARAH CURRAN. | History of England in the Eighteenth Century, by W. E. H. Lecky—History of the Irish Rebellion, by W. H. Maxwell—Curran and His Contemporaries, by Philips—Life of John Philpot Curran, by W. H. Curran—Life of Curran, by Thomas Davis—Life and Times of Robert Emmet—Manuscript Notes—Memoir of Robert Emmet, by T. Davis—Biography of Robert Emmet, by Comtesse d'Haussonville—Librarie Contemporaine Notice of Robert Emmet—Illustrious Irishwomen, by E. Owens Blackburn—Personal Recollections, by Lord Cloncurry—Life of Petrie, by W. Stokes—Secret Service of Pitt, by Fitzpatrick—Life and Times of Grattan, by his Son—Yesterday and To-day, by Cyrus Redding—My Lords of Strogue, by Honourable Lewis Wingfield—Hibernian Magazine—Memoirs, Journal and Correspondence of Thomas Moore—Dictionary of National Biography, Vol. XIII., page 332-340. |

MELESINA CHEVENIX ST GEORGE TRENCH. — The Remains of the late Mrs Richard Trench, edited by her Son—Notes on Admiral Nelson—The Annals of Ballitore, by Mrs Leadbeater—Contemporary Notices.

MARGUERITE POWER, COUNTESS OF BLESSINGTON. — Literary Life and Correspondence, by Robert Madden—Letters and Journal of Lord Byron—The Greville Memoirs—Chorley's Authors of England—Reminiscences, by Captain Gronow—The Gorgeous Lady Blessington, by Fitzgerald Molloy—Fraser's Magazine—New Monthly Magazine—Colburn's Magazine—Dictionary of National Biography.

SYDNEY OWENSON, LADY MORGAN. — Memoirs, etc., of Lady Morgan, edited by Hepworth Dixon—Lady Morgan, Her Career, Literary and Personal, by W. J. Fitzpatrick—Fifty Years' Recollections, by Cyrus Redding—The Croker Papers—Englishwomen of Letters, by Julia Kavanagh—Recollections of Society, by Lady C. Davies—Authors of England, by Chorley—Celebrities I have Known, by Lord W. Lennox—Notices in Newspapers and Periodicals—Dictionary of National Biography, Vol. XXXIX., pages 27-29—Athenæum for 1850—Private Information—Original Unpublished Letters, etc.

CAROLINE ELIZABETH NORTON. — Lives of the Sheridans, by P. Fitzgerald—D'Israeli's Letters—Memoir of Lady Gifford, by the Earl of Dufferin and Clandeboye—Lady Granville's Memoirs—Lady Eastlake's Memoirs—The Greville Memoirs—Diary of Crabb Robinson—Englishwomen's Domestic Magazine—Temple Bar, Fraser's Magazine, 1835, 1836—Contemporary Notices and Criticisms—Dictionary of National Biography, Vol. XL., pages 206-208.

ELIZA O'NEILL, LADY WRIXON BECHER. — Illustrious Irishwomen, by E. Owens Blackburn—Kilkenny Theatricals—Private Theatre, Kilkenny—Celebrities I have Known, by Lord W. Lennox—Personal Recollections, by Mrs Baron Wilson—Familiar Epistles of John Wilson Croker—Account of the English Stage, by P. Genest—Hazlitt's Memoirs—Contemporary Notices—Dictionary of National Biography, Vol. IV., pages 74-75.

MARIE DOLORES GILBERT, LOLA MONTEZ. — Les Contemporaines for 1890—Eugène de Mirecourt—Blaues Blut, by E. M. Varano—Lola Montez et les Jesuites, by Paul Edermann—Anfang und Ende—Lola in Bayern: Autobiography and Letters by Rev. Chauncey Burr—You have heard of them by Q——The Art of Beauty—Story of a Penitent—Temple Bar Temple Bar Magazine—Living Age—Illustrated London News—Dictionary of National Biography, Vol. XXI., page 332.

# INDEX

THE END

*Colston & Coy. Limited, Printers. Edinburgh.*

www.ingramcontent.com/pod-product-compliance
Lightning Source LLC
Chambersburg PA
CBHW021218270326
41929CB00010B/1181